The International Criminal Court and the Lord's Resistance Army

This book interrogates the sharp contrast that emerged between demands of the norms of international rule of law and the interests of conflict resolution at a local level in northern Uganda.

Examining how the nature and character of complex conflict situations like that of northern Uganda confounds the application of transitional justice mechanisms, *The International Criminal Court and the Lord's Resistance Army* reveals the enduring dilemmas of transitional justice. Scrutinising the competing interests of punitive approaches to contemporary transitional justice and the political considerations for peace that may entail entering into dialogue with criminals, this book approaches such concepts from the perspective of international standards and the standpoint of the victims. While exploring the complexities of transitional justice processes, the book interrogates prevailing assumptions, proposing a broader conception that places at the centre local structural conditions associated with a conflict.

The International Criminal Court and the Lord's Resistance Army will be of interest to scholars and students of international law, African politics and conflict studies.

Joseph Otieno Wasonga is a Lecturer and Chair of Department of Diplomacy and International Relations at Kenyatta University, Kenya.

Routledge Contemporary Africa Series

Open Access to Knowledge in Nigeria
A Framework for Developing Countries
Kunle Ola

Contesting Inequalities, Identities and Rights in Ethiopia
The Collision of Passions
Data D. Barata

Contested Criminalities in Zimbabwean Fiction
Tendai Mangena

Foreign Direct Investment in Large-Scale Agriculture in Africa
Economic, Social and Economic Sustainability in Ethiopia
Atkeyelsh G. M. Persson

Borders, Media Crossings and the Politics of Translation
The Gaze from Southern Africa
Pier Paolo Frassinelli

Life Writing from the Margins in Zimbabwe
Versions and Subversions of Crisis
Oliver Nyambi

Complex Adaptive Systems, Resilience and Security in Cameroon
Manu Lekunze

The International Criminal Court and the Lord's Resistance Army
Enduring Dilemmas of Transitional Justice
Joseph Otieno Wasonga

For more information about this series, please visit: www.routledge.com/Routledge-Contemporary-Africa/book-series/RCAFR

The International Criminal Court and the Lord's Resistance Army

Enduring Dilemmas of Transitional Justice

Joseph Otieno Wasonga

Routledge
Taylor & Francis Group
LONDON AND NEW YORK

First published 2020
by Routledge
2 Park Square, Milton Park, Abingdon, Oxon OX14 4RN

and by Routledge
52 Vanderbilt Avenue, New York, NY 10017

Routledge is an imprint of the Taylor & Francis Group, an informa business

British Library Cataloguing-in-Publication Data
A catalogue record for this book is available from the British Library

Library of Congress Cataloging-in-Publication Data
Names: Wasonga, Joseph Otieno, author.
Title: The International Criminal Court and the Lord's Resistance Army : enduring dilemmas of transitional justice / Joseph Otieno Wasonga.
Other titles: Routledge contemporary Africa series.
Description: New York : Routledge, 2019. | Series: Routledge contemporary Africa series | Includes bibliographical references and index.
Identifiers: LCCN 2019011590 | ISBN 9780367086060 (hardback) | ISBN 9780429023323 (ebook) | ISBN 9780429662782 (epub) | ISBN 9780429660061 (mobipocket)
Subjects: LCSH: Lord's Resistance Army–Trials, litigation, etc. | International Criminal Court. | War crimes–Uganda. | Peace-building–Uganda. | Transitional justice–Uganda. | Uganda–History–1979-
Classification: LCC KZ1208.U33 W37 2019 | DDC 320.01109676109051–dc23
LC record available at https://lccn.loc.gov/2019011590

ISBN: 978-0-367-08606-0 (hbk)
ISBN: 978-0-429-02332-3 (ebk)

Typeset in Times New Roman
by Wearset Ltd, Boldon, Tyne and Wear

To my family

Contents

Acknowledgements

I thank Professor Sheila Meintjes, whose insightful suggestions contributed in giving form to this book. I acknowledge the support of Locor Seminary for facilitating my research in northern Uganda. I thank Matthew Odong, Charles Odwar, Charles Olweny and Crispin Opio who supported me as I conducted research through the Gulu, Amuru and Kitgum Districts of northern Uganda. I thank reviewers whose critical insights sharpened the focus of this book. I acknowledge the contribution of Leanne Hinves, Henry Strang, Matt Deacon and the entire Routledge editorial team who administered the production of the book. I wish to thank Angela Valente for her contribution in copy-editing. I cannot mention all individually, but I sincerely acknowledge each and every person who contributed to the production of this book.

1 Introduction

One of the outstanding issues on the global stage since the end of the Cold War is the kind of justice appropriate for post-conflict transitional situations, highlighting the enduring conflict between the goals of universal standards of justice and the interests of peace. The kind of justice applied in situations making transition from mass atrocities to peace and stability is what Teitel (2000) referred to as 'transitional justice'. The mainstream transitional justice discourse and processes are concerned with how a stable and just political order can emerge from a state of instability, repression and injustices or with how a society composed of groups which have committed heinous crimes against each other in the past are better able to face and deal with the past atrocities (Crocker, 1998; Kritz, 1995, p. xx; Teitel, 2002; Teitel, 2000, p. 213).

The International Criminal Court (ICC) intervention in northern Uganda as a transitional justice mechanism following atrocities committed by the Lord's Resistance Army (LRA) is a critical case in point. From the late 1980s, the LRA, a rebel group led by Joseph Kony, staged a rebellion against the Ugandan Government. The rebels had waged a brutal battle against the government of Uganda for over 20 years by directing acts of torture, mutilation, murder, abduction and sex slavery at the civilians residing in northern Uganda. The crimes were committed as part of a systematic attack against the local population (Akhavan, 2005, p. 405). The Ugandan Government under President Yoweri Museveni had made several unsuccessful attempts to bring an end to the conflict. These attempts included military strategies and non-violent options such as amnesty. In December 2003, President Museveni took an initiative to refer the situation to the ICC as an option for bringing an end to the conflict. This was the first situation to be referred to the International Court. In response to the referral, the court intervened to investigate and prosecute individuals occupying the topmost echelons of the LRA, led by Joseph Kony, for war crimes and crimes against humanity committed by the rebels since 1986. But the court was immediately faced with critical challenges regarding the appropriateness of its role in a transitional situation characterised by an ongoing conflict. A section of the local population, especially traditional leaders and the broader civil society, proposed alternative models of justice to that of the ICC, as being more suitable to the northern Ugandan context. This was in contrast to the enthusiasm with which the

ICC was met on its establishment in 1998 when it was described as a paradigm shift in relation to earlier developments in the area of international accountability for serious crimes committed against humankind (Ernesto, 2004, pp. 329–30; Bassiouni, 2006, p. 421; Conso, 1999, p. 572).

Although it was the president of Uganda who initially invited the ICC to investigate alleged war crimes and crimes against humanity committed by the LRA, his position changed when, in May 2006, Joseph Kony sought peace talks (Allen, 2006). The president not only responded positively, he further stated that the Government of Uganda was willing to extend total amnesty to Joseph Kony and other LRA leaders. Moreover, he undertook not to hand them over to the ICC providing they renounced violence. This development was widely welcomed by a cross-section of Ugandans as a viable route to a peace that had been elusive for several years. They hoped that as a result, millions of internally displaced people would be able to return to their homes.

The ICC came to be seen as the central obstacle to ending the brutal civil war and its prescription as exacerbating conflict in Uganda, since the LRA had asked for talks with the Ugandan Government to end the 20-year civil war. Those who rejected the court's intervention argued that the need for peace justified engaging the LRA leaders in dialogue so that the people would have the opportunity to air their grievances, an element they considered important in the search for peace. Moreover, the LRA leadership had vowed not to surrender unless the prosecutor of the ICC withdrew the targeting of their top commanders (Liu Institute for Global Issues, 2006). Thus, the ICC intervention might have the effect of exacerbating the violence. Opponents of the court argued that, the situation in Uganda was one of ongoing war rather than the result of limited criminality, as had persistently been claimed by the Ugandan Government. The ICC, as an international institution, did not have its own military and for this reason it would have no means of enforcing its warrants other than through the cooperation of states party to the Rome Statute (Allen, 2006). This would give government forces a free hand to pursue military objectives when executing the warrants. In the process, the military might kill Acholi children who had been abducted by the LRA and were still in the bush (ibid.).

Members of the civil society and Acholi traditional leaders, though cognisant of the need for justice, thought that the best route for ending the suffering in northern Uganda was to pursue the path of forgiveness and reconciliation. Peace would bring immediate benefit to all the parties affected by the conflict (ibid., pp. 102–3). Against this backdrop the victims, civil society, community leaders and government representatives opted for amnesty and *Mato Oput*, a traditional Acholi approach to justice and the reintegration of offenders (Afako, 2002). *Mato Oput* is a voluntary process that involves, according to Afako (ibid.), [the] 'mediation of truth; acknowledgement of wrongdoing; and reconciliation through symbolic acts and spiritual appeasement'. The ritual was used in traditional Acholi communities in cases of murder and sought to embody the principles of truth, accountability, compensation and restoration. The elders played a vital role as mediators in the process. Initially following a dispute, the elders engaged with both sides of the conflict in order to ascertain the relevant facts of the crime and to administer justice through compensation and reconciliation, as the case might be. This was followed by a ceremony of 'drinking the bitter root' which aimed at reconciling and facilitating the reintegration of the offender back into the community.

Accordingly in its first intervention, the ICC encountered critical challenges regarding its appropriateness in a situation of ongoing conflict with alternative models of justice being proposed as more suitable in the northern Uganda context. This situation raises critical questions about the competing goals of transitional justice. Whereas the establishment of the ICC was applauded as a turning point in the history of transitional justice, the court encountered opposition in its first intervention in northern Uganda. The encounter between the ICC and local preferences presented a conundrum in the pursuit of peace and justice in northern Uganda. Traditional leaders and civil society members advocated the use of traditional approaches to justice as the panacea. But the ICC insisted that the indicted LRA leaders had to be made accountable for their crimes. The ICC Prosecutor, Luis Moreno-Ocampo, maintained this on the grounds that war crimes and crimes against humanity cannot go unpunished. Any form of settlement that would preclude prosecution, including amnesty, was rejected by the ICC on the grounds that it would encourage a culture of impunity. Failure to prosecute the perpetrators would be interpreted as a triumph of impunity over human rights and a frustration of justice, might be a recipe for continued systematic atrocities and send a message to the effect that violators of human rights are always free to act with impunity. At the same time ICC's insistence on the punishment of blatant violations of human rights occurring within a context of ongoing war complicated the prospects of peace and the end to conflict. And how would political leadership in Uganda spearhead and foster the process of truth and reconciliation when some of them were perceived as being culpable in the perpetration of past abuses and responsible for the prevailing miserable social conditions of the Acholi? These issues constitute some of the enduring challenges to the pursuit of a global standard of justice and are central to transitional justice.

This work thus interrogates the sharp contrast that has emerged between demands made by the norms of international justice and the interests of conflict resolution and peacebuilding at a local level by focusing on the ICC intervention in northern Uganda. It scrutinises the competing interests of punitive and retributive approaches to contemporary transitional justice and the political considerations for peace that may entail entering into dialogue with criminals. In the context of the atrocities perpetrated by the LRA, this work interrogates the notion of peace and justice from the perspective of international standards and the standpoint of the victims, within the context of an ongoing conflict. The book explores the complexities of the transitional justice processes while interrogating prevailing assumptions on transitional justice. The work further proposes a much broader conception of justice that embraces local structural conditions and broader questions about transitional justice. It is hoped that this work will contribute to new theory-building and policy options in relation to the intersection of peace and justice.

This book begins in Chapter 2 by exposing the context and trajectory of the northern Uganda conflict, highlighting its historical dimensions and the extent of atrocity crimes allegedly committed by the LRA against the civilian population. It does this in order to show the complex nature of the northern Ugandan conflict, and its implications on transitional justice processes. Doing this allows us to argue that the nature and character of conflict in northern Uganda complicates the application of any transitional justice mechanism, and reveals the enduring dilemmas of the transitional justice processes. Chapter 3 discusses the intervention of the ICC and subsequent opposition from the local community and political actors. In this chapter the reader encounters the problems international criminal justice has in situations making transition from conflict to stability. Chapter 4 looks at the various non-prosecutorial peace initiatives in response to the protracted conflict in Uganda. The chapter focuses particularly on *mato oput*, the traditional Acholi conflict resolution mechanism, as an alternative to the international criminal justice intervention. Chapter 5 analyses the nexus between the competing transitional justice mechanisms on the one hand, and sustainable peace and stability in northern Uganda on the other. Chapter 6 concludes by highlighting the key problematic points in transitional justice processes, the limitations of individual mechanisms and some proposals for encompassing an approach to transitional justice.

2 Conflict trajectory in northern Uganda

Its development and nature

Introduction

The conflict situation in northern and the ICC intervention therein is one of those spaces where transitional justice complexity manifests. The dynamics of this conflict can inform our understanding of the dilemmas associated with this transitional justice situation. Readers therefore need to understand the factors associated with the start and duration of the conflict. Some explanations have been offered by scholars. Ofcansky (1996, p. 37) has suggested that the colonial system of divide and rule in Uganda left behind a deeply divided society with differential access to economic development, political power; and a legacy of ethnic stereotyping and manipulation. Omara-Otunnu (1987) points to a militarised culture that emerged in post-independence Uganda whereby the military became a key instrument for securing political power and access to resources. To explain the above suppositions we offer a synoptic presentation of the trajectory of violence in Uganda, beginning immediately after independence and continuing until the LRA insurgency in northern Uganda in 1986. The dynamism and complexity of the conflict helps assess the ICC intervention as an instrument of transitional justice and issues that arise thereby.

The colonial legacy

Uganda, like most postcolonial African countries, was a colonial construct. British colonial rule in Uganda was established by the 1890 treaty with the Buganda Kingdom. This was followed by the 1894 declaration of a British protectorate over the whole area of Uganda. A protectorate within the British sphere of influence abroad was nominally distinct from a colony in that the former was semi-autonomous whereas the latter formed part of the British State. The country was created from the historical kingdoms in the south, such as the Buganda and the Bunyoro kingdoms, and the less centralised polities, such as chiefdoms among the Acholi headed by *rwodi* (rulers) in the north (Hansen & Twaddle, 1995; Mudoola, 1996). Generally, the southerners were Bantu speakers while the northerners were Nilotic speakers. The Buganda Kingdom, which was more centralised and had well-organised traditional administrative structures and institutions, became a key player in the protectorate compared to other polities and was used by the British colonial administration to administer the protectorate (Apter, 1961, pp. 84–116). It is upon these traditional cleavages that the British colonial administration built their system of indirect rule in Uganda.

This British indirect rule is one of the factors that historians have pointed to in trying to account for the conflict in northern Uganda. Indirect rule consisted of the integration of local chiefs into the administration of local governments in the colonies on behalf of the colonial power. It also involved using certain chiefdoms or kingdoms to assist in conquering, pacifying and ruling over others. This system was consolidated by the protectorate status granted to Buganda under the 1900 Agreement which defined relations between British colonial authority and Buganda, as well as between Buganda and the rest of the Uganda Protectorate (Ofcansky, 1996, p. 22; Kisamba-Mugerwa, 1991, pp. 311–21). According to the Agreement, the Buganda Kingdom was considered to be a province of the Uganda Protectorate. The kingdom was granted special status with a considerable degree of autonomy and was granted preferential status over other polities by the British. In return, the Buganda Kingdom recognised British sovereignty and divided their land equally between the British, in the form of crown land, and the Buganda chiefs, many of whom held the land in private ownership and leased plots to tenants (Kisamba-Mugerwa, 1991, pp. 311–21). This was known as the *mailo* (native) system – a form of feudal authority with structured, hierarchically-based subordination. The Buganda also paid taxes for their privileges.

The preferential consideration given to the Buganda Kingdom and Baganda (the people of Buganda Kingdom) contrasted with the British policy towards the Nilotic tribes in northern Uganda. The northern region was not economically developed during the colonial period and served mainly as a reservoir for cheap labour for the south, although the local population also carried out some small-scale, but significant, cotton and cattle farming. The British deliberately reserved the introduction of industry and cash crop production to the south. However, as a kind of quid pro quo, and consonant with the system of divide and rule, recruitment into the army was reserved for northerners and people from the east who, the British claimed, were naturally martial in nature (Lwanga-Lunyiigo, 1989; Omara-Otunnu, 1987). Amii Omara-Otunnu (1987), underscoring the prevalence of northerners in the army, notes that:

> …the African sector of the Army was not very representative of the ethnic composition of the country as a whole. The largest contingent was recruited from the north, especially from the people of Acholi…. By 1914, Acholi had become the main recruiting ground for the KAR (King's Africa Rifles), a pattern which was continued in the postcolonial period.
>
> (Omara-Otunnu, 1987)

At the time of independence in 1962, the Ugandan army was comprised predominantly of northerners, and the rapid expansion of the army during the first government of Milton Obote (1962–1971) continued to rely primarily on recruits from the northern regions of Acholi, Teso, Lango and the West Nile (Brett, 1995, p. 135). Behrend (1999, p. 19) attributes the continued dominance of people from the north of the country in the army before and after independence to the fact that there were limited economic opportunities in that part of the country since the British had excluded the region economically.

The significance of these divisions was that the British managed to maintain distinctive authoritative roles and powers between the southern civilian elites, whose role was administrative and political, and the largely northern military elites (ICG, 2004, p. 2). Thus, the British instituted a system of indirect governance in Uganda, which relied on Buganda to administer and rule other Ugandan kingdoms and dominated sectors such as the civil service. The British relied on the use of northern troops to keep control. This meant the southerners received education to prepare them for administrative posts in the protectorate while northerners were prepared for employment in the military and other fighting forces or were recruited as labourers (Behrend, 1999, p. 19; Jackson, 2002, p. 29). Thus, a deliberate and conscious structure was created by the British colonial administration, which Behrend (1999, p. 19) refers to as the 'ethnic division of labour'.

The British colonial policy in Africa, observes Young (1994, p. 97), was motivated by economic goals and had to be as self-sustaining as possible. To realise their goals the British had to depend on the local elites in the affairs of the colony (Mungeam, 1966). The strategy was successful in Uganda where the British found a strong structure of social control and where those in charge of these structures were willing to collaborate (Young, 1998, pp. 42–3). Gardner Thompson (2003, p. 22) notes that when the British introduced indirect rule it was not because they respected the feudal states but because, throughout the colonial period, they did not have sufficient human or financial resources to sustain a team of British bureaucrats in Uganda. In 1955 there were only three white officials, including the District Commissioner, in the whole of Lango District, yet the day-to-day running of colonial affairs remained successful (ibid.).

Researchers have argued that one of the causes of the perennial conflicts in Uganda in general, and northern Uganda in particular, was the manner in which the British colonial administration structured and manipulated pre-existing cleavages for their own goals (Jackson, 2002, p. 29; Omara-Otunnu, 1987, p. 35; Apuuli, 2005; Allen, 2006, p. 28). The Ugandan state was constructed in line with the British divide and rule system (Jackson, 2002, p. 29; Omara-Otunnu, 1987, p. 35). This system meant that the traditional patterns of social organisation were instrumentalised and bolstered in order to enhance the efficiency of the colonial administration. By adopting precolonial social organisational structures, the British deliberately kept the different traditional polities within the colony from forming alliances across the ethnic divide and challenging British hegemony. The result of this process was that the population in a given colonial territory were not integrated into a single centralised system of formal bureaucratic control. In effect, the British cultivated factional ethnic rivalries among the different ethnic communities within the colony as a means of maintaining their control (Blanton et al., 2001, pp. 479–80).

Accordingly, the Buganda Kingdom was given preferential treatment compared to the Nilotic and Sudanic polities in the north of the territory which worked against national integration. The British colonial administration did not develop the northern region, reserving it instead for cheap migrant labour to the south and for military recruitment, a process that would continue in the post-independence period (Lwanga-Lunyiigo, 1989; Omara-Otunnu, 1987). The British also relied on Buganda to subdue and administer other groups and kingdoms (Jackson, 2002, p. 29). Given the people of the Kingdom of Buganda played a central role in colonial administration, they were advantaged in comparison to other groups in the protectorate (Mutibwa, 1992, pp. 8–9). This meant that they received education and were exposed to opportunities that bolstered their dominance. These form the basic elements of social and political structures upon which Ugandan society was constructed as a result of the British colonial system of indirect rule.

The policies resulted in uneven development across the protectorate and led to the development of the state along markedly ethnic lines, empowering some while disempowering others in the process. The fact that development by the British colonisers in Uganda was uneven led to the theory of the 'north-south divide' – the north being poor and the south being prosperous. The trend has also been used to provide an explanation for why the Acholi, in particular, came to predominate in the army. The inevitable consequence was inequality and structural difference, which in turn generated and sustained intense and disruptive tensions and conflicts between the different ethnic groups after the fall of colonialism (Omara-Otunnu, 1987; Brett, 1995, p. 135).

These policies created deep divisions which fractured attempts to build a unified nation-state after independence. These divisions were already evident on the eve of independence as certain polities, such as the Baganda, were not enthusiastic about being part of an integral unitary state. The dominance of the Baganda elite in the colonial era straddled independence. Obote's move to undermine the dominance of the Bangada in the civil service and in the economy engendered bitterness. In the same vein the northerners, with their advantage of military dominance, would earnestly seek a political stake in the new system to end their political exclusion. Independence was followed by increased ethnic tension between Nilotic-speaking northerners and the Bantu-speaking southerners in competition for political dominance. Thus, with the exit of British colonial rule, the social cleavages and structures provided forums for the mobilisation of aggrieved minorities around collective action (Hansen & Twaddle, 1995; Mudoola, 1996).

Post-independence political upheavals and legacies

In 1962 Uganda acquired independence from British colonial rule under a coalition government and constitution. The independence constitution incorporated semi-federal features which gave the traditional political elites in the Kingdoms of Buganda, Bunyoro, Toro and Ankole some scope (Asowa-Okwe, 1994, pp. 133–64). The coalition government consisted of Milton Obote's predominantly Protestant party – the Uganda People's Congress (UPC) and the Buganda traditionalist political party, the *Kabaka Yekka* (KY), translated as 'The King Alone'. When Uganda became a republic in 1963, Milton Obote, who was from the northern part of Uganda, became prime minister with Kabaka Mutesa II as the president.

It is critical to note that this was largely a coalition of convenience which was bound to collapse within a relatively short space of time. The Buganda diehards had not been willing to let their identity and ceremonious kingdom be swallowed by the nation-state initiated by the Protectorate's Governor, Sir Andrew Cohen in the 1950s (Wrigley, 1988, pp. 30–3). For this reason, Kabaka's party entered into a coalition with Obote on condition that the Kabaka would become the president. For his part, Obote needed support since his party faced internal division and external threats from the Democratic Party, DP, which was predominantly a Catholic party (ibid.). Soon afterwards, the ruling coalition broke up due to disagreements over the Bunyoro territory. This territory had been annexed and transferred to the Baganda by the British as reward for their loyalty and collaboration (Lwanga-Lunyiigo, 1989, pp. 24–43). Obote called for a referendum in November 1964, the outcome of which led to a return of part of the disputed territory to the Bunyoro. The consequence was resentment on the part of the Buganda Kingdom, especially the elite. In the same year there was an attempt by the then UPC Secretary General Ibingira to push Obote out of power by accusing Obote and the Deputy Army Commander Idi Amin of involvement in a gold and ivory scam. In response, Obote arrested the main plotters of the attempted coup, suspended the independence constitution and promoted Idi Amin to army Chief of Staff. Most significantly, he deposed the Kabaka from the presidency. In April 1966, Obote convened a national assembly to write a new republican constitution, which then entrenched a strong executive presidency and substantially reduced the powers of the traditional leaders (Omara-Otunnu, 1987). Accordingly, given the sectarian interests of the coalition partners, the independence government and constitution collapsed after only four years into leading the country to a new turning point that would later shape Uganda's post-independent violent history.

The new constitution led to increased tensions between the new government and the traditional Buganda parliament, the *lukiko*, which rejected the new constitution and the limitations it imposed on Buganda federal powers. The *lukiko* passed a motion ordering the central government to leave Buganda. Obote responded swiftly and declared a state of emergency ordering the army to attack and occupy the Kabaka's palace. The attack is estimated to have cost more than 100 lives. Kabaka Mutesa II managed to escape to exile in London, where he later died (Lukwago, 1982). Obote promoted a new constitution which transformed Uganda into a republic with a strong presidential regime (Omara-Otunnu, 1987). Over the next few years Obote consolidated his powers by introducing yet another constitution in 1967 which abolished the traditional kingdoms and further strengthened executive powers. Following an assassination attempt on Obote in 1969, the UPC banned all opposition groups and effectively created a one-party state (ibid.).

Two significant points arise from these unfolding of events. First, the actions of Obote against the Buganda Kingdom created an enduring resentment that would be a key factor in later conflicts. Kabaka Mutesa II, who had been disposed by Obote, was seen as a victim of Obote's despotism which resulted in a crisis of legitimacy for the UPC Government. The Baganda felt humiliated and alienated, leaving a sense of abiding hostility and heightened ethnic animosity against the people from the north of the country. According to Omach (2003, p. 68), these actions created a tendency in Ugandan politics to apply negative labels to whole communities and hold them liable and guilty for the actions of leaders from their region, ethnic group or with whom they shared religious affiliation. As a result of these events the Baganda harboured grievances against Obote and anybody associated with him.

Second, military power proved to be a key factor in settling political disputes. The effect was to legitimise the instrumentality of militarised politics. Under the colonial government, the military had been used as a divide and rule instrument. The structuring of a militarily strong north vis-à-vis an economically powerful south, weakened the possibility of uniting opposition forces. As Omach suggests, the events of the 1966 crisis entrenched the culture of violence and militarism in the politics of Uganda. The consequent use of the military as a key political tool against the Government's opponents resulted in increased reliance on coercive state instruments to resolve conflicts and to consolidate state power (Omach, 2003, p. 69). Politicians or parties employed military might to impose their standpoint. In this context, Obote came to rely on the personal allegiance of troops, becoming dependent on soldiers whom he had to pay lavishly in order to buy their loyalty (Wrigley, 1988, p. 34). Idi Amin, who came from the West Nile region, was the person in charge of the attack on the Kabaka's palace and was promoted to army commander after the action. This experience led him to understand the instrumentality of military power. Once he took control, Amin's strategy was to recruit and promote West Nile people into strategic positions, sacking Acholi officers and even executing them (Doom & Vlassenroot, 1999, pp. 8–9).

As Obote became preoccupied with consolidating his own political power, Idi Amin consolidated his control over a considerable proportion of the Ugandan armed forces. Between 1969 and 1971 tensions developed between Obote and Amin as the former attempted to neutralise Amin's power base within the army. Just before leaving for Singapore in January 1971 to attend a summit of Commonwealth leaders, Obote had asked Amin to account for £2.5 million (GBP) spent by the army. In Obote's absence Amin deposed him on 25 January 1971. Many Ugandans, especially those living in Buganda and other areas, who had grown dissatisfied with Obote's oppressive government, at first welcomed Amin's military coup with jubilance. The same instrument, the military, which

Obote had used to topple the Kabaka was used against him by Amin, the very person who had led Obote's onslaught on the Kabaka.

Amin initially gestured towards tolerance and compromise. He released many detainees and allowed Kabaka Mutesa II's body to return from England for burial in Uganda. The Kabaka had died in exile in England where he had fled when Obote attacked his palace. These initial overtures were short-lived. Amin soon ordered the Acholi and Langi soldiers, who constituted the backbone of the army, to surrender their arms and return to their barracks only to have them killed there (Gersony, 1997, p. 7). While Amin's regime tortured and killed indiscriminately, Acholi officers were among those most likely to be targeted for murder (Doom & Vlassenroot, 1999, p. 9). As I have said earlier, at the time of independence in 1962, the Ugandan army had been predominantly northern, and this would continue until 1971 when Obote was deposed by Amin. Having witnessed the effects of military seizure and the consolidation of political power, Amin would not feel secure with members of the army whom he perceived to be loyal to Obote.

Amin's Government extended its control over Uganda by attacking all potential opposition. Highly educated and influential members of the Acholi and Langi were arrested, detained and killed (Ofcansky, 1996, p. 44). He created several new security organisations which reported directly to him, including the Public Safety Unit and the State Research Bureau. Along with the military police, these two organisations wrought terror on Uganda. Within three months of taking power Amin had suspended all democratic rights, had given the army dictatorial powers of arrest and punishment and had set up a military tribunal to try political offenders. Over the next few years, tens of thousands of Ugandans fell prey to Amin's henchmen. Ofcansky (ibid.) states that by the end of Amin's first year in office, his security forces had murdered approximately 10,000 Ugandans and, during his eight-year rule, between 100,000 and 500,000 Ugandans lost their lives or disappeared. These included not only the Langi and the northern groups, which had formed the backbone of the Obote Government, but also many Baganda intellectuals as Amin began to target people he perceived as disloyal from other parts of the country (ibid.).

Amin recruited new soldiers into the national army, largely from West Nile, in order to protect the regime, which lacked political legitimacy. However, according to Ogenga Otunnu (2002), he appointed prominent Bantu to important positions in his Government. The regime largely maintained the dominance of southerners in the civil service and commerce, while the northerners largely controlled the Government and army (Mutibwa, 1992, pp. 8–9).

To escape Amin's repressions many Ugandans fled the country including those who later established various liberation movements. In April 1979, the exiles formed the Uganda National Liberation Army (UNLA), members of which were overwhelmingly from the Acholi and the Langi. Assisted by the Tanzanian army and Yoweri Museveni's Front for National Salvation (FRONASA), they overthrew the Amin regime in 1980. The new military administration organised general elections in December 1980. Political parties which participated in the election included the UPC, whose presidential candidate was Milton Obote, the Democratic Party (DP), led by Paul Kawanga Ssemogerere, and the Uganda People's Movement led by Museveni (Odongo, 2000, pp. 53–4). The elections were won by the UPC led by Milton Obote. This ushered in what has been referred to as the 'Obote II period'. Accusations of widespread irregularities and pervasive political violence undermined the legitimacy of the elections. According to Onyango Odongo, the 1980 elections were actually won by the DP but were rigged in favour of Obote's UPC. Thus the DP, the main opposition, rejected Obote's victory. Museveni also rejected the results.

After the disputed election of Obote, a number of armed groups declared war against Obote's Government. These included Museveni's Popular Resistance Army, later renamed the National Resistance Movement/Army (NRM/A) among others. Museveni claimed that the rigged elections and the corrupt military-dominated system which returned Obote to power inspired him to form the NRA and wage a guerrilla war. He argued that his call to arms was a legitimate response to undemocratic practices. He wrote, 'once again, a minority, unpopular clique was imposed on the people of Uganda, leaving them with no option but to take up arms in defence of their democratic rights' (Museveni, 1990, p. 3). Museveni (ibid.) perceived his struggle against Obote as more than a struggle for power, describing it as a struggle '[…] to free Uganda from the political manipulation of elitist and non-representative political parties and to create a more democratic and representative system of governance'.

Significantly, Museveni launched the guerrilla war against Obote's Government in the Luwero Triangle in central Uganda close to Kampala. The Luwero Triangle, formed by roads leading north and northwest out of Kampala, is situated between three lakes, Victoria, Albert and Kyoga. This region is inhabited by the Buganda from whom Museveni received popular support. In retaliation, in January 1983, Obote launched 'Operation Bonanza' against the Luwero Triangle Baganda for their perceived support of the rebels (Ofcansky, 1996, pp. 54–5). Operation Bonanza was the name given to the relentless and murderous military operation that Obote's Government forces launched to mop out the NRA rebels within the Luwero Triangle (Mutibwa, 1992, pp. 138–45; Ofcansky, 1996, pp. 54–5). The attacks launched by Government soldiers were characterised by serious disregard for human rights, military excesses and a massive loss of life. The UNLA troops destroyed small towns, villages and farms and killed or displaced hundreds of thousands of civilians (Mutibwa, 1992, pp. 138–45). When the war ended in 1986, around 300,000[1] people had died in the Luwero Triangle and a third of the region's population were unaccounted for (Ofcansky, 1996, p. 54). Twenty-four years later, human skulls were still reported to litter the Luwero Triangle.

Although the UNLA was a national and multi-ethnic army, the NRM/A held the Acholi exclusively responsible for the atrocities committed. This perception was to shape subsequent attitudes towards the conflict in Luwero, the conflict in northern Uganda and the Acholi population in general. This attitude towards northerners is reflected in President Museveni's autobiography, *Sowing the*

Mustard Seed (Museveni, 1997). In his autobiography, where he portrays himself as servant leader, Museveni provides an account of his life, the country's post-independence regimes, the struggles against Amin (1971–1979), Obote's second regime dictatorship (1981–1985), the eventual overthrow of the brief rule of President Tito Okello in 1986, and his struggle to build a country which was on the verge of collapse. Various remarks made in this book by Museveni about the Acholi and other northerners reflect a rather negative attitude towards northern Ugandans.

The circumstances of the Luwero Triangle in the early 1980s provide us with a significant analytical point. It is a pointer to the manner in which ethnic differences are manipulated as a mobilisation strategy and helps us grasp the dynamics of the conflict in northern Uganda and why it has taken so long to quell. The Luwero Triangle region was a popular support base for the NRA rebels. The inhabitants around the Luwero Triangle supported the NRM because they were all fighting against bad leadership and poor governance. More significantly the Baganda who resided in the Luwero Triangle supported the NRM because they were promised the restoration of the kingship in Buganda and the entitlements that went with it. The Baganda had felt humiliated and resented the destruction of their kingdom in 1966 by President Obote's first regime. So they supported the war against Obote to ensure restoration of the kingdom. Gersony (1997, p. 30) suggests that, during the NRA insurgency, Museveni allegedly promised to restore the Bunganda kingship. This promise of restoration would be quite appealing since the kingdom was so dear to their culture and way of administration. So the expectation was created that joining the struggle would lead to the re-emergence of Buganda's deserved pre-eminence in Uganda's governance (ibid., pp. 20–36). By launching his war in Luwero, among the Baganda to whom he promised the restoration of their kingdom destroyed by the northerner Obote, Museveni exploited the hatred of the people for northerners. In this case, although the events in the Luwero Triangle were the immediate triggers of the war, the Luwero events were preceded by the mobilisation and rekindling of ethnic hatred.

Despite the repressive measures of the UNLA, the NRA/M continued to make significant progress in its guerrilla campaign against the Obote Government. The strong anti-Obote feelings in Buganda, where memories of Obote's first repressive government remained strong, guaranteed the NRA/M the region's support. Obote depended on a small core of his own sub-ethnic group, the Langi officers, to take command of the army and defend his political regime (Ofcansky, 1996). Captain Ageta who was a relatively junior officer was put in charge of a newly created *Reconnaissance Unit*[2] that was equipped with mounted guns to operate within the Central Brigade where Luwero was located (ibid.). The Acholi commander Bazilio Okello who led the Brigade was unable to control Captain Ageta's activities. This rift between the Obote core group, the Acholi officers and troops in the army led to their alienation. Obote made a number of promotions which favoured the Langi officers in the army (ibid.). Obote's overstepping of his political mandate was an indication of how, in a militarised society such as Uganda, the boundary between political office and the military becomes blurred. The military had been turned into instruments for maintaining state power, as mentioned earlier.

By 1985, Milton Obote had gradually set the stage for the elimination of Acholi officers from the Uganda army. The National Security Agency (NASA) was essentially an anti-Acholi intelligence organ. The Special Forces became an alternative army aimed at by-passing or replacing the UNLA Acholi-dominated officer corps (Pain, 1997). By 1984, Obote had virtually handed over responsibility for the Luwero Triangle to NASA. The Acholi officers retreated to the north and challenged the activities being carried out by these Special Forces (ibid.). By 1984 the Acholi officers had lined up behind the then Vice-president Paulo Muwanga, a Muganda, in opposition to Obote. Muwanga used this support to establish links with Museveni who was then in exile in Sweden. With the support of Baganda factions in the ruling UPC, the DP and the NRA/M, Brigadier Bazilio Okello and General Tito Okello, both Acholis, staged a coup against Obote in May 1985 (ibid.). This coup by the Acholi officers against Obote could be interpreted as a pre-emptive self-defence move by Bazilio Okello and Tito Okello to prevent Obote's plans of eliminating them from the armed forces. According to Pain (ibid.), Obote, for his own political survival, had begun to perceive the Acholi officers in the UNLA as being too independent of his political control and therefore a danger to his rule.

The Okellos seized power on a platform of national reconciliation, urging all political parties and insurgent groups to join the new government. Although many insurgent groups joined them, the NRA/M refused to join partly because Museveni was dissatisfied with the number of seats on the ruling Military Council offered to the NRA/M (Omara-Otunnu, 1987). There were also more fundamental reasons, including the fact that Tito Okello was a northerner. The NRA, however, engaged the regime in protracted peace negotiations in Nairobi. In December 1985, the Nairobi Peace Agreement was signed under the chairmanship of President Moi of Kenya. Meanwhile, Museveni continued fighting against the Okello Government. The Okello Government was defeated when the NRA/M marched into Kampala and effectively established itself as the Government of Uganda on 25 January 1986. Thus the Nairobi Peace Agreement was never implemented (Omara-Otunnu, 1987).

The NRA revenge mission and cultic warfare in northern Uganda

After the NRM/A captured power in the coup in Kampala, the Acholi military officers retreated to Acholiland to defend themselves. They were haunted by the memory of the massacres of Acholi soldiers by Amin in the early 1970s and feared that these would be repeated. Indeed, as soon as the NRM took over the main urban areas inhabited by the Acholi around March 1986, the regime launched a crackdown on Acholi UNLA soldiers who had fled Kampala. At this stage the NRA's perception was that all the UNLA were Acholi. The new

Government's move was to hold former government soldiers responsible for the atrocities committed in the Luwero Triangle, the massacre of about 300,000 people (Gersony, 1997, p. 9). It was also meant to halt any threat to the consolidation of the NRA power. However, it turned into a revenge mission as the NRA committed almost an equal measure of atrocities as the former government soldiers. Behrend (1991, p. 165) observes that the 35th Battalion of the NRA, which was sent to Kitgum to pursue the UNLA soldiers for their atrocities in Luwero, took the opportunity to loot, rape and murder. According to a number of sources, terrible atrocities were committed during these operations. The NRA buried many people alive in northern Uganda in 1988 and forced men and women into sexual acts in front of their families in order to humiliate and degrade the Acholi community as a whole (Van Acker, 2003, p. 6). According to Lumwaka (2002), in August 1986, a Baganda militia, operating with the NRA, the Federalist Democratic Movement of Uganda (FEDEMU), massacred 40 civilians in Tito Okellos's village of Namokora in Kitgum, partly in retaliation for UNLA killings in Luwero. FEDEMU had not been part of the original NRA, but was a fighting group that forged an alliance with it when the latter was about to take power. In July 1987, the NRA executed some 97 civilians at Kona Kilak in Gulu. In June 1988, 40 civilians were massacred at Koch Goma in the Amuru district (ICG, 2004, p. 2). These events in the north, in the immediate aftermath of the NRA victory, reinforced prejudices and created perceptions that led to the next phase of the conflict. The NRA's atrocities fed suspicions that a southern war of revenge was being undertaken against the Acholi (ibid., pp. 3–4). Many Acholis, and others, believed that sending the most brutal elements of the 35th Battalion of the NRA to the north was a deliberate strategy of revenge and subjugation (Apuuli, 2006).

These retaliatory operations created a breeding ground for guerrilla reactions (Allen, 2006, p. 30). Against the background of this mistrust and violence, in May 1986 the new Government ordered all former UNLA soldiers to report to barracks. The order was met with deep suspicion and fear because it was reminiscent of the massacres of Acholi officers by Amin in 1971 (Allen, 1991, p. 371). As a result, some ex-UNLA soldiers decided to go underground; others took refuge in Sudan and some resorted to engage in counter-insurgency. The ex-soldiers who decided to take up arms were soon joined by a stream of youths fleeing from the NRA revenge operations.

In August 1986, some Acholi refugee combatants, led by Brigadier Odong Latek, formed a movement with its military wing, the Uganda People's Democratic Movement/Army (UPDM/A) in Juba, Sudan. Some of Okello's ex-soldiers were incorporated into the new guerrilla army (UPDA). According to the International Crisis Group (ICG), the UPDA's emergence in 1986 was generally seen across the Acholi region as a struggle to recapture power, although it lacked a coherent programme since its political wing, the UPDM, was based in London (ICG, 2004, p. 4). Allen suggests that there seems, ironically, to have been little sympathy for the former government soldiers among the Acholi population. The ex-soldiers were given a difficult time when they returned to their villages, taunted for their failures and castigated for their brutal action in Luwero (Allen, 1991, p. 371). Moreover, the local population feared that the presence of former soldiers would encourage NRA forces to take revenge on the broader population for what had happened in Luwero (ibid.). Thus the UPDA did not manage to mobilise broad-based popular support among the Acholi and failed to register meaningful success in their insurgency.

In late 1986, as UPDA's capacity to stage a sustained rebellion dwindled, a new, somewhat cultic movement emerged to guide military operations, led by a 27-year-old Acholi woman by the name of Alice Auma (Allen, 2006, p. 31). Auma claimed to have been possessed by a Christian spirit called Lakwena which had called upon her to topple Museveni's Government not simply to restore power to the Acholi people, but to prevent the extinction of her people at the hands of Museveni. Auma, who later came to be popularly known as Lakwena, formed the Holy Spirit Mobile Forces (HSMF) in 1987 to guard against the annihilation of the Acholi community. The fear of annihilation was reinforced by the scale of the NRA massacres of the Acholis. This development marked a new chapter in the war, a development built on the interaction between Christianity and traditional Acholi beliefs in the power of protective charms and traditional anointment. The HSMF was explained as a social rebellion against the newly established order, and portended nationalist revival in the context of the restoration of ethnic identity (Behrend, 1999). Lakwena argued that the Acholi would soon find themselves marginalised due to their dominance in the national army that had fought Museveni in his guerrilla campaign to attain power (Lomo & Hovil, 2004).

Alice Auma had started her career as a healer after having been possessed by the Lakwena and her cult grew rapidly in significance. She performed healing rituals for UNLA soldiers after their retreat from the south. She claimed to have been directed to resort to a military campaign to defend the Acholi for there would be no call to heal those who would be killed in the end (Allen, 2006, p. 35). Lakwena, however, adopted unconventional military strategies, anointing her soldiers with oil, promising that if they were pure, bullets would not penetrate them. Purity meant, among other things, abstinence from sexual intercourse and alcohol (ibid.). Thus, the HSMF soldiers had to be cleansed, initiated, and introduced to new and unorthodox methods of fighting (Doom & Vlassenroot, 1999).

In her military campaign she initially had a large following and achieved some successes. According to Allen (ibid., p. 37), 'at the end of 1986 she claims to have had 18,000 soldiers'. In November 1986 the HSMF carried out a major attack on the NRA position in a place called Corner Kilak, 40 miles south of the town of Lira. According to Tim Allen the soldiers were taken by surprise and were terrified to behold hundreds of men coming out of the bush singing and walking upright without taking cover. Panic ensued and the NRA fled. However, between Christmas and mid-January 1986 the movement suffered serious casualties. The NRA had killed 700 of their fighters. On 18 January a further battle was fought at Corner Kilak. Again the soldiers were confronted by charges of men singing hymns (Allen, 1991, p. 372). This time the Government forces simply mowed down their attackers leaving some 400 dead. The battlefield was littered with magical objects made from wire, including models of helicopters and tankers (ibid.).

Although the HSMF employed unconventional military tactics, it was successful for a short period, even coming within 100 kilometres of Kampala. Lakwena was finally defeated at Jinja and fled to Nairobi in October 1987 (Allen, 2006, pp. 35–6). She lived the rest of her life in Kenya where she died in 2005. However, Lakwena's movement did not disappear immediately after her escape to Kenya. Sevarino Lukoya Kiberu, Lakwena's father, claimed to have been possessed by his daughter's spirits. Thus he attracted some of Lakwena's followers to lead the resistance (ibid., p. 36). His resistance movement was called *Lord's Army*, based on religious purity. He encouraged his followers to be possessed by pure spirit. Lukoya's resistance was defeated by the NRA in 1989.

Lakwena's tactics, on face value, may be dismissed as lunatic, but one striking aspect was the manner in which the tactics and convictions became a rallying point for ethno-political mobilisation. Although the HSMF may have been a peasant cult, it was nonetheless able to attract broader support than the UPDA, extending even beyond the Acholi to most tribes in northern and eastern Uganda (Allen, 1991, p. 372). Alice Lakwena invoked the fear of Acholi annihilation which needed to be faced through a fundamentally new strategy. To achieve this she exploited the spiritual world, which formed the core of the Acholi identity, as a rallying point (Behrend, 1999). As a mobilisation strategy, she played on fears of ethnic extinction which evoked a degree of ethnic renewal in response. Moreover, Lakwena's movement and its spiritual underpinning were rooted in the social milieu at the time. In the early 1980s the phenomenon of spirit messengers (or divination) and spiritual healing had emerged in Acholiland. As mentioned earlier, this spiritual intervention may have arisen because of fears that were beyond people's powers: the memories of the massacre of Acholis by Amin in the early 1970s; mass atrocities committed at Luwero purportedly by Acholi soldiers; and the mass killing of Acholi by the NRA soldiers. The spiritual healers were consulted in search of answers to problems that bedevilled the people and, in the upheaval that followed the victory of NRA in 1986, many diviners emerged. This religious intervention came to be used as an instrument of military campaigns (Allen, 2006, pp. 31–7).

Meanwhile, the UPDA, who had been unsuccessful in its military campaign, resorted to negotiations with the NRM. This led to a peace agreement in 1988. However, this agreement was followed by NRA military operations to finish off recalcitrant Acholi rebels, during which a number of renowned UPDA Acholi leaders were killed (ICG, 2004, p. 4). The 1988 NRA counter-insurgency was brutal, including the deliberate destruction of civilian food stocks and domestic animals. Suspicions re-emerged and the whole operation was interpreted as being geared towards the extermination of all Acholi (ibid., p. 4).

From spiritual redemption and political emancipation to self-extermination: the LRA insurgency

The LRA and their command structure

Joseph Kony sought to continue fighting for the emancipation of the Acholi. He operated in Acholiland, and recruited some of the Acholi army veterans into his force. Kony revitalised the Holy Spirit Movement and radicalised its teachings and methods. Like Lakwena, Kony incorporated Christian principles and a strong religious component with apocalyptic tones into the Movement, while adding his own dimensions of terror and coercion (ibid.). Kony combined spiritual redemption and political opposition with the goal of moulding Uganda into a country, 'ruled in accordance with the Biblical Ten Commandments' (Jackson, 2002, p. 49). According to Doom and Vlassenroot, Kony offered spiritual redemption to the Acholi people who feared genocide and destruction with the rise of Museveni. The war in Acholiland was thus portrayed as being based on fear of ethnic extinction (Doom & Vlassenroot, 1999, p. 22). Kony provided an opportunity for frustrated Acholi citizens to mobilise against the new southern leadership in Kampala.

Because of the obscure nature of its operation, no clear facts are available about the structures, ideology, and membership of the LRA. At first, in 1988, Kony called his movement the Uganda Peoples' Democratic Christian Army (UPDCA), which he later changed to the Uganda Christian Democratic Army (UCDA) before renaming it the Lord's Resistance Army (LRA) in 1991. In terms of its ideological orientation, the LRA sought to rule Uganda in accordance with the Ten Commandments, the restoration of multiparty politics in Uganda and a federal system of governance. The LRA also called for impartial national socio-economic development, the inclusion of the Acholi in national politics, the enjoyment of human rights, promotion of peace and security and an end to corruption (Finnström, 2003). The LRA manifesto also called for free and fair elections, the separation of judicial and executive powers from the military, and the reform of parliament to tackle these issues (ibid.).

Membership of the LRA was often fluid and changing since, as new members were recruited, other were constantly escaping (Allen, 2006). Estimates of LRA numbers fluctuated from time to time. Weeks (2002, p. 8), writing in 2002, puts the number at 2,000. At the beginning of the Juba Peace Talks in July 2006, numbers given ranged from a few hundred to at least 10,000, depending on the source (Schomerus, 2007, p. 12). The Uganda People's Defence Force (UPDF) portrayed the LRA as a group of a few hundred scattered fighters. The LRA claimed that they have over 10,000 members, including fighters and non-combatants (ibid.). Reliable estimates of LRA numbers in the history of their insurgency are impossible to come by and it is unclear whether the LRA kept any records.

The command structure of the LRA is referred to as 'control alter', though there is not much information about it. The control alter had five levels of seniority. The topmost level was the Chairman, who was also the Commander-in-Chief. This

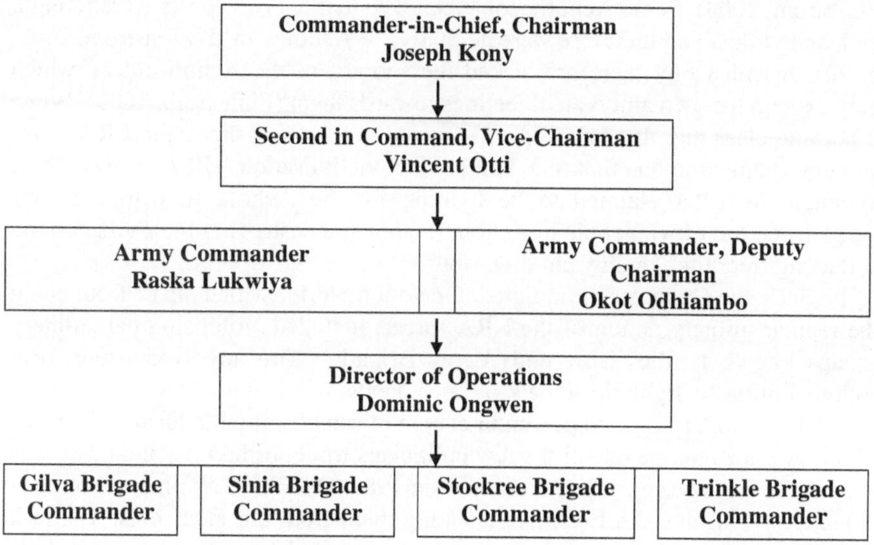

Figure 2.1 The LRA command structure: the control alter.[3]

position was occupied by Joseph Kony. Second in Command was Vice-Chairman Vincent Otti. The third level of command was that of the Army Commanders. Okot Odhiambo held the position of Army Commander and Deputy Chairman. The other Army Commander was Raska Lukwiya. Below the Army Commander was the Director of Operations, Dominic Ongwen. At the lowest level of the control alter were four brigades referred to as Gilva, Sinia, Stockree and Trinkle, headed by commanders.

Although the above command structure did exist, the LRA troops were constantly on the move and spread out across the vast jungles of southern Sudan and northern Uganda from where they operated and it is doubtful whether they kept track of every group of fighters. Some sources claim that field commanders operated with a certain degree of autonomy.

Kony fully expected the Acholi people to give him their popular support since he had taken-up their cause and had links with Lakwena's HSMF, which had enjoyed popular support. However, the people saw it as '[having] something of a schizophrenic or disjointed nature about it' (Westbrook, 2000, p. 5). For instance, to accomplish its goals all members of the LRA had to be formally initiated, cleansed and be predisposed to violence. This created an organisational culture predicated on exceptional cruelty, terror and fanaticism. The initiation rites included clubbing, stamping and beating friends and relatives to death, then licking their brains, drinking their blood and even eating their flesh as part of the indoctrination process following abduction (Doom & Vlassenroot, 1999).

Because of this, many Acholis questioned Kony's spiritual and military objectives. This deprived the LRA of the kind of enthusiastic support the Acholi had offered to Alice Lakwena and her HSMF/M (Westbrook, 2000, p. 5; Finnström, 2003). Some Acholi people believed that Kony's spirits were foreign, evil, and violent and therefore were not native to Acholi world (Finnström, 2003, p. 20). Joseph Kony therefore lacked the support of the Acholi elders, which may explain his own ambivalent feelings towards them (Finnström, 2003). When it became clear that the Acholi people would not support them, the LRA's war strategy changed to one that relied on civilian victimisation (HRW, 1997). Thus, although the LRA claimed to be fighting for the Acholi, they turned their weapons on their own people in Acholi, looting and destroying their villages and abducting 'recruits', mainly children (ibid.).

In 1991, the Government initiated 'Operation North' which, apart from being the regular military action of the NRA forces, included mobilising paramilitary groups known as the 'Bow and Arrow Brigade'. This involved using local Acholi militia to fight the rebels by any means, even with bows and arrows (HURIFO, 2002, p. 7). The person in charge of establishing the local militia was Betty Oyella Bigombe one of the few politicians from northern Uganda who was incorporated in Museveni's Government in 1986. Operation North was aimed at completely crushing the LRA and isolating them from the grassroots. The lack of popular support for the LRA among the local population seems to have made this possible. The Government also resorted to recruiting children to serve in Local Defence Units (LDUs), which amounted to vigilante groups.

These strategies did not succeed in rooting out the LRA but did have rather negative repercussions. The participation of the Acholi in the Bow and Arrow Brigade and LDU was interpreted by the LRA as an attempt to put the population against the rebel group (HRW, 2003b). As indicated, the LRA therefore resorted to a policy of civilian victimisation, as described above, in order to coerce the Acholi people to support them (Doom & Vlassenroot, 1999). Until 1991, the LRA had not engaged in civilian victimisation. They had carried out raids for supplies in which they forced captive villagers to carry for them and then released them. The LRA also engaged in sporadic but large-scale attacks, which may have been meant to expose the Government's incapacity to offer security to the people (Sanchez, 2007). Though Operation North may appear to be a failed military strategy, it managed to create bad blood between the LRA and the local population thereby destroying the popular support base for the insurgents. In this respect, LRA brutality against its own people could be understood to be a response to what it considered was the betrayal of the people the organisation had sought to emancipate.

Bigombe peace talks of 1994

In 1994, after the failure of Operation North, Betty Bigombe initiated peace talks between the Government and the LRA in an attempt to restore peace (Doom & Vlassenroot, 1999). According to the Human Rights and Peace Centre, (HURIPEC 2004, pp. 92–3), this was the first face-to-face peace negotiation between the Government and the LRA. Bigombe initiated the talks through

Yusuf Okwonga Adek, who was based in Gulu and was one of Kony's most trusted people. He had been detained previously at Luzira prison on charges of collaborating with rebels, but was released and returned to his home near Gulu town (O'Kadameri, 2002). Previous intermediaries, who were not genuine, had claimed to have close contacts with the rebels so as to get goods such as money and bicycles in return for letters purportedly written by rebel commanders. Adek, however, had genuine contact with the rebels. He initiated genuine negotiations between Bigombe and the LRA (ibid.). As part of their demands the LRA asked for a blanket amnesty for their combatants stating that they would not surrender but were willing to come home. As the negotiations were taking place between the Government and the LRA, Kony was also talking to, and seeking support from, the Sudanese Government. This caused the Government to disregard Kony and claim that he was simply buying time. During a meeting held on 10 January 1994, Kony demanded that he be given six months to consolidate his fight for demobilisation. But in February of the same year, the LRA walked out of negotiations claiming that the NRA were trying to ensnare them. Four days later, President Museveni announced a one-week ultimatum for the LRA to surrender, bringing an end to the negotiations (Doom & Vlassenroot, 1999, p. 24). Immediately after Museveni gave the ultimatum of February 1994, LRA fighters crossed over to Sudan to escape the Government's anticipated counter-insurgency.

It is not clear who really undermined the peace deal. Some commentators think that it was President Museveni who jeopardised the prospects of a peace deal when he abruptly announced his seven-day ultimatum (Westbrook, 2000). Doom and Vlassenroot (1999, p. 24) believe that the Acholi diaspora may have been pulling strings from abroad in order to undermine the peace deal. Some army officers in the NRA may have thought that there was no need to sign a truce with a weaker enemy who was already virtually defeated. What is significant is that neither party wholeheartedly embraced the peace deal in entirety. Since most Acholi had been very enthusiastic about the peace talks and were ready to settle with Museveni's Government, Kony yet again passed a collective guilty sentence, turning against his own people and drastically intensifying his policy.

The collapse of the 1994 peace talks and the seven-day ultimatum marked a turning point in the history of the war. It was around this time that the LRA moved to southern Sudan to seek refuge from NRA counter-insurgency. The LRA, with the support of the Sudanese Government, established their base in Sudan which they used as a base from which to launch their civilian atrocities for over a decade. They also received the much-needed supplies of weapons to continue fighting the Ugandan army. In Sudan, Kony found a base conducive to establishing his rebel group. Southern Sudan had been the seat of rebel activity carried out by the Sudanese Liberation Movement/Army (SPLM/A), led by John Garang, against the Khartoum Government. The military environment of Sudan in the 1990s was so muddled that it was not easy to distinguish between armed rebel groups and civilians (Schomerus, 2007, p. 19; Apuuli, 2005, p. 39). This made it easier for the LRA to gain root in that country, especially among the

Sudanese Acholi who considered the LRA to be their brothers (Branch & Mampilly, 2005). The LRA also found some support among the Acholi of Sudan. The Acholi of Sudan supported the LRA to demonstrate their rebellion against the SPLM/A. The SPLM/A was dominated by the Dinka, one of the dominant ethnic groups in southern Sudan, and alienated other groups such as the Acholi and Madi from Equatoria Province in South Sudan (Schomerus, 2007, p. 19).

For its part, the Khartoum Government found an opportunity to retaliate against the Ugandan Government's support of the SPLM/A by giving sanctuary and military support to the LRA to fight the Government of Uganda (Allen, 2006, pp. 48–9). The Ugandan Government had been giving support to the SPLM/A through the Acholi districts of northern Uganda (Weeks, 2002, p. 7). The involvement of the Government of Sudan through the provision of military support to the LRA was one of the most devastating and complicating contributions to the conflict and played a significant role in the longevity of the northern Uganda conflict (Prunier, 2004, p. 359). Indeed the conflict situation in Sudan played a significant a role in the northern Uganda conflict, to the extent that some northern Ugandans even thought that the long-standing war was a proxy war between Uganda and Sudan (ibid.).

The Carter Peace Agreement and Operation Iron Fist

The year 1998 was yet another turning point in the history of the war. Both the Sudanese and Ugandan governments had decided to ease the tension that had existed between them. The two countries thus decided to enter into an agreement in 1998. The agreement was brokered by former US President Jimmy Carter through the American Carter Center (Neu, 2002). Sudan had been particularly keen to improve its diplomatic relations with its neighbours and the US. The Clinton administration had branded Sudan a terrorist state following its alleged role in the assassination attempt on Egyptian President Hosni Mubarak on 26 June 1995 and its hosting of Osama bin Laden, the mastermind of the 1998 terrorist attacks on the US embassies in Kenya and Tanzania (Deng, 1995; Neu, 2002). In 1998 the US bombed an alleged chemical weapons factory in Khartoum. Sudan thus sought, through Jimmy Carter, to influence US policy on Sudan and improve their diplomatic ties.

Uganda may have envisaged that improved diplomatic relations with Sudan would make the latter withdraw its support for the LRA, thus making it easy to deal with the LRA (Neu, 2002). In the late 1990s, the Ugandan Government was already weighed down by three wars. The UPDF were fighting against the LRA in the north of the country; in the West Nile Bank Front the forces were engaged against the Allied Democratic Forces (ADF) and the Uganda National Rescue Front II (UNRF II). In the Democratic Republic of Congo (DRC) Ugandan forces were engaged in fighting in the war involving Angola, Namibia, Zimbabwe and Rwanda. Thus Museveni may have wanted to redeploy troops from the north and west to fight in the DRC (ibid.).

Following the talks brokered by the Carter Center, an agreement was signed between the Ugandan and Sudanese governments on 8 December 1999. According to the agreement, Sudan was to stop supporting the LRA while Uganda was to reciprocate by withdrawing its support for the SPLA. This agreement seems to have led to a change in political climate in the region since a considerable calm was achieved in northern Uganda after 1999. But the calm that had started to return to northern Uganda disappeared in March 2002, when a new counter-insurgency operation, dubbed 'Operation Iron Fist', was launched by the UPDF in Sudan. The aim of this operation was to eradicate the LRA from their bases in southern Sudan. The operation followed an agreement between the governments of Uganda and Sudan, which allowed Ugandan troops into the Sudanese territory in order to deal with the LRA rebels (Apuuli, 2005, p. 40). According to Apuuli (ibid.), the president was at that time very upbeat about finally defeating the insurgents.

Operation Iron Fist had mixed results. Schomerus (2007, p. 22) observes that, Operation Iron Fist was one of the bloodiest periods of the war, marked by regular helicopter gunship attacks by the UPDF on the LRA. The LRA, in retaliation, launched ground attacks. The battle left a good number of LRA and UPDF dead. The civilian population in Eastern Equatoria, where the LRA were based and which became the battleground, also suffered enormously. The expected routing of the LRA by the UPDF did not actually take place, and the LRA remained in Eastern Equatoria for a further four years until the Juba Peace Talks began in Juba. Even though the LRA was not completely dislodged from its base, Kony no longer had fixed bases in the southern Sudan area near the Uganda border from which he could launch attacks on Uganda (Apuuli, 2005, p. 40).

Overall, Operation Iron Fist did not bring positive results. The LRA in fact expanded its area from the original Gulu, Pader and Kitgum districts to other northern Uganda districts such as Lira, Apac and the two districts of Katakwi and Soroti in the Teso region. Since the LRA base in southern Sudan was destabilised through the operation, some LRA troops returned to northern Uganda (HRW, 2003d). The Acholi Religious Leaders' Peace Initiative (ARLPI) remarked that Operation Iron Fist was one of the worst security miscalculations of the Government as it had doubled the number of displaced persons (Apuuli, 2005). According to the United Nations Office for the Coordination of Humanitarian Affairs (UNOCHA) the number of internally displaced persons (IDPs) shot up from 800,000 to 1.2 million or more (HRW, 2003d). The fact that the Government referred the situation in northern Uganda to the ICC in December 2003, one year after the operation, also meant that the operation was not completely successful in clearing the LRA.

The LRA human rights abuses in northern Uganda

Abduction of children

The protracted conflict in northern Uganda was characterised by massive human rights violations suffered in the hands of the rebels as well as government soldiers. One of the hallmarks of the LRA atrocities in the northern region was the abduction of children. The rebels abducted children, boys and girls alike, mostly between the ages of 12 and 16 years old, but at times as young as 8 or 9 (UNHCHR, 1999). The rebels carried out these abductions by invading camps, villages or schools in large numbers and rounding up the people living in the settlements. In this way they captured as many as 30 children in a single raid (HRW, 2003d, p. 7). There were numerous cases of abductions during the 20 years of insurgency. But the most infamous of all abduction cases is that of St. Mary's College in Aboke, in the northern Apec district. The incident took place on 10 October 1996 when about 200 armed men broke into the school and captured 139 secondary school girls who were between 13 and 16 years of age. Later, 109 girls were released. By 2006, 5 of the remaining 30 children had died; all except 2 were eventually released (Foundation for Human Rights Initiative, January 2007, p. 14; UNICEF, 2005).

A semblance of calm seems, nonetheless, to have fallen over northern Uganda between 1999 and 2002, largely the result of international factors, especially the diplomatic agreement between Khartoum and Kampala brokered by Jimmy Carter in 1999. But the level of abductions rose sharply from the moment the LRA returned from Sudan following the UPDF's Operation Iron Fist launched inside Sudan in 2002. In 2002, the United Nations Human Rights Commission (UNHRC) reported that since the inception of the conflict in the north, it was estimated that over 26,833 people had been abducted, including more than 10,000 children destined to become child soldiers, with girls being especially targeted to become sex slaves (UNHRC, 2003). According to the report, most of the so-called combatants in the LRA were children who were abducted or fathered by rebel commanders. They formed 85 per cent of the LRA forces (ibid.). UNICEF estimates that some 20,000 children were abducted in 19 years of war (UNICEF, 2005). In 2004, the United Nations (UN) Department of Public Affairs estimated that in the 18 years since the inception of the war in 1986 about 30,000 children had been abducted (UNDPA, 2004). The World Development Report of 2007, estimated that up to 66,000 children may have been abducted by the LRA, the majority of whom remained unaccounted for (World Bank, 2006, p. 182).

There is a certain lack of clarity with regard to the information on abduction records. The uncertainty vis-à-vis the number of children abducted is due to the lack of accessible information about the LRA as well as the dislocation of the families concerned. Much of the available information was obtained through interviews of ex-abductees or their families. Since some families may have been entirely wiped out by the LRA or because some children may have died in the bush, it is possible that not all the information about abductions was discovered.

Apart from abductions themselves, the process of converting the abductees into soldiers was itself very inhuman. Since the LRA relied almost entirely on abductions to provide them with fighters, they devised a peculiar method of training and retaining their forces. They used extreme violence as a means of achieving psychological control over the abductees (HRW, 2005). Children were subjected to brutal treatment as child soldiers, labourers, sexual slaves and were even forced to kill others (HRW, 2003a; McKay & Mazurana, 2004). The abductees were intimidated and brutalised to such an extent that they were often too frightened to return home. According to the UNDPA (2004) report,

> [o]ver half of the children surveyed – over 300, all [of whom] had been abducted at an average age of 12 – had been severely beaten, 77 per cent had witnessed another person being killed, 39 per cent had killed another person and 39 per cent had abducted other children. Over one-third of the girls had been raped while 18 per cent had given birth while in captivity.

The indoctrination process began from the moment a child was abducted. The abducted child would be forced to beat and kill their own parents, sisters or brothers. The killing of a child's own relatives was intended to cut the child off from his or her family roots and ordinary life and also to predispose a child to commit any form of violent act. After having been incorporated in the LRA ranks, the abductees were required to engage in combat actions against government soldiers, capture new recruits, loot and work long hours for their commanders. They received training in combat actions, the handling of light firearms, such as AK-47s, and in how to launch hand grenades.

Combat actions were the most dangerous encounters for the newly abducted boys. According to one of the ex-LRA abductees, they would be placed in the front line to test the strength of their opponents, and in such cases the casualties were severe given the boys' lack of experience in combat actions. This meant that children were used by senior combatants to shield themselves. Those badly wounded would be shot dead by their fellow rebels as they were no longer useful. Kony believed that those who were wounded were impure and did not deserve to be a member of the group. Since the LRA did not have proper doctors and medical supplies, the conditions of the wounded were deplorable. According to Joseph Okwera (Interview, 17 March 2008), who was abducted in 1997 and escaped from the bush in 2007, those fighting in the bush did not even have medical supplies. While in combat with the UPDF, a bullet lodged in the left side of Okwera's abdomen. Since there were no medical facilities in the bush, he had to rely on his friends to operate and remove the bullet using a sharp hooked piece of metal. His wound was disinfected with hot water (ibid.). Apart from their involvement in direct combat action, the children were commanded to undertake other unimaginably risky tasks such as creeping into villages to interact with other children of their age in order to gather information for the rebels (Okulu, Interview, 30 March 2008). In this respect child soldiers became instrumental in undertaking rebel activities.

Generally girls were not assigned to combat, looting, and abduction tasks. Following their abductions, many younger girls were reported to have been assigned as brides to commanders in forced marriages, having to carry out gruelling domestic tasks and endure long hours and continuous beatings (HRW, 2003d). The abducted girls were responsible for cooking, cleaning, fetching water and food and for caring for any of their children who may have been born in the bush. In this respect girls served as sex slaves or wives to high-ranking LRA commanders. However, according to the LRA code of conduct, subjecting the girls to sexual activities against their will did not constitute rape. For them, rape consisted in having sexual intercourse without the approval of the LRA top commanders (Okidi, Interview, 17 May 2008). Rape was therefore institutionalised in the LRA code of sexual conduct and considered normal practice in the bush where a sexual act with a girl against her will was approved as a reward for those who had qualified for sexual intercourse (ibid.). Rape was also approved as a punishment. According to one ex-abductee (Interview, 17 May 2008), gang rape was permitted as punishment when a girl tried to escape and was caught. This 'control' of the sexual act was due to the LRA belief system that sexual intercourse was considered impure unless socially sanctioned. Moreover, the LRA soldiers believed that Kony had supernatural powers to know when someone had engaged in an 'illicit' sexual act (ibid.). This attitude towards sex informed the abduction of younger girls who were considered to be virgins and hence pure.

Discipline was enforced either through the death penalty or through other cruel and violent acts. Children who did not follow directives as required had parts of their bodies – hands or lips – chopped off or were killed by their fellow abductees. The chopping of body parts was, according to one former abductee, part of the LRA doctrine, probably a fundamentalist application of the Biblical phrase that 'if a part of your body leads you to sin then you must chop it off' (JB, Interview, 18 May 2008). When abductees attempted to escape, those intercepted would be punished severely by being killed or forced to kill their fellow abductees as an example to other abductees. One woman, abducted by the LRA in 2004 and later rescued by the UPDF, told the author of this book how a girl who was abducted together with her attempted to escape:

> They [LRA soldiers] pursued the girl and captured her. When she was brought back to the camp, the captors beat her to death using crude weapons. They hit her on the head, neck and back until she succumbed. When she died, the one who was in charge of the killing commanded me to carry the body away to bury. This was meant to be a warning to me and others not to try the same.
>
> (Anonymous ex-abductee, Interview, Kitgum 18 May 2008)

Since any insubordination carried with it the death penalty, the level of allegiance to the LRA command was very high. Through this kind of training, the LRA managed, to a large extent, to instil psychological detachment vis-à-vis the abductees' previous lives at home and developed an organisation founded on a cruel and torturous mode of operation.

The child soldiering adopted by the LRA was clearly an example of child abuse and immoral. Child soldiering became a common trend in guerrilla warfare in the last part of the twentieth century and the beginning of the twenty-first century, practised not only in Africa but also in other conflict zones around the world. The phenomenon was prevalent in Uganda, Liberia, Sierra Leone, Burundi, Rwanda, Congo-Brazzaville, the Democratic Republic of the Congo, Sudan, Ivory Coast as well as Afghanistan and Burma among others (Coalition to Stop the Use of Child Soldiers, 2004). In Uganda, child soldiering first gained prominence during Milton Obote's repressive reign following the disputed 1980 elections. When President Yoweri Museveni was a rebel leader, the NRA/M movement included an estimated 3,000 child soldiers, boys and girls under the age of 16 and known as *kadogos*[4] (Keitetsi, 2002).

The phenomenon of child soldiering was a product of certain factors associated with failed states in most African countries which made children easy prey for recruitment into rebel or militia groups. These factors included the situation of protracted conflict and instability, poverty and the demographic dominance of children (Fuller, 2003, p. 2). The protracted conflict resulted in a shortage of soldiers either among government forces or rebel groups. As an alternative these groups resorted to recruiting child soldiers. Given the conflict situation, most families were likely to have been displaced or the parents killed, leaving children destitute and vulnerable. Poverty was likely to prevail in conflict-ridden regions, which meant that there were few opportunities for education and limited future prospects. All of these factors meant that children were more susceptible for recruitment (Singer, 2002). Some children joined rebel groups to revenge the killing of family members (Keitetsi, 2002; Brett & Specht, 2004). The factors associated with child soldiering were prevalent in northern Uganda and Kony's enlistment of child soldiers is therefore to be seen within the wider context of child soldiering in Africa. However, Kony's extremely brutal methods of recruitment, training and discipline call for particular parameters when interpreting the LRA's use of child soldiers.

We can recall that Kony claimed that he was inspired by Alice Lakwena. Lakwena herself had called for an ethnic renewal. It is likely, therefore, that Kony was also motivated by the desire for ethnic renewal. Indeed Kony sought to cleanse the Acholi community, which he considered impure. According to Human Rights Watch, the LRA targeted Acholi children as the next loyal generation, the *tabula rasa* that would be raised in accordance with Kony's commandments, remain loyal to Kony's ideology and breed a loyal generation (HRW, 2003c, p. 20; Human Rights Watch, September 2005). Moreover, the fact that the LRA did not enjoy popular support among the Acholi people, not only exacerbated his anger against the Acholi, but also gave him a reason to resort to abductions as a means of enlisting their personnel.

Torture, mutilation and killing of civilians

Apart from the abduction of children, the LRA tortured, mutilated, maimed and killed civilians. Victims' hands, feet, noses, ears, lips and breasts were cut off, often as punishment. These brutal tactics promoted fear and deterred people from cooperating with the Government (HRW, September 2005). Margaret Oyella (Interview, 18 April 2009), a 55-year old woman who lived in Kitgum, told this author that in 1993 rebels attacked her home and forced her to watch as they killed her brother. Her only son was severely injured when his head was hacked open. He never recovered fully. In her words, 'his head is neither straight nor stable' (ibid.). She also watched as her nephew was killed. She said,

> The rebels cut all over his body until he died. Then they piled his body parts in a heap. The sight was disgusting as the body parts looked like red meat. Since that time, I always experienced nightmares and always thinking of some people coming to kill me.
>
> (Ibid.)

The year 2005 was one of the worst periods. In March 2005, the *New Vision* daily newspaper reported that seven civilians had been beaten to death with hoes in Adjumani district in an attack on the Dzaipi trading centre (Allio & Moro, 2005). The Adjumani district, which is situated northwest of Gulu district on the right bank of the Nile bordering Sudan, was soft sport for LRA attacks. The district's vicinity to Sudan meant that it was a strategic place for the LRA to raid and then escape into Sudan. In May 2005, ten civilians were killed in a raid near Koch Goma camp in the Gulu district (Wallis, 2005). These are just a few of the numerous cases.

The LRA abducted adult persons to transport their loot. Refusal to cooperate would result in severe beating and death. Those who were unable to carry the loads for lack of strength were likely to be killed. Two young men, who were members of the LRA between 1997 and 2007 and chose to remain anonymous, narrated the horrors of the LRA actions. An old man was killed simply because he was unable to carry a load of loot for the rebels. The man was very old and frail with the result that he fell under the weight of the load. This seemed to have angered some of the boys who beat him to death (Two anonymous returnees, Interview, 18 May 2008). However, in most cases those who cooperated and managed to deliver the goods to the bush would be released soon afterwards.

The mutilation of the body parts of civilians started in the early 1990s. Matthew Odida reasoned that mutilation was a reaction to the Government's decision to deploy local militia against the LRA in 1991. The LRA interpreted this as a betrayal by the community (Odida, Interview, 12 April 2008). To retaliate they resorted to cutting off the hands, feet, noses, ears, lips and breasts of victims. Thus, mutilations were part of the LRA strategy to discourage people from cooperating with the Government. According to one of the local dailies, *The Monitor*, one of the LRA commanders, Same Kolo, surrendered to the Government in early 2005. After his surrender, President Museveni became very excited and, on 17 February 2005, announced that the LRA was finished since its top commanders had started to surrender (Nyakairu, 2005). This would appear to have annoyed the LRA which set about mutilating civilians. A few days after the publication of Kolo's surrender, 11 women were abducted, driven into an abandoned hut where they were stripped naked, and mutilated (Kirunda, 2005).

The brutality of the LRA combatants, according to an ex-abductee, was attributable to Kony's successful indoctrination of abductees which stripped them of any human feeling. Having alienated the children from their families, social surroundings, social formation skills and social networks, the abductees lost their moral bearing and acquired a new form of social and moral universe. This predisposition transformed the LRA into lethal, violent and brutal, soldiers.

Social effect of the war on the community

Apart from cases of abduction, rape, mutilation and torture, other adverse predicaments, arising from LRA activities, were suffered by families and the wider society. These included the socio-economic dislocation resulting from the war, especially the phenomenon of protected villages and a general lack of security. One of effects of LRA activities was the phenomenon of 'night commuters'. Fearing the too common nightly abductions by the rebel LRA, thousands of children travelled at night from rural villages into Gulu town and the Lacor trading centre to escape this fate. They slept in hospitals, on verandas, in bus parks, on church grounds, and in factories. In the mornings, they returned to their homes (HRW, 2003c, p. 6). Another predicament was the loss of property through LRA destruction. The ICC (2004) estimates that, by 2004, the LRA had burnt at least 1,946 houses and 1,600 storage granaries and looted at least 1,327 houses, 116 villages and 307 shops, leaving the people destitute.

The population of northern Uganda was also displaced from their homes to IDP camps. The uprooting of the people was basically a government programme. Although the researcher of this work discovered that in Gulu, Kitgum and Amuru some people had moved voluntarily to the camps, the majority were forced by the Government. According to one district leader (Interview, 10 April 2008), the Government opted to take the people to these camps in order to facilitate its own military operations and to deny the LRA access to villages. The Government reasoned that it would be easier to protect the civilians if they were concentrated in camps. For Matthew Odida (Interview, 12 April 2008), a resident of the Pabo IDP camp, under the Government's 'scorched earth policy', the intention was to cut off any lifeline to the rebels. The scorched earth policy is a military strategy adopted since ancient times and consists of destroying anything that might be helpful to the enemy as it moved through or retreated from an area. Initially, it was limited to the burning of crops in order to deny the enemy food resources, but its contemporary application includes destroying, not only food stocks, but also any other infrastructural facility – shelter, transportation, communications and industrial resources that could assist the enemy. The scorched earth policy was one of the war tactics successfully adopted by the Soviet Republic against German invasion during the Second World War.

The Ugandan Government's use of the scorched earth policy against the LRA entailed moving the population to protected camps. The Government envisaged that, by doing this, it would deny the LRA not only the possibility of recruiting child soldiers, which had formed a key source of their personnel, but also food supplies. As a result, all homes were destroyed and the people displaced. According to the HRW (2003c, p. 5), between the years 1996 and 2000, up to 400,000 civilians, predominantly from Gulu district, were forced into IDP camps by government soldiers. The HRW (2003c) further reports that, in 2002, the LRA returned to Uganda from Sudan where Ugandan forces had launched a counter-insurgency operation, ‘Operation Iron Fist’, to flush out the LRA. Following this return another 400,000 were forced to leave their homes and to relocate in camps, mainly in the Kitgum and Pader districts. By 2003, up to 800,000 people out of an estimated total population of 1,100,000 in Acholiland were living in IDP camps (HRW, 2003c, p. 5). According to figures given by Global IPD in December 2003 up to 1.5 million people were displaced in northern Uganda and resided in IDP camps; the majority were mainly from the districts of Gulu, Kitgum, Pader and Lira (Global IDP Database, December 2003). Displacement in Gulu, Kitgum, Pader in general accounted for more than 80 per cent of the population in Acholiland and ranged from 70 to 80 per cent of the 1.5 million IDPs in northern Uganda (ibid.).

When all crops were burnt and all cattle taken away ‘to be kept safely’, the message given to the people was that the cattle would be returned once stability had returned. This, however, never happened. According to Dominic Ochar (Interview, 3 June 2008) the scorched earth policy programme was devastating. Cattle were the main source of income for the people and allowed them to educate their children and manage other financial needs. According to Kizito Odhiambo (Interview, 5 May 2009), cattle were also a source of milk and meat. As stockholders, the people of northern Uganda traded in livestock and livestock products, such as milk, ghee, skin and hides. Livestock also provided them with manure for their farms. Removing the cattle meant that the people were completely disempowered and destitute, forced to rely on donors. Because of the security situation, camp dwellers were not able to travel to their fields to till their land for fear of being attacked by the LRA. The UPDF was unable to provide people with adequate protection when they worked fields. Moreover, if the civilians had to travel a significant distance to work their farms, they would be labelled LRA collaborators and severely punished by the UPDF (ibid.). This experience was interpreted by many people whom I talked to as a scheme by Museveni’s Government to fight and exterminate the Acholi. The scorched earth policy seemed to be a policy not so much against the LRA as against civilians. This is captured by Adam Branch (2004, p. 23):

> The displaced people’s camps themselves were created through a government campaign of displacement, including bombing and burning down entire villages. Those in camps cannot leave because the UPDF kills civilians outside them. The government does not protect the camps, so they are easy targets for the predation of the LRA – and often of underpaid, undisciplined UPDF soldiers. The failure to provide food, medicine, decent housing, and protection, in direct contravention of the Geneva Conventions, has led many Acholi to see the camps not as ‘protected villages’ (the

government's euphemism), but as a calculated effort to destroy the Acholi as an ethnic group – as genocide.

As mentioned early, the displacement phenomenon resulted in severe humanitarian conditions. Food insecurity posed a serious threat to the people's well-being and resulted in high levels of malnutrition. For some time food security was mitigated by the international donor agencies, such as the World Food Programme (WFP) which supplied people with food. By 2005 the WFP was catering for around 1.4 million people in the region, providing about 75 per cent of daily requirements per person (World Food Programme, 2005). This programme, according to Fr Crispin Opio (Interview, 29 May 2008), made the situation bearable but only for some of the time. But donor fatigue would ensue eventually afterwards. Benson Otto (Interview, 20 March 2008) observes that, '[w]e used to receive good food rations from organisations, but now it is not there, we are really suffering'. Even with sustained donor support, adds Otto, relying on donations was not befitting for people who could till their own land, produce their own food and keep their own cattle. This sentiment was shared by many informants.

The scorched earth policy also failed because it did not prevent the LRA from recruiting through abduction. Although the camps were meant to make it easy for government forces to stave off the LRA, government forces failed to protect the camps adequately. The camps made it even easier for the LRA to round up abductees and take them away. Moreover, any single attack was likely to result in many deaths since the camps were very congested (ibid.). According to a survey carried out by the World Health Organization (WHO) (2005), it is estimated that, between the months of January and July 2005, about 12,000 were abducted from the camps. Thus, the camps did not adequately serve their purpose.

Generally, the conditions in these camps were deplorable. Camp dwellers lived in dehumanising conditions, in tiny, densely-built, grass-thatched mud huts, with poor sanitation, no toilets, no water and no heath facilities. Human waste spread all over the pavements. This was yet another form of threat to human security. Moreover, Pabo, one of the largest camps in Amuru and probably the largest in the Acholi region, had a population of about 62,000 people without facilities (Bosco, Interview, 4 April 2008). Over-population meant that the grass-thatched huts were very close to each other which made incidences of fire outbreak very common and exacerbated security risks. Fire outbreaks were also common because of the hot and windy weather, especially during the dry season. Camp life therefore subjected people to health hazards.

Fr Charles Odwar (Interview, 16 March 2008) observed that, from the moment the people moved to the camp, having left their farms and had their crops destroyed and cattle taken away, people's health deteriorated. Malaria was prevalent. Poor sanitation in the camps brought about widespread cases of cholera and diarrhoea. In a survey conducted by WHO in 2005, mortality rates were very high, calculated as over 1,000 deaths per week in the region, commonly resulting from malaria, fever, cholera, AIDS and violence (World Health Organisation, 2005). According to a report produced by the Norwegian Refugee Council/Global IDP Project (12 December 2005, p. 1):

> [a]ccess to health care, water, education, land and shelter and the denial of freedom of movement [...] have contributed to a situation which has yielded a mortality rate which is above emergency thresholds and nearly double the mortality rate of Darfur, the conflict generally considered the worst humanitarian crisis in Africa.

Given this dislocation and poverty, education was seriously affected, there were no schools and parents had no resources to pay school fees for their children. Most mothers were widowed or their husbands shirked their responsibilities through lack of ability (Oyella, Interview, 18 April 2009). Girls were easily lured out of school by sexual predators, especially the UPDF. Soldiers were among the few people to have a regular salary in the camps. Accordingly, they often took advantage of the poor conditions suffered by young women and girls (ibid.).

Atrocities committed by government soldiers

Apart from atrocities committed by the LRA there were also claims of atrocities committed by government forces, the UPDF, formerly the NRA. The atrocities by the UPDF amounted to human rights violations and violation of international humanitarian law (HRW, 2003a). HRW reports that the UPDF, especially the 11th Battalion of the NRA, killed civilians in northern Uganda. People found outside the IDP camps were commonly assumed by the army to be rebels or rebel collaborators and were shot at by the army. Several victims were even shot inside the camps (HRW, 2003a). Many shootings occurred at night, at close range, and were deliberate, not merely cases of mistaken identity as the army often asserted in its defence (HRW, September 2005). The UPDF soldiers beat or tortured people almost every day for the first two months of 2005 (ibid.). The HRW adds that the 11th Battalion treated civilians, whom they were supposed to protect, in a heartless and brutal manner. Civilians alleged to be 'rebel collaborators' were commonly detained and sometimes tortured or severely beaten with sticks as part of the interrogation process (ibid.). Rape and other sexual violence were also frequent occurrences in and around the camps. A UNICEF report released on 15 June 2005 concluded that rape was the most common form of violence in the sprawling Pabo IDP camp in Gulu district (UNICEF, 2005). The lack of discipline within the army and the almost total lack of accountability contributed to an environment in which women were extremely vulnerable to abuse from the UPDF.

The foregoing account has not only revealed the criminal aspects of the conflict in northern Uganda, but also the social, economic dimensions of the war in a broader perspective. These included destabilisation, torture, loss of family members, loss of material well-being and work, and uncertainties associated with IDP camp life. Parents and relatives did not escape the extreme trauma associated with the predicaments of their children. Thus, all the populations living in northern Uganda and the Acholi, in particular, suffered not only physical injuries inflicted on individuals but also very serious social injuries inflicted on the community as a whole. Chris Dolan (2009) refers to such suffering as 'social torture'. According to Dolan, when directed at individuals, torture directly affects only a minority and the majority does not feel the impact of it, but in social torture only a minority will escape its impact. Social torture may constitute the cumulative impact of multiple violations, triggering a visible symptom, the impact of which cannot be traced back to any one of those violations in particular (ibid.). In the case of northern Uganda, these multiple violations include the human rights violations committed by the NRA in the north after it had seized power, the multiple human rights violations committed by the LRA and the phenomenon of being forced to abandon one's home. These inhuman conditions in northern Uganda affected the very core of human well-being and constituted serious human rights violations.

Conclusion

What emerges from this overview and analysis of the LRA insurgency in northern Uganda is that there is a multiplicity of factors that contributed to the start and continuation of the conflict in northern Uganda. One of the major underlying factors of the war was the deep-seated divisions between northern and southern Uganda, a divide that engendered a fear of being dominated by other regions and ethnic groups. This served as a barrier to national unity. By inheriting and exploiting the economic and political structures established by the British colonial administration under their divide and rule policy, Uganda's postcolonial leaders, from the very beginning, built the country upon ethno-political fault lines. Obote, Amin and Museveni all exploited ethnic differences to win support from the respective groups. The civil war that raged in the Luwero Triangle between 1981 and 1985 and the atrocities that characterised it were the result of this propensity of political leaders to manipulate ethnic divisions. In this respect, the Ugandan political elite continued the politics of divide and rule, especially the politics that increased the divide between the south and the north of the country. An enduring political culture characterised by animosity, deep-seated hatred and distrust developed. Another important element worth noting was the militarisation of politics. A militarised culture was established, a culture that became an instrument of domestic politics for the following decades. The use of the military was instrumentalised in the solving of political disputes. The colonial government had implanted this culture as a divide and rule instrument to weaken the possibility of uniting opposition forces. They did this by building a militarily strong north while empowering an economically strong south. Obote too made use of the military following independence; Amin did the same in his endeavour to seize and consolidate state power; and Museveni used the military to seize and sustain political power. It therefore makes sense to argue that the

LRA believed they would not be able to realise political and economic emancipation for the north except through a military option. Thus, the foregoing has exposed the nature and extent of the conflict in northern Uganda and its ramifications. We have exposed the dynamics of the war in terms of its various aspects, exploring the criminal, sociopolitical and moral dimensions of the conflict. This chapter has demonstrated how the violence ran deeper than the phenomena of abduction and looting and pervaded all other aspects of people's lives. The victimisation was extensive, and the line between victim and perpetrator blurred. The perpetrators of vicious acts such as sexual torture, mutilation and murder were themselves the products of the very same kinds of acts. Dealing with this complex situation would certainly generate critical conundrums. It is against this background that this work has explored the appropriateness of the ICC, or alternative systems of transitional justice.

Notes

1 One, however, needs to be cautious not to attribute the mass death to massacres by UNLA since the Luwero Triangle was also a battlefield where both the government soldiers and rebels suffered serious casualties, a good number of NRA fighters being child soldiers.

2 In military terms, a reconnaissance unit is a unit tasked with conducting research to find out information about the enemy.

3 This LRA command structure is adopted from Enough (n.d.) Wanted by the ICC: The LRA's leaders: Who they are and what they've done. Enough, the project to end genocide and crimes against humanity. Available at www.enoughproject.org/files/pdf/lra_leaders.pdf.

4 The term *kodogos* was a derivation from Kiswahili word 'kidogo' which means small.

3 The International Criminal Court

A judicial response to LRA atrocities

Introduction

The anguish in northern Uganda remained largely ignored or over two decades. Tim Allan (2006, p. xiii) observes that only occasional media reports about strange cults, healing rituals, abducted children, night-commuting children and women mutilated by the LRA attracted attention. The international community had not, during these years, seriously grappled with the question of how to bring lasting peace and stability to the region. It was only when Jan Egeland, the United Nations Under-Secretary General for Humanitarian Affairs and Emergency Relief Coordinator, was appalled by the humanitarian conditions in northern Uganda upon visiting the region in November 2003 that the issue came to into the international limelight. Egeland, after visiting northern Uganda, declared that 'the situation is intolerable and we must agree as an international community, the UN and donors that this is totally unacceptable. Northern Uganda is the most forgotten crisis in the world' (*The Monitor*, November 2003). Following this revelation, the President of Uganda, Yoweri Museveni referred the matter to the ICC in 2003 (ICC, 2004). This referral was based on the allegation that the LRA had committed gross human rights violations, thereby contravening international humanitarian and human rights law. The LRA case was consonant with those crimes against humanity punishable according to the standard of the international rule of law. The grave crimes that had been committed by the LRA against the civilian population in northern Uganda for over 20 years gave the court a practical test case. Even though the atrocity crimes in northern Uganda had called for intervention for some time, the ICC intervention apparently met critical opposition from a section of the community. In this chapter we expose the judicial responses to the atrocities. This allows to us expose contradictions and complexities which emerge in the search for peace and justice in post-conflict situations.

Historical precedents in international criminal accountability

In retrospect, the stage for international accountability had already been set by the International Military Tribunal (IMT) established in Nuremberg by the Allied

Powers – France, Great Britain, USSR and USA – to try individual senior German and Japanese officials in the aftermath of the Second World War (Greenawalt, 2007, p. 590; Schabas, 2004, p. 5). Article 6 of the IMT Charter mandated the tribunal 'to try and punish persons who, acting in the interests of the European Axis countries, whether as individuals or as members of organisations' committed crimes against peace, war crimes, or crimes against humanity (Schwelb, 1949, p. 181), especially the German war criminals (Morris & Scharf, 1998, p. 3). The Nuremberg trials initiated the move towards the deconstruction of absolute sovereign power. Prior to 1945, the state was sovereign in an almost absolute sense, exercising supreme legal authority within its jurisdiction (Forsythe, 2006, p. 21). Events within a state were almost entirely outside the jurisdiction of international law, and criminal law was dominated by principles of territoriality and nationality (Tomuschat, 2006, p. 837). Accordingly, the way a government treated its citizens was considered to be a domestic affair. With the Nuremberg Tribunal, the international community came to understand that a government's treatment of its citizens, even in peace time, needed to be a matter of international concern (Ratner & Abrams, 2001). Slowly the protective umbrella of state sovereignty began to be questioned (Gowlland-Debbas, 2000, p. 312). Thus the Nuremberg Tribunal represents a benchmark in the development of international criminal justice (Schabas, 2004, pp. 1–2; Ratner & Abrams, 2001, p. 6).

Its novelty notwithstanding, critical voices among Germans argued that the IMT had violated the principle of legality according to which nobody should be prosecuted in respect of conduct of which he was not aware and which he could not be expected to have been aware of at the time of committing the offence. The tribunal was formed after the crimes had been committed, and its laws were written in retrospect. Until that time no leading statesman had ever been held accountable for launching a war (Tomuschat, 2006, p. 832). According to some of these German critics, there were also questions about IMT's impartiality. The fact that justice was being dispensed by prosecutors and judges from the four main victorious powers, with no single judge from a neutral country or from Germany, made the prosecutions a form of 'victor's justice' where the victorious punished the vanquished (Chaney, 1996; Tomuschat, 2006, p. 832). Given the political nature of the world wars, vengeance on the side of the Allied Powers could not be ruled out, and this was bound to influence German perceptions vis-à-vis the tribunals and to undermine the legitimacy of the tribunal. Moreover, the tribunal did not bring within its jurisdiction the crimes committed by the Allied Powers (Tomuschat, 2006, p. 833). The atomic bombings of Japanese civilians at Hiroshima and Nagasaki, which constituted violations of the laws of armed conflict, were ignored (ibid.). These voices already revealed the tenacity of the contestations between the aspirations of international justice and the interests of politics.

The ensuing Cold War frustrated the achievements that had been made in the field of human rights protection through international standards of justice. Ruti Teitel (2005, p. 837) observed that the post-Second World War trials which set such an important precedence in international criminal adjudication found no further parallels. The ensuing period was characterised by polarised international relations, suspicion, distrust and lack of friendly relations, none of which was conducive to nurturing the protection of human rights. While the USA and the Soviet Union remained suspicious of each other, each side supported allied developing countries to maintain, according to Teitel (2003b, p. 70), '... a stable bipolar balance of power'. This involved supporting dictatorial leaders in a clientele relationship in an endeavour to undermine each other.

However, the end of the Cold War in late 1989 dramatically changed the matrix of international relations. The demise of the Cold War and the collapse of the Soviet Union led to the collapse of authoritarian and totalitarian states in the former USSR and Eastern Europe (Shatzmiller, 2005). It also meant that dictatorial leaders in Africa who were sustained by their usefulness in balancing the Cold War equation became dispensable as they were no longer useful. As a consequence, many domestic, regional and international orders were suddenly open to challenge (ibid.). Cassese (2006, p. 724) observes that the collapse of the model of international relations that had characterised the Cold War brought about the fragmentation of the international community, leading to disorder. Far-reaching ethnic tensions and new forms of nationalism occurred, particularly in Central Europe, Eastern Europe and Africa. These tensions resulted in serious violations of human rights such as the ethnic cleansing in Bosnia from 1992 to 1995 and the genocide in Rwanda in 1994.

These developments led to an urgent need for the further development of international criminal justice and establishment of a permanent international criminal justice institution. The bloodshed characterising the post-Cold War periods pointed to the urgent need for not only an international human rights instrument but also a united international response to such crimes (Philipp, 2003, p. 334; Cassese, 2006, p. 723). Moreover, while serious crimes increased, the atmosphere that characterised the post-Cold War era in the 1990s created conditions that were conducive to the development of international criminal law to act against such crimes. The end of the Cold War meant a reduction in the animosity and mutual suspicion that had dominated international relations (Cassese, 2006, p. 724). The formation of the International Criminal Tribunal for Yugoslavia (ICTY), the International Criminal Tribunal for Rwanda (ICTR) and the ICC under the Rome Statute are to be understood in this light.

The horrific atrocities committed in the former Yugoslavia and Rwanda in the early and mid-1990s motivated many governments, prompted in particular by the United States, to seek criminal accountability through the creation of two international tribunals (Ratner & Abrams, 2001, p. 6). The ICTY constituted a significant advance on its predecessor, the Nuremberg Tribunal. In contrast to Nuremberg, it was created neither by the victors nor parties to the conflict, but by the United Nations (UN) representing the international community of states. Whereas the Nuremberg Tribunal judges were appointed by the victors, the ICTY judges came from across the world to ensure the international character of the ICTY (Morris & Scharf, 1998, p. 38; Chaney, 1995, pp. 57, 60). The Yugoslavian

Tribunal Statute would in turn influence the Rwanda Tribunal because both were driven by the spirit of international humanitarian law.

On 8 November, 1994 it was envisaged that prosecuting persons responsible for the 1994 genocide in Rwanda would contribute to the process of national reconciliation and to the restoration and maintenance of peace (UN, 1994). One of the significant contributions of the ICTR was the legal innovation of extending international humanitarian law to an internal conflict (Mose, 2005). According to customary international law, war was defined as a state of armed conflict between two or more states, but the 1994 Rwandan genocide constituted an internal armed conflict. The inclusion of Article 3 of the 1949 Geneva Convention regulating armed conflicts which are not of international nature and of the Nuremberg concept of crimes against humanity, made the ICTR Statute to transcend customary international law (ibid.). In doing so the Rwandan Tribunal represented an important extension of international humanitarian law to internal conflicts.

Further, the ICTR enjoyed supremacy over national courts and territories regarding crimes committed in Rwanda during the 1994 genocide and had the prerogative to request that any neighbouring state's court defer certain cases of indicted genocide criminal to its jurisdiction (UN Security Council, 1994). This request carried with it the threat of a penalty for non-compliance given that the Security Council would consider sanctions against any state for such non-compliance. This provision was crucial because states had offered safe sanctuary to perpetrators of serious atrocities. In addition, the ICTR provided an opportunity for evaluating the political impact of international criminal justice on post-conflict peacebuilding. The charging of individual leaders suspected of criminal liability played a significant role in discrediting, neutralising and destabilising the genocidal forces and delegitimising their role in political arena (Obote-Odora, 1999). Moreover, focusing on individuals, including high-powered state agents, lifted the burden of guilt that would rest on the Hutus as a group and had the effect of neutralising collective guilt.

Regardless of their achievements, both the ICTR and the ICTY encountered operational and institutional limitations which undermined their effectiveness (Mose, 2005). These limitations were associated with the absence of an established institutional model as the tribunals were ad hoc. Investigators, lawyers, judges and prosecutors came from varying legal and linguistic backgrounds. It became difficult to reconcile various legal traditions, making the process both time-consuming and costly. In addition, the costs of the tribunals were extremely high and they lacked sufficient resources for investigation and the employment of sufficient judicial personnel. These led to trial and prosecution delays (Human Rights Watch, 1999). Inadequate compensation, the overwhelming nature and scale of the work, and the risks involved in prosecuting war criminals caused the judicial personnel to fail to perform at maximum efficiency. These limitations became some of the motivating factors for expediting the establishment of the ICC. The international community understood that a permanent International Court would mitigate the above institutional challenges which had dogged the ad hoc tribunals.

The ICC was established following a UN diplomatic conference held between 15 June and 17 July 1998 in Rome, Italy where a statute was developed (Ratner & Abrams, 2001, p. 9). At this conference, governments overwhelmingly approved the statute to establish a permanent International Criminal Court. In total, 120 nations voted in favour, 7 against and 21 abstained. On 1 April 2002 the Rome Statute received more than the required 60 ratifications and entered into force on 1 July 2002 (Philipp, 2003, p. 331). The Rome Statute, Article 1(3) provides for the establishment of an International Criminal Court sitting in The Hague, The Netherlands and charged it with 'exercising its jurisdiction over persons for the most serious crimes of international concern, as referred to in this Statute' (UN, 1998). Crimes within the jurisdiction of the court, according to Article 5 of the Rome Statute, are the most serious ones and of concern to the international community as a whole. These include the crime of genocide; crimes against humanity; war crimes; and the crime of aggression.

The court has two important features which are relevant to the application of the international rule of law. First, the court grounds its mandate upon the principle of universal jurisdiction which overrides sovereignty in situations where gross human rights violations have been committed (Aukerman, 2002). This principle makes international intervention possible in situations where leaders violate the rights of their own citizens (Nardin, 2000). However, the principle of universal jurisdiction is quite controversial and constitutes one of the dilemmas of transitional justice. Second, the court focuses on individual responsibility in the case of gross human rights violations. This is important because it pursues peace, not by focusing on groups that engage in mass murder, but by criminalising acts committed by individuals. This approach, according to its advocates, has the capacity to contribute to future peace by neutralising tensions between groups; making atrocities appear to be less ethnic, racial or religious, thus assisting the entire population to realise peace in their political community.

Upon the ratification of the Rome Statute on 11 April, 2002, many world leaders heralded the maturation of international criminal law enforcement (Burke-White, 2003, p. 5). The establishment of the ICC epitomised the development of international criminal law, raised international justice to a higher level and represented what was considered a magnificent leap forward in the struggle against impunity, surpassing the benchmark set by its predecessors (Ernesto, 2004, pp. 329–30). Former Director of the Codification Division of the UN Office of Legal Affairs, Roy Lee (1999), remarked that the ICC Statute was a tremendous historical success. Giovanni Conso (1999, p. 472), the President of the Rome Conference that formulated the ICC Statute, observed that the ICC was a success story because the statute was adapted in a record time during the course of the Rome conference as compared to the long and arduous codification process as a whole, which lasted from 1948 to 1998. On 11 April 2002, when 60 states signed their membership of the Rome Statute, the then UN Secretary General Kofi Annan is reported to have remarked that impunity had 'been dealt a decisive blow' (Manjunath & Sharma, 2005, p. 3). Bassiouni (2006, p. 421) described the ICC as an institution that befitted the nature of international relations characterised by competing interests. Against the background of this optimistic view of the ICC, certain questions could be raised. To what extent would the ICC be able to operate without being conditioned by the social world around it? Would the court be able to overcome the political and institutional hurdles that were encountered by the previous judicial endeavours? These concerns became real when the ICC Statute had its first opportunity to adapt to the real world of competing interests – when President Museveni referred the situation of northern Uganda to the International Court.

The Ugandan Government referral of the situation in northern Uganda to the ICC

The atrocities allegedly committed by the LRA were in violation of international law applicable to non-international armed conflicts. The conscription or enlisting of children below 15 years of age in the army, wilful killing, rape, sexual slavery, forced pregnancy, forced displacement and mutilation of body parts of civilians constitute crimes against humanity according to Article 7 of the Rome Statute and war crimes under Article 8 of the same statute. Thus the ICC intervened in the situation having been triggered by the Ugandan Government referral. President Museveni referred the 'situation concerning the Lord's Resistance Army' to the Prosecutor of the ICC in December 2003 (ICC, October 2005). This initiative fell within the category of self-referral, which was in line with the ICC's mandate and particularly Articles (13) (a) and 14 of the ICC Statute (ICC, January 2004). These articles permit State Parties to the Treaty to refer, to the ICC Prosecutor, a situation in which one or more crimes falling within the jurisdiction of the court may have been committed.

Uganda's referral was the first one to be submitted to the ICC subsequent to the Rome Statute entering into force. Other referrals were made in subsequent years, predominantly from Africa (Bekou & Shah, 2006). These included those submitted by the Democratic Republic of Congo (DRC) in April 2004 and the Central African Republic (CAR) in January 2005 (Grono, 2006). The DRC referral targeted violations allegedly committed by the various parties in the DRC between 1998 and 2002, which included the killing of civilians, forced recruitment of child soldiers, destruction of villages, internal displacement, cannibalism, rape and torture. In early 2006, Thomas Lubanga was already in Congolese custody pending prosecution under national court for crimes against humanity and genocide (Politi & Gioia, 2008). The ICC, in February 2006, preferred charges of enlisting child soldiers against Lubanga, who was to be transferred to The Hague.[1] The situation in the CAR pertained to the cases of sexual violence and rape suffered by hundreds of victims, allegedly at the hands of Jean-Pierre Bemba Gombo's *Mouvement de Libération du Congo* (MLC). Bemba was eventually found guilty by the ICC for crimes committed by his forces in the CAR. It is noteworthy that while Uganda was the first referral to the ICC, the first trial was in the DRC. There was also the Security Council referral of the situation in Darfur in Sudan in March 2005 (Bekou & Shah, 2006). The ICC

Prosecutor eventually issued a warrant of arrest for Al Bashir in 2009, accusing the Sudanese president of genocide, crimes against humanity, and war crimes in Darfur. Other countries in which the international ICC intervened were Kenya; Libya; Côte d'Ivoire; Mali; Georgia; and Burundi. These referrals provided the first opportunity for the ICC to demonstrate its capacity in relation to situations of human rights violations and impunity.

The referral of the situation in northern Uganda followed several failed attempts to find a peaceful solution to the conflict and bring it to an end through military action and dialogue with the LRA, such as the peace initiative by Betty Bigombe and the adoption of the Amnesty Act of 2000 by the Ugandan parliament. Under this act, the Government of Uganda had granted the LRA rebels pardon and full immunity from prosecution provided that they renounced rebellion (Uganda Government, 2000, Cap 294, Law of Uganda). The LRA leadership refused to honour this offer. Even though President Museveni had signed the Amnesty Bill, he still had confidence in a military solution. This preference for a military option to end the conflict was, in all likelihood, inspired by the military credentials he earned in the bush war that brought him to power in 1986. It was also likely to have been reinforced by his disdainful opinion of the LRA commanders, whom he referred to as 'empty-headed criminals' (*The Monitor*, October 2003). But President Museveni's confidence in a military option did not bear fruit, a failure he justified by claiming that Sudan had continued to support LRA rebels in disregard of an agreement reached earlier. This was a reference to the agreement brokered in 1998 by former US President Jimmy Carter in terms of which the Ugandan Government was to stop supporting the SPLA/M and the Sudanese Government the LRA/M (Allen, 2006, p. 72). Even though he defended his failure, the prolonged and devastating humanitarian conditions in northern Uganda raised international concerns and President Museveni's international reputation began to wane.

Given the constant failure of military strategies to bring the conflict to an end, some of Uganda's key development partners, like the European Union and the United Kingdom, began to express their reservations about a continued military option following Jan Egeland's comment that the humanitarian conditions in northern Uganda were unacceptable, and needed to be dealt with (ibid., p. 73). It was in response to this international pressure that, in December 2003, the Ugandan President, Yoweri Museveni, shifted from his strategy of a military solution and referred the situation in northern Uganda to the ICC prosecutor to investigate crimes committed by the LRA in accordance with Article 14 of the Rome Statute of the International Criminal Court. The article permits state parties to 'refer to [the International Criminal Court] Prosecutor a situation in which one or more crimes within the jurisdiction of the court appear to have been committed' (UN, 1998, Art. 14).

Admissibility of the situation in northern Uganda

Once President Museveni referred the situation in northern Uganda to the ICC Chief Prosecutor, Luis Moreno-Ocampo, one of the key difficulties was ascertaining whether there were reasonable grounds for an investigation into the atrocities allegedly committed by the LRA (ICC, July 2004). When the ICC intervenes in a particular situation, one of the crucial and sensitive considerations is whether a case is admissible or not. This consideration helps the prosecutors to intervene in a situation without interfering with the prerogative of state sovereignty. Thus the prosecutor had the task of determining whether the case referred to the ICC was admissible in accordance with the statute's principles of gravity, interest of justice and complementarity (ICC, September 2007).

Accordingly, the ICC Chief Prosecutor indicated that he would determine whether the case was admissible according to the Rome Statute (ICC, September 2007; Glassborow, 2006). Article 1 of the Rome Statute states in part that, a case 'being investigated by a State which has jurisdiction over it' is inadmissible 'unless the state is unwilling or unable to genuinely carry out the investigation or prosecution' (Art. 17 (1) (a)). This article safeguards against the possibility of the court usurping the role of national courts. According to legal experts, such as Kress, the Ugandan self-referral was admissible since it was not in disagreement with Article 17(1) (a) (Kress, 2004, pp. 944, 946). At the time of the referral, the Ugandan Government had not launched any national judicial investigations or court proceedings against the LRA, strengthening the case for admissibility before the ICC pursuant to Article 17 (1) (a) and (b) (Akhavan, 2005, pp. 412–15). In this connection, when issuing warrants of arrest for the LRA, the Pre-Trial Chamber II made reference to a letter of 28 May 2004 from the Ugandan Government which stated that 'the Government of Uganda has been unable to arrest ... persons who may bear the greatest responsibility' for the crimes within the referred situation; that 'the ICC is the most appropriate and effective forum for the investigation and prosecution of those bearing the greatest responsibility' for those crimes; and that the Government of Uganda 'has not conducted and does not intend to conduct national proceedings in relation to the persons most responsible' (Nouwen & Werner, 2010; ICC, 27 September 2005).

This initiative taken by the Ugandan Government was in accordance with the spirit of the international obligation to end the impunity of perpetrators committing what is referred to in the ICC preamble as the 'most serious crimes of concern to the international community' (UN, 1998). The preamble to the Rome Statute stresses 'the duty of every State to exercise its criminal jurisdiction over those responsible for international crimes' (Preamble to the Rome Statute, 1998). Article 18 of the statute is equally explicit on the obligation of state parties to cooperate with the court in bringing violators of international human rights to justice. Even though the legality of the referral appeared clear and that there was no impediment to the ICC intervention to bring the LRA to justice, the fact that President Museveni, who referred the situation, was a party to the conflict, raised the issue of impartiality.

It also remained important to clarify the question of whether the LRA, as a non-state actor, fell within the jurisdiction of the ICC or that of the national courts. The relevance of this question lies in the fact that this was the first time in history that an international tribunal was to deal with non-state actors. The

Nuremberg Trials, the ICTY and the ICTR had as their primary concern acts of violence committed or sanctioned by state actors. The LRA however was not a state actor. According to some lines of thought, non-state actors operate outside the political and public realm and are judged at the level of free and autonomous parties, and hence should not be subjected to international human rights standards (Wood & Scharffs, 2002, pp. 531, 544–5). Such an application and interpretation of the standards of human rights would exclude the LRA from being accountable in accordance with international human rights standards which form the fundamental guiding principles of the ICC. The LRA would, instead, be liable under ordinary national criminal justice and not international human rights standards. The crimes committed by the LRA would be judged not as extraordinary but rather as ordinary crimes.

Criminal responsibility of non-state actors under international law has generated debate in scholarship. One of the lines of reasoning is that if non-sate actors have some right under international law, then they must also have obligations under the same law. For instance, the right to resist tyranny allows individuals to guard themselves against the abusive state (Selbourne, 1997; Razmetaeva, 2014). In such instances, non-state entities assume actions that would otherwise be the domain of the state, such as apparatus of power. It can then be argued that these entities should be called upon to respect human rights obligations towards individuals. A logical implication is that if these actors contravene prescriptions of international law through a systematic attack against a civilian population then they are liable under international law. Another line of argument is that international criminal justice target individuals who have rights but also obligations under international law enjoyed under various treaties, for instance, the obligation not to commit the crime of genocide, crimes against humanity or war crimes. These responsibilities do not discriminate whether the individual is a state or non-state actor. According to the UN General Assembly, 1970, human rights 'continue to apply fully in situations of armed conflict' (UN General Assembly, 1970) such that any actors, whether state parties or armed opposition groups or rebel movements, are bound by the international human rights standards (Robinson, 2003, pp. 5–6). Consistent human rights protection would require both state actors and non-state actors to uphold international human rights standards.

This line of reasoning provided a basis for the inclusion of the LRA within the sphere of international human rights standards. The LRA, or any other armed opposition group, cannot be precluded from being responsible for upholding international human rights standards. Since the *raison d'être* of the ICC is anchored on the international human rights values, the LRA case fell within the domain of the ICC's jurisdiction. The LRA atrocities, as such, fell within the prescriptions of international human rights. The rebel group committed systematic, massive and serious human rights violations, especially against women and children during the armed conflict. Thus, the ICC proceeded on the basis of the fact that the crimes allegedly committed by the LRA leadership fell within its jurisdiction in accordance with Article 5 of the Rome Statute. Further, the crimes were allegedly committed within Uganda, that is, within a territory of a state party to the Rome Statute (UN 1998, Art. 12(2) and Art. 11). In addition, as already mentioned, the case was admissible in accordance with Article 17, since no investigation or prosecution had been initiated by the Ugandan authorities in response to crimes allegedly perpetrated by the LRA leadership. In its decision to issue arrest warrants for the LRA leaders, the Pre-Trial Chamber II simply stated that,

> [b]ased upon the application, the evidence and other information submitted by the Prosecutor, and without prejudice to subsequent determination, the case against Joseph Kony, Vincent Otti, Raska Lukwiya, Okot Odhiambo and Dominic Ongwen falls within the jurisdiction of the court and appears to be admissible…
>
> (ICC, 8 July 2005, p. 3)

Notwithstanding the foregoing, there still remained some critical questions. There was no evidence of an initiative from the Ugandan Government to investigate or prosecute the LRA for allegations of causing atrocities in northern Uganda (HRW, September 2005). Uganda's court structures were intact and working at the time of the referral. A significant question is why did Uganda turn to the ICC when its national judicial capacity was strong? The issue seemed to turn on political relevance. A possible reason could be linked to the claim that practical difficulties had made it impossible for the Ugandan Government to capture the LRA leadership and bring them before the local court. The LRA operated largely from Sudan and was supposedly supported by the Sudanese Government, making it practically impossible for the Ugandan Government to apprehend them without causing an international incident. Given this scenario, the ICC, as an international body, became the most appropriate instrument.

Were an element of inaction on the side of the Ugandan Government to be revealed, would this constitute a justifiable reason to stop the court from intervening? According to the ICC Prosecutor, Moreno-Ocampo (2003a, p. 5), in some cases 'inaction by states is the appropriate course of action'. The ICC prosecutor noted, to quote at length, that,

> [t]here is no impediment to the admissibility of a case before the Court where no State has initiated any investigation. There may be cases where inaction by States is the appropriate course of action. For example, the Court and a territorial State incapacitated by mass crimes may agree that a consensual division of labour is the most logical and effective approach. Groups bitterly divided by conflict may oppose prosecutions at each others' hands and yet agree to a prosecution by a Court perceived as neutral and impartial.… In such cases there will be no question of 'unwillingness' or 'inability' under Aart 17.
>
> (Moreno-Ocampo, 2003b, p. 4)

Finally, given that at the time of the referral the Ugandan Government had passed the Amnesty Act of 2000, was this to be considered a local judicial initiative? The thrust of the Amnesty Act of 2000 was in essence forgiveness and did not enshrine investigation and prosecution. The Act ran contrary to the very fundamentals of the ICC. Moreover, given the nature of crimes that call for international judicial intervention, international obligations prevail over national law should there be any conflict between international obligations and national law and domestic law may not be invoked to justify non-fulfilment (Denza, 2006, p. 425). In this regard, Uganda's international obligations under the ICC Statute would prevail over national amnesty law and practice, particularly in dealing with crimes against humanity. The Amnesty Act, therefore, was not an obstacle to the ICC enforcing its warrants of arrest. The above lines of reasoning formed a reasonable basis for admissibility of the situation of northern Uganda.

Warrants of arrest for the top LRA commanders

After establishing that the crimes allegedly committed by the LRA fell within the jurisdiction of the ICC and that the Ugandan Government had not initiated any formal investigation and prosecution, the ICC decided to issue warrants of arrest against the LRA leadership. According to the Rome Statute, Article 58, warrants of arrest can be issued by a pre-trial chamber when there are reasonable grounds to believe that the arrest of a person suspected of committing a crime falling within the jurisdiction of the court is necessary to ensure the person's appearance for trial (Rome Statute 1998, Art. 58 (1)). Accordingly, on 6 May 2005, the Prosecutor applied to the Pre-Trial Chamber II for warrants of arrest against Joseph Kony and four other LRA leaders after establishing that there were reasonable grounds to do so (Moreno-Ocampo, 2005). The warrants were issued by the Pre-Trial Chamber II on 8 July 2005 but were kept under seal (ICC, 13 October 2005).

The request for the arrest and surrender for indictment of the LRA commanders was transmitted to the Government of Uganda, although the Government was advised not to reveal the warrants (Happold, 2007). On 9 September 2005, the Prosecutor made an application to the Chamber to unseal the warrants (ibid.). On 27 September 2005, following this application by the Office of the Prosecutor, the Chamber ordered the Registrar to transmit, under seal, the requests for arrest and surrender to the governments of the DRC and Sudan (Happold, 2007). Eventually, on 13 October 2005, the Chamber ordered the unsealing of the warrants (Happold, 2007; Allen, 2006).

On 14 October 2005, it was finally announced that arrest warrants had been issued against the five leaders of the LRA top command (ICC, 14 October 2005). According to the warrants, these LRA leaders had allegedly committed multiple counts of crimes against humanity and war crimes as defined in the Rome Statute, Article 7(1) and Article 8(2) (c) (ibid.). The warrants charged the LRA leaders with a total of 33 counts of crimes against humanity and war crimes. These included sexual enslavement, rape, enslavement, murder and inhumane acts. They were also charged with war crimes committed in a non-international armed conflict which included attacks against the civilian population, the enlisting of children, cruel treatment, pillage and murder (ICC, 8 July 2005, pp. 12–20). The offences, according to the ICC warrants, were allegedly committed by the LRA on IDP camps and other places in northern Uganda between 2003 and 2004 (ibid., pp. 6–9). These charges were limited to crimes committed between 2003 and 2004, whereas in fact the LRA atrocities date back to the late 1980s and early 1990s. The reason for this is that the ICC's mandate only allowed it to consider crimes committed after 2002.

The top five members of the LRA leadership targeted by the warrants were referred to as members of the LRA 'control altar', the group in charge of executing LRA strategy (ICC, 14 October 2005, p. 4). This is the group presented in Chapter 2 of this book under the 'LRA Command Structure: the Control Alter'. Seated at the top of the control alter was Joseph Kony, who was listed as the Chairman and Commander-in-Chief of the LRA. He was alleged to have committed, ordered or induced 33 counts of crimes against humanity and war crimes. These included 12 counts of crimes against humanity: murder, enslavement, sexual enslavement, rape, and inhumane acts of inflicting serious bodily injury and suffering; and 21 counts of war crimes – murder, cruel treatment of civilians, intentionally directing an attack against a civilian population, pillaging, and enforced the enlisting of children (ibid., pp. 12–19).

Vincent Otti was the LRA Vice-Chairman and the commander of LRA operations in Uganda between 2003 and 2004. He was charged with 32 counts of crimes against humanity and war crimes. These included 11 counts of crimes against humanity – murder, enslavement, sexual enslavement, rape, and inhumane acts of inflicting serious bodily injury and suffering; and 21 counts of war crimes – murder, cruel treatment of civilians, intentionally directing an attack against a civilian population, pillaging, and the enforced enlisting of children (ibid., pp. 12–20). Otti was reportedly killed on Kony's orders in October 2007 because of his interest in pursuing peace and the potential threat he posed to Kony (BBC, 21 December, 2007).

Raska Lukwiya was the LRA deputy army commander. He was charged with four counts including enslavement, cruel treatment, attacks on civilians and pillaging (ICC, 8 July 2005, pp. 8–10). Lukwiya was later killed in fighting against the Ugandan army in northern Uganda in 2006 (*The New Vision*, 13 August 2006). Specific details of his death remain obscure. Okot Odhiambo, an LRA brigade commander, was charged with ten counts and on the basis of his individual criminal responsibility. These included two counts of crimes against humanity, that is, murder and enslavement; and eight counts of war crimes, namely, murder, intentionally directing an attack against a civilian population, pillaging, and the enforced enlisting of children (ICC, 14 October 2005, pp. 10–12). Dominic Ongwen, another LRA brigade commander, was charged with seven counts (ibid.). The warrant of arrest for Dominic Ongwen lists seven counts on the basis of his individual criminal responsibility including: three counts of crimes against humanity – murder, enslavement, and inhumane acts of inflicting serious bodily injury and suffering; and four counts of war crimes – murder, cruel treatment of civilians, intentionally directing an attack against a civilian population, and pillaging. Ongwen is reported to have escaped from a detention camp at the end of 2014. The media reported that Ongwen escaped the camp near Songo, in Kafia Kingi, CAR, and that nomadic cattle herders who handed him over to Seleka, a rebel group near Sam Ouandja in CAR. The Seleka group commander later handed him over to the American Special Forces in Obo, CAR, through some non-governmental organisation worker in Obo. The American forces later handed him over to Ugandan forces. The Ugandan Government ultimately handed Ongwen over to the ICC (BBC News, 9 January 2015; BBC News, 14 January 2015; Daily Nation, 13 January 2015). Over ten years after the warrants of arrest, Dominic Ongwen was the only LRA member to have been arrested.

As a follow-up to these warrants, the International Criminal Police Organization (Interpol) issued Red Notices for the arrest of the five LRA commanders named in the ICC arrest warrants (Mukasa, 2006a). The Interpol Red Notice system is part of its global network as a law enforcement agency, created to assist in tracing and arresting internationally wanted fugitives. This is the only effective instrument for international arrest warrant in use today. Interpol circulates notices to member countries listing persons who are wanted for extradition. The names of the persons in the notices are placed on watch lists. When a person whose name is listed comes to the attention of the police abroad, the country that sought the listing is notified through Interpol and can request either his provisional arrest, if there is urgency, or file a formal request for extradition. These notices were instrumental in ensuring that the descriptions of the persons pursued by arrest warrants were known globally and in facilitating the international obligation to pursue and arrest people accused of committing crimes against humanity. The ICC made use of the Interpol Red Notice as it did not have its own police force and had to rely on other established international institutions.

The ICC prosecutor, however, did not consider the atrocities allegedly committed by the UPDF. The Prosecutor explained that his decision to target the LRA leaders and not members of the UPDF was guided by the gravity criterion laid out in Article 53 of the Rome Statute. According to this criterion, focusing on those who bear the greatest responsibility for the most serious crimes would be more feasible than bringing charges against all apparent perpetrators (ICC, September 2003, pp. 6–7). According to the ICC Chief Prosecutor, the accused were selected on the basis of who was responsible for the decisions. The Prosecutor indicated that the selection was carried out on the basis of careful analysis in accordance with the principles of objectivity and impartiality, and in accordance with the criterion of gravity set out in Article 53 of the statute (Moreno-Ocampo, 24 October 2005, pp. 5–6). With specific reference to the situation in northern Uganda, the Prosecutor noted that:

> In Uganda, the criterion for selection of the first case was gravity. We analyzed the gravity of all crimes in Northern Uganda committed by all groups

> – the LRA, the UPDF and other forces. Our investigations indicated that the crimes committed by the LRA were of dramatically higher gravity. We therefore started an investigation of the LRA.
>
> (Ibid., p. 7)

In the context of criminal justice, the gravity of the crimes committed by the LRA called for the prosecution of the perpetrators. This was ultimately expected to have a deterrent effect, reduce hostilities and provide greater accountability worldwide (Punyasena, 2006, p. 57). The Prosecutor nonetheless gave the assurance that his office had not closed its books on investigations, and that it had simply made a positive decision to seek arrest warrants against certain LRA leaders, a decision which did not rule out subsequent charges against members of other parties to the conflict (Schabas, 2007, p. 246). The Prosecutor stated that, the ICC would '[... continue] to collect information on allegations concerning all other groups, to determine whether other crimes meet the stringent thresholds of the Statute ...' (Moreno-Ocampo, 24 October 2005).

These assurances notwithstanding, the apparent impartiality and the expected cooperation from the Ugandan Government, combined with the political dimensions of the conflict in northern Uganda, were bound to shape the attitude of the local Acholi population towards the ICC intervention. It was bound to raise questions as to whether the court was being used by the state to fight its battle and whether the Government would still assure the court of its support if persons associated with it were targeted. Paola Gaeta's research showed how this mode of operation posed a potential problem for ICC legitimacy (Gaeta, 2004, pp. 951–2). Gaeta argued that the Ugandan state might be seeking to use the court as a political weapon against its opponents and willing to cooperate with the court only when the court scrutinised the activities of their opponents and not those of the actors on the Government's side (ibid., p. 952). Accordingly, with issuance of warrants of arrest against the LRA, while ignoring the atrocities allegedly committed by Government forces, the stage was set for subsequent processes and debates on the northern Uganda situation.

State's obligation and the ambiguity of self-referral

The ICC did not have its own police force and had therefore to rely on the support of the state party to the ICC to arrest the LRA suspects. In this respect it was expected that Uganda, itself being a state party to the Rome Statute, would provide all necessary support to facilitate the investigation and provide protection to investigators and witnesses (ICC, September 2003, p. 5). Indeed, for the ICC to execute these warrants, it was essential that, in accordance with the international obligation to end impunity, all states respected the demands for justice and international criminal accountability not only in northern Uganda, but wherever such crimes occurred. Thus, on 15 September 2006, the Pre-Trial Chamber requested

> [t]he Prosecutor to submit to the Chamber, on or before Friday 6 October 2006, without prejudice to his powers and functions under the Statute, information and comments in writing on the status of cooperation with the relevant states and with the Registry as regards the execution of the Warrants.
>
> (ICC, 15 September 2006)

The ICC Prosecutor, Moreno-Ocampo, maintained that states party to the ICC were expected to respond positively as part of their obligation to assist in combating and eradicating the culture of impunity which could undermine the democratic order. Since the LRA was a regional problem, its elimination required greater regional cooperation and sustained support from the international community. Thus, arresting the indicted LRA/M leaders was not only a challenge for Uganda, Sudan and the DRC, but also a challenge for the international community, especially those which were party to the ICC Statute (Ahere & Maina, 2013). The anticipated cooperation in arresting the LRA was probably based on the fact that the referral was made by the President of Uganda, Yoweri Museveni. In the Prosecutor's eyes this seems to have demonstrated political will on the side of Uganda and to have reassured the Prosecutor that the national authorities would cooperate in the investigation and enforcement of the warrants of arrest. But this was not really as obvious as it may have appeared. The human rights abuses by the LRA had existed in northern Uganda for close to two decades, since the war begun in 1986, yet the Government of Uganda had failed to deal with it.

The fact that the case was taken to the ICC by the Government, the assumption would that these LRA were beyond the capacity of the state to apprehend and prosecute; otherwise they would have been investigated, arrested and prosecuted through national judicial organs. The ICC was to do what the Government had failed to do. It did not make sense therefore to hope that the Government would be effective in enforcing the warrants of arrest. Moreover, the State was itself a party in the conflict and asking the ICC to intervene meant that the State was asking the ICC to fight its battle. Another consequence of the process was that the Government was likely to be jittery to have the forces associated with it investigated for any malpractice during the conflict. The question was, therefore, whether the International Court's intervention in northern Uganda was a case of the law being made to serve as the handmaid of politics. This seemed to have been the case when the ICC targeted the LRA but left out the UPDF. Evidence to the effect that the LRA had committed atrocities was not difficult to come by. Child soldiers were in the bush; girls raped and held as sex slaves were still in the bush; and cases of mutilations were evident across the region. These stood as testimonies. But would international criminal justice be able to isolate legally pertinent issues without getting caught up in the politics of the conflict? These emerging issues were highlighted in the reaction that ICC intervention elicited among a cross section of Ugandans.

Reaction to the ICC

Although the atrocities allegedly committed by the LRA constituted war crimes and crimes against humanity and fell squarely within the realm of the ICC, the ICC's appropriateness was questioned by sections of Ugandans including the victims, civil society and community leaders. These groups challenged the relevance of the ICC intervention and instead opted for alternative instruments of justice and peacebuilding. Immediately after the Kampala Government's announcement of the indictments, the LRA leadership offered to negotiate with the Government for a peaceful settlement of the conflict on condition that the ICC dropped the warrants of arrest (UN IRIN, November 2005). In the ensuing years the LRA stated that withdrawal was a prerequisite for the signing of any peace deal. This offer by the LRA was embraced by a section of the local population, especially traditional leaders and civil society. The leaders based their argument on the fact that, during the years of war, the predominantly Acholi population had borne the brunt of the suffering inflicted by the LRA, despite several attempts by the Ugandan Government to bring the war to an end by military means. Given that the LRA had agreed to negotiate with the Government, this offer should have provided the point of departure for reaching a feasible solution to the conflict (Allen, 2006). The ICC intervention therefore elicited a number of objections from victims, civil society, community leaders and some government representatives. The author's own field research in northern Uganda revealed various views of the people on the ICC intervention.

The first objection was that the ICC was not balanced. This was an issue of particular interest to the local population. Key concerns in this respect arose from the manner in which the referral was made to the ICC and from the fact that the ICC did not target the UPDF, also accused of atrocities against the civilian population. It did not escape the attention of the Acholi population that it was President Museveni who made the referral, and yet the president was one of the protagonists in the conflict (Opio, Interview, 29 May 2008). There was also no evidence of consultations between political leaders in President Museveni's Government and political leaders in northern Uganda. Thus the impression was created that the ICC was part of the political manoeuvring carried out by President Museveni. The impression first arose when the ICC Chief Prosecutor, Luis Moreno-Ocampo, held a joint press conference with President Museveni in London on 29 January 2004, when the Prosecutor announced his decision to begin investigating crimes allegedly committed by the LRA. Although the joint conference may have been a gesture on the part of the Ugandan Government to assure the ICC of cooperation, it turned out to be a political mistake given the dynamics in northern Uganda. Furthermore, the ICC intervened at the request of the Ugandan Government, but the Government had been a party to the conflict and was also accused of human rights violations. This would make many northerners who were familiar with the dynamics of the war suspect that the ICC was operating at the behest of the Ugandan Government, a suspicion corroborated by the ICC decision not to investigate the alleged UPDF atrocities. These led to conclusions about the main intention of the referral and to the perception that the Ugandan Government was using the court as a weapon against the LRA. According to Fr Charles Olweny, a Catholic priest working among IDPs living in the Pabo camp in the Amuru district and a native Acholi,

> [i]f a balanced trial were to be realised then both the LRA and the UPDF must be tried for their atrocities. We agree that LRA have committed serious atrocities, but there is equally enough evidence that the UPDF have committed [serious] atrocities. The government is only using the ICC to score his political goals against the Acholi.
>
> (Olweny, Interview, 3 April 2008)

Fr Charles Olweny referred to some IDP camps as 'death dens for eliminating the Acholi'. In Pabo, Fr Olweny pointed out two sites which he said were mass graves. He told the author how the UPDF battalions had killed the Acholi in Pabo. The people, according to him, were simply collected together, killed and buried in the camp. He spoke about the mass graves and how whoever spoke about them would mysteriously disappear. He also claimed that there were cases of torture and rape by UPDF forces (ibid.). The government forces had been accused of raping women and torturing anyone they suspected of being rebel collaborators. According to a respondent, Caroline Auma (Interview, 31 May 2008), 'the LRA abducted children, but the UPDF also committed very grave human rights abuses on our people like raping, torturing and killing'. Some of the interviewees had personally experienced violations. One informant, Ochola, told the story of how his father was pulled out of his vehicle and killed by government soldiers manning road blocks. The other occupants who were from the south of the country were spared and allowed to proceed (Ochola, Interview, 2 June 2008).

Experience and knowledge of these UPDF violations and the fact that the ICC did not target the UPDF brought the court's impartiality into question. The local population maintained that both the UPDF and LRA were equally responsible for serious human rights violations in northern Uganda (Allen, 2006, p. 95). Some of the informants demonstrated an understanding of the complex nature of the conflict in northern Uganda. According to Charles Abok (Interview, 23 April 2008), interviewed in Pabo IDP camp,

> [t]he conflict in northern Uganda is complex and it is difficult to state who was really fighting for the people and who was against the people. Both the government and the LRA claimed to have been fighting for the interests of the Acholi, yet both had committed very serious and vengeful crimes against the Acholi people.

The above view was corroborated by Christine Labogo (Interview, 23 March 2008) who argued that,

> [b]oth the LRA and UPDF should face justice in equal measure. The warrants should not be lifted. Both sides have caused suffering. Both sides should face justice. How can the government be the accuser while it is an accused? The government killed civilians; looted property of the civilians, raped women, looted cows. The people through the paramount chief have asked the government to compensate them for the losses.

The years of conflict since Amin and the persecutions that accompanied these conflicts left painful memories in the minds of many northern Ugandans. The Acholi people seemed to have suffered extremely in the hands of successive governments especially that of Amin (see Chapter 2 of this work). The role of President Museveni's Government in the conflict brought back painful memories. One respondent remarked that it was necessary for the ICC to pursue

> those leaders in Museveni's government who [had] killed innocent people and buried them in mass graves. As long as the ICC does not pursue those who committed such atrocities, there will be no justice since justice should apply to all parties.
>
> (A young man, Interview, 25 May 2008)

According to popular understanding, the beginning and continuation of the war should not have been blamed on the rebels alone and 'if there were any prosecution, the government should also be prosecuted' (Anonymous Man (b), Interview, 24 May 2008). A man living in Pabo IDP camp in Amuru district recalled how a government soldier allegedly killed over 30 people in Pabo. He reasoned that justice demanded that all parties to a dispute be treated according to how much responsibility they held and anyone who carried any responsibility should be held accountable. He wondered why the ICC was not concerned with government soldiers. Another anonymous participant said,

> [b]oth sides have caused suffering to innocent people. Both sides should face justice. How can the government be accused while it is the accuser? If Kony wins the case, the government should be accused. The government killed civilians; looted property of the civilians, raped women, looted cows.
>
> (Anonymous Man (a), Interview, 15 April 2008)

This perception impressed itself strongly on the minds of both the local Acholi population and their leaders. In October 2004, the Acholi Religious Leaders' Peace Initiative (ARLPI) and the Acholi Paramount Chief, Rwot Onen David Acana II, wrote to the court stating that,

> [w]hile we recognise your need to investigate the crimes committed by the LRA against humanity, we would strongly suggest that the investigation

> encompasses the whole of the situation of the war in northern Uganda in order for true justice to be done…
>
> (ARLPI cited in Allen, 2006)

Such deep-seated feelings reinforced the position that, within the context of the northern Ugandan situation, consideration had to be given to all the parties involved in the conflict if any justice initiative was to have a popular impact. For the local population, the failure to target the UPDF was the result of it being protected by the Ugandan Government (Allen, 2006, p. 97). Thus any judgement would not be perceived as just if the government forces were not also held accountable for their actions (Okidi, Interview, 17 May 2008).

The ICC, however, justified exclusion of the UPDF, by maintaining that one of the parties to the conflict, the LRA, had committed worse atrocities than the other. In this respect, if members of only one group were prosecuted, a number of undesirable results might ensue, especially in situations characterised by political polarisation. The court sought to prosecute the worst offenders on one side of the conflict and excluded, at least initially, offenders on the other side whose crimes it did not consider sufficiently serious to prosecute. This omission foregrounded the political dimensions of the conflict. People's perceptions were that the process was uneven and therefore unjust. Even civil society organisations raised concerns about the ICC's apparently partial decision. Amnesty International (30 January 2004), for instance, remarked that '[a]ny court investigation of war crimes and crimes against humanity in northern Uganda must be part of a comprehensive plan to end impunity for all such crimes, regardless of which side committed them and the level of the perpetrator'.[2] It is for this reason that the apparently selective prosecution by the ICC led people to believe that the court was a tool of government. The above objection reveals that the message to the ICC was to charge the UPDF as well. For ordinary people it was not whether the crimes committed by parties to the conflict were equally serious, but whether the court allowed impunity or not.

The second objection was that the ICC process might exacerbate the violence and become a stumbling block to the peace process (Allen, 2006, p. 102). Political and religious leaders from northern Uganda contended that pursuing the LRA top command for prosecution could exacerbate violence and lobbied for the withdrawal of the ICC case against the LRA leadership. Reagan Okumu, a Member of Parliament for Aswa County in Gulu district, contended that prosecuting the LRA top commanders would not be healthy since the threat of prosecution would have the effect of making Kony resort to killing innocent people in protest (Musinguzi, 2004). Other leaders who lobbied for the dropping of the charges include, among others, Archbishop Baptist Odama, of the Catholic Diocese of Gulu, Bishop McLeod Baker Ochola, Bishop of the Anglican Church and the Acholi Paramount Chief, Rwot David Onen Acana (*The Monitor*, 14 April 2005). Rwot Acana argued that pursuing the LRA would not work in the interests of peace since it would hamper the ongoing peace negotiations between the rebels and Government (*The Monitor*, 18 February 2005). Many doubted that the LRA leadership would surrender freely without the prosecutor of the ICC withdrawing the indictments against the five commanders (Liu Institute for Global Issues, 2006). Abel Ojara, an ex-rebel soldier whom I interviewed, said that it was impossible for a rebel leader who knew that he had committed serious crimes and who was being pursued by a warrant of arrest to give himself up, surrender his weapons and sign a peace deal (Ojara, Interview, 16 May 2008). The fear that the ICC indictments would exacerbate the conflict was shared by most of the people interviewed. Betty Akello, in response to whether she knew about the ICC and whether she thought it would bring peace by pursuing the LRA, said:

> Yes, I have heard about the ICC. I know that they have released warrants of arrest for Kony and the LRA commanders. But that should be withdrawn because it will derail peace processes. The war is enough and no one would wish to go back to the bush. What the people are for is peace no matter what it costs.
>
> (Akello, Interview, 25 March 2008)

Local leaders too expressed their awareness of the fact that, without its own military to enforce the warrants of arrest, the ICC would have to rely on the very government forces, the UPDF, for this purpose (Group of Elders, Interview, 11 March 2008). A further concern about the UPDF was that it had not been able to defend the people from attacks and abductions by the LRA (Ojara, Interview, 16 May 2008). This sentiment is captured in the remarks of Matthew Odong, Secretary General of ARPI:

> It has taken the government of Uganda 21 years to do away with Kony to no avail. How will the ICC arrest them? Does it have its own military or is it going to rely on the UPDF which have failed to defeat the LRA, protect the people against the LRA and have themselves caused atrocities comparable to those of the LRA. How long will it take the ICC to arrest Kony? The people have questioned the ability of the ICC. In the case where the ICC sits on the way of dialogue with the LRA it is merely perpetuating the conflict. The best way is to allow the LRA back.
>
> (Odong, Interview, 27 March 2008)

Locals were cognisant that that Ugandan Government had moved almost the entire Acholi population into IDP camps ostensibly to protect them from the LRA. However, as one respondent observes, government soldiers had not managed adequately to protect the camps from being attacked by the LRA (Auma, Interview, 31 May 2008). These camps were also characterised by very poor conditions and posed serious health hazards. The camps had no clean water or infrastructure, and the people were completely dependent on food aid (ibid.). Benson Otto, who had been residing in Lacor IDP camp for four years, told me that he was driven to the camp where his community were told they would receive maximum protection. Over the years, they had become completely incapacitated, had no land to plough, no food, no water, no school fees for children, no clothes and relied entirely on donations from NGOs. His desire was to go back to his homeland (Otto, Interview, 20 March 2008).

Such adverse experiences partly explain why any offer on the part of the LRA to negotiate received immediate positive response.

> What the people want is simply peace, they have pardoned the rebels. They want to forget the past and start a new life. Many people have lost their properties and relatives. The government does not have the capacity to bring the war to an end except through negotiations. They have fought for over 20 years. The civilians are the ones suffering.
>
> (Ibid.)

What people harboured in their minds was that the Government had wilfully neglected the northern Ugandan situation. For the ICC, failure on the part of the Government to act decisively against the LRA would not be an impediment to intervention. But for the Acholi population, this inaction was a political issue. Given its extensive machinery and intelligence, the people questioned the apparent inability of the Government to put down the war in the north as it had done elsewhere in Uganda. According to some reports in the media, the failure of the UPDF to defeat the LRA was attributed to a myriad of factors such as lack of resources, prevalence of HIV/AIDS, low morale, indiscipline and drunkenness among troops (*The Monitor*, February 1998). But this situation in the army was not a strong enough reason to explain why the Government failed adequately to protect its civilians against the LRA. Because of its military profile and advantages, the Government's failure to protect its civilians was interpreted not simply as incapacity but as negligence. The UPDF should have been able to defeat the rebels given their numerical dominance over them. According to Chris Dolan (2009, pp. 72–3), throughout their insurgency, the number of rebel soldiers was estimated to range between 1,000 and 5,000 while government troops were estimated at between 50,000 to 60,000 troops – excluding ethnic militia deployed in the north such as the LDU whose number was estimated at 20,000. It was therefore incomprehensible how government forces could be defeated by a ragtag rebel group surviving on abduction and looting from a very poor neighbourhood (ibid.). Moreover, the UPDF had guerrilla-fighting credentials which they could apply in understanding LRA operations. They had registered military successes against other insurgencies across the country, notably the ADF in Western Uganda in the late 1990s (ibid., p. 73). Within southern Sudan, where the LRA were based, the UPDF had the support of the SPLA. Moreover, the UPDF had military support from the US in the form, for example, of training and information. Thus factors such as lack of resources, prevalence of HIV/AIDS, low morale, indiscipline and drunkenness among troops were not compelling enough to justify the UPDF's failure, at least in the judgement of the victims.

This apparent inability on the side of the Government led to speculation that fostered radical interpretations of the Government's role in the war and shaped people's attitudes towards various peace initiatives. One of these radical views was that the continuing insurgency of the LRA gave Museveni an opportunity to exterminate the Acholi. According to Otto (Interview, 20 March 2008), since Museveni was well aware of the conditions in the camps, letting the people live in them for over a decade was a '[d]eliberate plan to make people die slowly'. According to Odwar, some interpreted the Government's incapacity as a lack of goodwill and revenge. Odwar noted that 'northerners were perceived as paying for the atrocities they had allegedly committed in the south' (Odwar, Interview, 16 March 2008). He attributed this lack of goodwill on the part of Government to what he referred to as the 'political usefulness of death' (ibid.). This, according to Odwar (ibid.) meant deliberately allowing people to suffer and die so that they would not rise up against Museveni's regime. The failure of the UPDF was also seen as the deliberate intention of the Government to prey on the people's suffering because continuation of the war was beneficial to personalities associated with Museveni. Odawar pointed to the popular belief, both within Uganda and abroad, that government soldiers were using the war for economic gain. Army officers used the situation to enrich themselves through the *ghost soldier* scandal. Ghost soldiers were non-existent soldiers within the military budget for fighting the rebels in the north (Mwenda & Tangri, 2005).

Thus, for many people in northern Uganda, the self-referral to the ICC was considered to be a political ploy presented as a genuine initiative. Odwar (Interview, 16 March 2008) suggested that it was meant to portray the LRA in a negative light to the international community and label the rebel group a terrorist gang, making it possible for them to be formally accused, and to make the Government appear to be resolving the conflict. In the process, argued Odwar, the Government would also have succeeded in covering-up the atrocities committed by the UPDF. The ICC was therefore faced with the enormous task of dealing with such perceptions and the dynamics which informed the conflict.

The third objection to the ICC intervention was in relation to the abduction of children. Respondents, especially those whose children had been abducted, were apprehensive of the manner in which the LRA would be arrested. They envisaged a military encounter which would place their children in the crossfire. In other words, the central issue was not the possibility of the LRA being prosecuted, but the manner in which Kony could be apprehended without harming the abducted children. During my interview with Matthew Odong, it emerged that the local leaders who advocated forgiveness were aware of the heinous nature of the crimes committed by the LRA except that the circumstances surrounding the commission of these crimes obscured straightforward legal redress:

> We acknowledge that the LRA have violated fundamental human rights such as right to life, right to education, right to freedom. But forgiving the LRA has some sort of ethical consideration, since the people are caught in

crossfire. You strike the LRA you arm the people who are already wounded in many respects. It is a problem of double effect.

(Odong, Interview, 27 March 2008)

Thus, a key concern here was that of the abducted children. The predicament of abducted children raised not only legal but also moral questions. The northern Uganda situation was an ongoing conflict, where pursuing the culprits implied military action which could possibly kill loved ones. These loved ones were initially abducted and later turned into perpetrators. International standards of criminal justice generally seem to assume that, in cases of war crimes, it is easy draw a clear distinction between perpetrators and victims such as the distinction between the Nazis and the Jews or between Hutu extremists and Tutsi victims. This was not the case in the northern Uganda situation. The majority of the combatants and/or perpetrators in the LRA were forcibly abducted and were themselves victims. This scenario elicited fears among the Acholi that the military apprehension of the LRA and their subjection to judicial processes would result in the death of abducted Acholi children. The abducted children may have turned into serious criminals, but the process that led them along such a path had deprived them of their agency. At the time of their abduction, the children were not yet capable of making informed choices about becoming involved in militia activities. The abductions and training of these child soldiers took place in contexts characterised by very limited choices. This concern of moral agency for criminal liability would emerge years later during the trial of Dominic Ongwen during his trial at the ICC after having been handed over to the court.

In the strictest sense, the objection to the ICC was not based on a justice issue, but rather on fears that the intervention would bring victims face to face with family perpetrators, possibly people's own children. A second factor had to do with exhaustion. People wanted the fighting to stop and peace to prevail. Apprehending the LRA would most likely involve a military operation. A further observation was that the immediate response to military attacks against the LRA was dependent on whether a child or relative had been abducted. Indeed, many of the responses relating to what should happen in a post-conflict environment differed not according to the extent to which individuals interpreted the conflict within a national and historical context but on a personal level, informed by personal experiences. Accordingly, those whose children or close relatives had been abducted immediately rejected military action against the LRA. This was not because of adherence to the LRA as an organisation but because such attacks might kill abducted children.

The final objection was that the ICC's methods of punishment might not make an immediately positive impression on those Acholi people who questioned its adequacy and relevance. This objection had two versions. The first was that the ICC mode of punishment was a punitive model. Concern about the ICC's punitive approach was motivated by an understanding of the need for a system that would be both restorative and integrative whereas the application of the legal system would simply isolate the individual from the community without necessarily bringing peace. A member of a group interview remarked that even if 'the ICC decided to condemn Kony it would not bring peace, it would leave a gap in the hearts of the people' (Group Interview, 2 April 2008). Traditional systems of justice would better serve the need for reconciliation and would make the people truly forget, leading to both reintegration and reform. Punishment, in the ICC manner would target an individual, but the conflicts had community dimensions in that the entire community was affected by the various aspects of the conflict such as abductions, killings, mutilations of civilians and dislocation. Moreover, people believed that, once peace was obtained, the criminals should be allowed to live in the community. By living together in the community people would come to accept and reconcile themselves with the past. According to many respondents the system of reconciliation was very successful in traditional society and was applicable in this context (ibid.).

The second version of this objection was that the ICC was an international instrument with international standards of punishment according to which persons sentenced by the ICC were not subjected to the harsh and dehumanising conditions prevalent in African jails. Pursuant to Article 77 of the ICC Statute, the LRA leaders, if convicted, would have life sentences imposed on them by the court. In the minds of a section of local population, such punishment was not the kind of punishment appropriate to the kind of atrocities committed by the LRA. According to Peter Onega (Interview, 13 March 2008), if Kony were arrested and handed over to the ICC, the court would impose a life sentence if he were found guilty. But the kind of treatment received by Kony in prison would be extremely lenient in comparison to the far harsher conditions he experienced in the bush and to those experienced by his victims. Corroborating this view, a local leader remarked that arresting Kony and taking him to The Hague, would not be much of a punishment for a culprit of his kind since he would watch TV in prison, read newspapers each morning, be examined by doctors and have his health regularly monitored, eat good food and no longer have to be worried about UPDF revenge (Cultural Leader, Interview, 8 March 2008). According to Jacinta Apola (Interview, 6 March 2008), a social worker who had worked with IDPs since 2002:

> Kony caused a lot of pain to the population and it would be important that he came out to see the pain he caused the people. If Kony is arrested and taken to The Hague, he will probably be jailed for life and in this case he will live in comfort not comparable to the pain he has caused the people. Even if he were to hang, he would not have had a personal experience of his atrocities.

This was echoed by a woman whose daughter had been abducted and raped by the LRA and who argued that it was important to reintegrate the LRA back into the community so that they would realise what they had done as killing them would not achieve this (Mother of abducted girl, Interview, 5 April 2008).

Underlying this sentiment was the view that Kony should be made to stay in the community in order to live with the consequences of his actions. Victims, in most cases, wished to be directly involved in the justice process in some way as they wanted justice to be seen to be done. Such sentiments have featured in various transitional justice processes in Africa, for instance in post-genocide Rwanda. During the proceedings of the ICTR in Arusha, Tanzania, the general public expressed interest in attending the court cases and judgements of some of the masterminds of the 1994 genocide. They were, however, distant from the proceedings and not actively involved in the tribunal processes. The tribunal was also seen, in terms of procedure, as foreign to Rwandese society (Human Rights Watch, 1999). This is one of the reasons why the *gacaca* court system was seen as relevant in filling the gap that arose between the ICTR and the Rwandan population. In similar respects, Ugandans who had suffered at the hands of Kony would feel even more detached if Kony were prosecuted and jailed in The Hague. International punishment for the perpetrators could be interpreted as a form of alienation which further severs relationships and harmony in a community already suffering from the impact of broken family relationships.

The views expressed by informants against the ICC reflect a diverse set of concerns. The first objection suggests a perceived lack of impartiality in the pursuit of perpetrators by the ICC. The second and the third objections focus on the fears that the ICC might bring more suffering. The underlying contention among ordinary people appears to be that if justice were to be seen to be done, then all sides needed to be held responsible. The final objection raises questions about how people conceived of the ICC. Some indicated that Kony needed to be more severely punished emotionally, so that he could feel the same pain that the LRA had caused the population. It appears that those who wished forgiveness for the LRA at the same time did not want a punishment that would be too lenient. What emerges is people's ambivalence and confusion about what they really meant when they spoke of forgiveness and punishment. This ambiguity highlights the complexity of what really should constitute the most appropriate of transitional justice mechanism.

Conclusion

This chapter shows that civilians living in northern Uganda suffered serious crimes at the hands of the LRA and government soldiers. These crimes were punishable according to standards of international criminal justice by following the rule of law, thereby justifying the ICC's intervention to bring the perpetrators to justice. But certain dimensions of the conflict, such as suffering inflicted on the entire society, did not directly fall within the legal jurisdiction of the ICC. Moreover, some of the perpetrators were initially victims of these same crimes. The issues raised here relate to the intersection of the nature of atrocities committed in northern Uganda, international justice systems and other forms of justice. What emerges is that it is not true that people did not want punishment or justice but that their concerns were complicated. They wanted the violence to stop, but they did not want their children to die. They may have been afraid of vengeance from the LRA, but did they really think about what it would mean to live with the perpetrators of violence in the future? Could they ever imagine what that would be like? Is this why they turned to the mechanisms of justice that they knew better? Were they sure that this form of justice would be the panacea? These questions are central to the contestations between goals of justice and interests of peace in societies making transitions from protracted conflicts characterised by serious atrocities.

Notes

1 Pre-Trial Chamber I Decision on the Prosecutor's Application for Warrants of Arrest (ICC-01/04-01/06-8), 10 February 2006.
2 Amnesty International, Public Statement 59/001/2004.

4 Local alternative approaches to transitional justice in northern Uganda

Introduction

The critique of the relevance of international criminal justice, as presented in the previous chapter, is based on the understanding that the nature and dynamics of the conflict in northern Uganda require more localised and context-specific approaches. Accordingly, civil society and traditional leaders called for a more restorative approach to the resolution of the situation. This entails a departure from strict adherence to the fundamental principles of the rule of law. This alternative system of justice would rely on reconciliation rather than punishment and would serve to heal the wounds caused by this devastating conflict to victims, offenders and entire communities. The present chapter builds on the previous chapter by exploring the nature and scope of local initiatives which were proposed as alternative responses to the incessant conflict in northern Uganda. Particular attention is paid to the attempts of truth commissions, the Uganda Amnesty Act 2000, the Juba Peace Talks and *mato oput*, the Acholi cleansing ceremony, all of which were advocated as alternatives to ICC intervention.

Earlier restorative justice mechanism: truth commissions in Uganda

The use of truth commissions in Uganda can be traced back to 1974 when Uganda under the regime of Idi Amin Dada established Commission of Enquiry into the Disappearances of People in Uganda since 25 January 1971. A truth commission is an official body, mandated by a national government, to investigate, document and report on human rights violation in a country over a specified period of time (Teitel, 2003b, p. 78). Generally truth commissions were constituted, following the fall of an authoritarian government, by a successor government to expose past injustices and facilitate the reconciliatory process (Rotberg, 2000, p. 3). Thus the goal of truth commissions was to make hidden truths public so as to help facilitate the reconciliatory process. The philosophy behind such attempts is that truth, not punishment, contributes to reconciliation.

Truth commissions were also used in Argentina to achieve reconciliation in post-junta Argentina following the collapse of the military regime in 1983 (Teitel, 2003b, p. 78). The use of truth commissions up-surged in the post-Cold War periods as a response to mass atrocities and became a dominant instrument in post-apartheid South Africa in the 1990s when the apartheid regime and its structures were dismantled. As a result of decades of conflict in South Africa, parties to the pre-1994 negotiation process agreed that, in order to deal with the challenges of the new democracy and face the future with confidence, the violence of the past had to be exposed and acknowledged – hence the South African Truth and Reconciliation Commission (TRC) (Maepa, 2005, p. 66).

The commission's key restorative goals included generation of in-depth information on the extent, nature and causes of human rights violations in South Africa under apartheid; identifying persons responsible for the violations; providing a platform for the victims to bring out their feelings. It was also aimed at granting amnesty to those who offered to disclose their involvement in such violations and giving recommendations on how to prevent future human rights violations (Graybill, 1998). An amnesty is a legislative undertaking by a state to pardon offences punishable by law and as such goes against the principles of the rule of law (Bhargava, 2002, pp. 1309, 1327).

The South African TRC stressed the importance of acknowledgement. This was based on the belief that acknowledgement of the truth would lead to healing, reconciliation and nation-building. According to Villa-Vicencio (2003, p. 235) the TRC provided the fragile South African context with an opportunity to explore an option for nation-building. The TRC was to promote peaceful co-existence while highlighting the need to understand the 'motives and perspective' of all involved in conflicts of the past, as the beginning of a process that could ultimately lead to national reconciliation (ibid.). As such, the TRC was a restorative transitional mechanism designed to allow a society characterised by conflicts, injuries and brokenness to make the step towards a future holding out the prospect of respect for human rights, democracy, peaceful co-existence and development opportunities (ibid., p. 237). Accordingly, the TRC, though quasi-judicial in terms of its operation, fulfilled the basic principles of restorative justice by focusing on truth, healing, reconciliation and reintegration.

The first attempt to deal with gross violations of human rights in Uganda is traceable back to 1974 when the Commission of Enquiry into the Disappearances of People in Uganda was established.[1] The commission was established under the reign of Idi Amin to enquire into the aspects of the disappearances of persons in Uganda since 25 January 1971. The commission was also expected to recommend what the government should do to stop the disappearances of people in Uganda. The establishment of the commission was in response to public pressure that demanded an investigation of the disappearances (Hayner, 1994, p. 612).

The commission was chaired by an expatriate Pakistani Judge, Justice Mohamed Saied, two Ugandan Superintendents and a Ugandan army officer. The Commission had power to compel witnesses to testify and to call for evidence from official sources, although access to information was frustrated by actors in the government, such as military police and intelligence (Carver, 1990, p. 612). The commission concluded that the Public Safety Unit and the State Research Bureau, special security bodies set by Amin, were the institutions mainly responsible for the disappearances (ibid., p. 356). It also condemned army officers, military police and intelligence for abuse of office (ibid.). The Commission recommended that police and security forces be reformed and law enforcement officials be trained in the legal rights of citizens. Ultimately, the commission had little impact and the commissioners were targeted for reprisal which led to the Pakistani Judge losing his employment with the government, one commissioner being framed with murder charges and subsequently sentenced to death and the third fleeing the country (ibid., p. 400). There was no positive impact of the commission and murder by Amin forces increased.

A better-intentioned attempt as a form of transitional justice is associated with the rule of General Tito Okello. After overthrowing Obote's second regime, General Okello made attempts to bring lasting peace to Uganda. As part of this peace initiative, Okello invited all rebel groups that had been fighting Obote's regime to join his Government. This invitation implied that the junta offered pardon to all the groups despite any serious crimes they may have committed in the course of their insurgencies (Apuuli, 2005, p. 43). He also initiated peace negotiations as part of the effort to bring lasting peace to Uganda. This took the form of comprehensive peace talks held in Nairobi with other rebel groups involved in insurgencies against Obote's Government, as mentioned in Chapter 2. Despite the peace talks resulting in an agreement signed in December 1985 in Nairobi, peace was short-lived as Museveni's NRA/M failed to honour the agreement. Museveni's guerrillas continued fighting and soon afterwards overthrew Okello's Government.

When Museveni came to power, his Government enacted certain legislation designed to encourage opponents to return from exile or to cease fighting. For example, in 1987 the National Resistance Council (NRC) passed the Amnesty Statute of 1987 (Jones, 2009, pp. 56–7). This was a presidential pardon which was aimed at rebels such as the UPDA/M and Ugandans who were living in exile and were reluctant to return to the country for fear of reprisals (ibid.). However, under the 1987 Amnesty Statute four offences were considered too heinous for the perpetrators to be granted amnesty. These offences were genocide, murder, kidnapping and rape (Afako, 2002). Thus, the 1987 Amnesty Statute did not provide a blanket amnesty but rather a selective one and failed to end rebel activities in the country.

The Amnesty Act 2000

A notable legislative initiative undertaken some years before the situation in northern Uganda was referred to the ICC was the Amnesty Bill introduced in 1998 by the Ugandan parliament with regard to the LRA. The bill was a product of pressure on the Government emerging both from within Uganda and from abroad to end the conflict (Apuuli, 2006, p. 44). At the international level, the Amnesty Act passed by the Ugandan Government was pressurised by negotiations taking place in Sudan between the Khartoum Government and the SPLM (Finnegan, 2005, p. 41). Peace in northern Uganda and peace in Sudan were intimately linked. The Ugandan Government agreed to stop supporting the SPLA who were fighting the Sudanese Government while Khartoum reciprocated by withdrawing support from the LRA (ibid.). This was consistent with the diplomatic agreement between Khartoum and Kampala brokered by Jimmy Carter. From within Uganda, local Acholi leaders began to put pressure on the Government to pass an amnesty act that would allow the rebels to surrender (Latigo, 2008, pp. 94–5). According to Ojara Latigo, Museveni had maintained a strong belief in the ability of his military response against the LRA and had not been willing to negotiate meaningfully with the LRA who he considered criminals (ibid.). Acholi leaders considered amnesty a more feasible option after it became apparent that the military response and formal criminal prosecution of all the LRA members for the atrocities allegedly committed would be impracticable. The amnesty initiative was designed to encourage the LRA fighters to surrender (Allen, 2006, p. 74). Even though the Amnesty Act was aimed primarily at the LRA, it offered a broad-based pardon to all Ugandans who had been engaged in acts of rebellion against the Government of Uganda since 26 January 1986 (Apuuli, 2006, p. 44).

The Amnesty Bill was introduced in 1998, but it was, however, not until 2000 that it was enacted as the Amnesty Act of 2000, Cap 294 of Uganda law, with the goal 'to provide for an Amnesty for Ugandans involved in acts of a warlike nature in various parts of the country and for other connected purposes' (Uganda Government, 2000, Cap 294, Law of Uganda). The Act was founded on what its preamble referred to as:

> The expressed desire of the people of Uganda to end armed hostilities, reconcile with those whom they have caused suffering and rebuild their communities and the desire and determination of the Government to genuinely implement its policy of reconciliation …
>
> (Ibid., Preamble)

The terms of the Act provided that those who had been accused of human rights violations would be, in effect, forgiven. In the Act 'amnesty' meant 'pardon, forgiveness, exemption or discharge from criminal prosecution or any other form of punishment by the state' (The Amnesty Act 2000, Law of Uganda, Cap 294, Section 1). In this respect, the Act provided that,

> An Amnesty is declared in respect of any Ugandan who [had] at any time since the 26th day of January, 1986 engaged in or [was] engaging in war or armed rebellion against the government of the Republic of Uganda by (a) actual participation in combat; (b) collaborating with the perpetrators of the war or armed rebellion; (c) committing any other crime in the furtherance

of the war or armed rebellion; or (d) assisting or aiding the conduct or prosecution of the war or armed rebellion.

(Ibid., Section 3(1))

In this respect, the objective of the Act was to forgive those involved in armed rebellion, bring an end to the conflict, promote reconciliation and prevent 'unnecessary suffering' (ibid.). According to the Act, any person falling within the category described in Section 3(1) of the Act, '[S]hall not be prosecuted or subjected to any form of punishment for the participation in the war or rebellion for any crime committed in the cause of the war or armed rebellion' (Uganda Government, 2000, Cap 294, Law of Uganda Law, Section 3(2))

To qualify for amnesty, the Act required that a person:

- a report to the nearest Army or Police Unit, a Chief, a member of the Executive Committee of a local government unit, a magistrate or a religious leader within the locality;
- b renounce and abandon involvement in the war or armed rebellion;
- c surrender at any such place or to any such authority or person any weapons in his or her possession; and
- d be issued with a Certificate of Amnesty…

(Ibid., Section 3(1))

Section 4(5) of the Act provided that in a situation where a person granted amnesty was living outside Uganda, such a person would have to '[report] to any Ugandan diplomatic mission, consulate or any international organisation which has agreed with the Government of Uganda to receive such persons' (ibid., Section 3(5) (b)).

If amnesty was accepted, it offered its recipients binding and lasting legal immunity from prosecution or punishment for crimes committed during insurgency activity during the period specified. However, new legislation was later introduced by the government, which held that, if, after receiving amnesty, a further insurgency offence were committed, the recipient would not be protected from prosecution for the new offence.

The Amnesty Act came into effect on the 21 January 2000 and was initially intended to remain in force for a period not exceeding six months subject to ministerial extension (ibid., Section 17). It was, however, later extended several times to enable rebels to surrender and continued to remain in force for a number of the years that followed. Before the Amnesty Act of 2000 was enacted, the Government had insisted that the 1998 Amnesty Bill should be consistent with the 1987 presidential pardon, which excluded certain offences such as genocide, murder, kidnapping and rape (Finnegan, 2005, p. 42). This proposal was rejected by the leaders from the northern part of the country, particularly members of the ARLPI who called for a comprehensive blanket amnesty. The ARLPI strongly advocated the adoption of a comprehensive amnesty, arguing that threats of prosecution to any of the combatants would pose an obstacle to the peaceful resolution of the conflict (ibid., pp. 40–2). Ironically the support for a comprehensive blanket amnesty emerged from the very communities which were directly affected by the conflict. This indicates that a strong desire for reconciliation existed within the victim community (ibid., p. 42). Given this strong desire for reconciliation, the extent of the role played by Acholi leaders in pressuring the Government's decision to adopt the Amnesty Act remains to be considered.

The Amnesty Act 2000 and the politics of the northern Uganda conflict

Tim Allen claims that the Act did not receive positive backing from President Museveni who only assented to it hesitantly (Allen, 2006, p. 77). Although Allen does not provide clear evidence in support of his claim, the claim is corroborated by some factors. First among these factors was President Museveni's general attitude towards the LRA which made him sceptical about the possibility of a peaceful end to the conflict. President Museveni had repeatedly declared that his Government forces would defeat the LRA militarily, yet the military option was a devastating failure putting the Government's military solution into question (Latigo, 2008, pp. 94–5). Moreover, the President did not consider the LRA a group with whom he could negotiate. Latigo observes that, in August 1986, Museveni went to Gulu to address the people of Acholiland about the rebel war and swore that he would never talk peace with the LRA who he described as criminals with no real cause (ibid.). In a 1987 speech President Museveni referred to the insurgency as a product of 'rear-guard actions of defeated, moribund, sectarian and neocolonial elements' (Museveni, 1987). He also referred to the insurgency as

> elements that have caused untold suffering to the people of Uganda, violated human rights, murdered people, destroyed the economy and violated the sovereignty of the people of Uganda [... and] fighting and annihilating these types of elements is a justified cause.
>
> (Ibid.)

Moreover, in early 2002, just as the amnesty process appeared to be bearing fruit with many members of the LRA returning from the bush, the Government seems to have frustrated the process by embarking on Operation Iron Fist: a military operation intended to conclude the war. This only served to worsen the situation as the rebels, in retaliation, intensified their attacks on the civilian population (Refugee Law Project, 2006, p. vii). The military could not deliver victory because the army was reportedly riddled with command and control problems, corruption and inefficiency, was unmotivated and, as a result of its past failures, lacked the support of local populations (Latigo, 2008, pp. 94–5). The military failure placed the President in an awkward position since it would mean embracing the alternative: the amnesty. However, embracing amnesty as a solution would mean conceding the failure of his military option which he had held in high esteem. While the President found it unpalatable to accept the failure, the Acholi leaders pressured the Government to pass the Amnesty Bill.

Other views held that President Museveni may not have wished the war in northern Uganda to come to an end through the amnesty so as to prolong the benefits of what can be referred to as the political economy of war in northern Uganda (Ongom, Interview, 11 January 2008; Odwar, Interview, 16 March 2008; Olweny, Interview, 3 April 2008). According to the theory of the political economy of war in northern Uganda, the persistent insurgency in northern Uganda served the interests of both the Government and the rebels. Kustenbauder (2008, pp. 3–4) argues that the persistent war offered significant political, economic and military advantages to Museveni's Government. According to Kustenbauder, the war in northern Uganda contributed to growth in the national economy because, when the LRA were declared a terrorist organisation by the US Government, fighting them became part of the larger war on terror justifying military assistance, foreign development assistance and relief aid especially from the US (ibid.). The third political advantage mentioned by analysts is that peace and stability in the north of the country would offer a strong opposition to Museveni's grip on power. These observations seem to corroborate the claim that President Museveni could not fully embrace the amnesty initiative. Since amnesty was intended to bring about peace and stability in northern Uganda it would not be a welcome idea for president Museveni. It is not easy to establish the authenticity of these views, however, they shaped some opinions regarding Museveni's attitude towards the amnesty.

Even though President Museveni's commitment to the amnesty was questionable, there was enthusiastic support for the Amnesty Act of 2000 from political activists, churches, non-governmental organisations (NGOs), traditional leaders and sections of the Acholi population in northern Uganda (Allen, 2006, p. 76; Refugee Law Project, 2004, p. 45). Those who supported the Act understood amnesty as forgiveness. Tim Allen observes that religious organisations and traditional leaders understood amnesty to mean forgiveness arguing that the traditional Acholi system of justice is based on forgiveness (Allen, 2006, pp. 76–7). The Refugee Law Project (2004, p. 45) suggests that the ARLPI and sections of the Acholi population held that amnesty was consistent with traditional Acholi dispute resolution mechanisms because it was anchored on the Acholi idea of forgiveness. The Acholi system of justice was based on a belief that revenge does not solve conflicts. Traditionally conflicts among the Acholi were solved through forgiveness and reconciliation. Given the understanding that the Amnesty Act resonated with the cultural values of the Acholi people, it was considered appropriate and relevant to the context of the LRA insurgency. In the spirit of amnesty, all LRA returnees would be accepted back into their communities and pardoned. For this reason the process was perceived as a positive strategy because the initiative would enable 'the Government to genuinely implement its policy of reconciliation in order to establish peace, security and tranquillity throughout the whole country' (Amnesty Act 2000, Cap 294, Law of Uganda, Section 4(1)).

Implementation of the Amnesty Act

To bring the Statute into effect, Sections 6–16 of the Act provided for an Amnesty Commission to encourage those who had been involved in systematic human rights abuses to seek amnesty. According to an undated document, *A Handbook for Implementation of the Amnesty Act 2000: Procedures and Principles of Operation*, the Amnesty Commission was to convince combatants of the advantages of surrendering and accepting amnesty and to encourage victim communities to reconcile with those who perpetrated atrocities against them. The commission was also charged with ensuring that the rebels conformed to the conditions of the amnesty and were received into the communities (Amnesty Commission, n.d.). The creation of a Demobilisation, Disarmament and Resettlement Team (DDRT) was also provided for under the Act. This team was commissioned to take charge of the disarmament process and facilitate the reintegration into the community of those who applied for amnesty under the legislation. The Amnesty Commission and the DDRT were expected to undertake relevant activities including, promotion of dialogue, sensitisation, drawing up programmes for decommissioning of weapons and resettlement of returnees (ibid.). In ordinary military terminology, demobilisation means either the dissolution of an armed unit, the reduction of the number of combatants in an armed group or temporary dissolution in an interim stage before the reassembly of the armed forces, be they regular or irregular forces. This often takes place when a new government or a dominant regime questions the political legitimacy of an armed group following a military stalemate which draws the warring parties to the negotiation table (Gleichmann et al., 2004, p. 15). In the 2000 Amnesty Act, demobilisation referred to the complete dissolution of armed groups. Disarmament forms an integral part of demobilisation in that it constitutes handing over of weapons used by the demobilised personnel to the authorities who take charge of the safeguarding, redistribution or destruction of said weapons (ibid.). Reintegration is a social and economic process by which ex-combatants take on civilian status and forms of work (ibid.). Reintegration of ex-combatants is necessary for sustainable peace because if ex-combatants are not incorporated into the community both economically and socially they are likely to turn to practices that threaten peace and security such as robbery or drug addiction.

As part of the Amnesty Act of 2000, the DDRT began following a disarmament, demobilisation and reintegration programme in 2005. The programme sought to support ex-combatants' efforts to start new lives and reintegrate into the community (ICG, 23 June 2005). Some of those who sought amnesty received a reintegration package as part of the DDR programme. The programme provided those who surrendered with resettlement packages which included the equivalent of US$150 and a home kit which included a mattress, a blanket, saucepans, plates, cups, a hoe, maize flour and seeds (Mugabi, 7 October 2009). The undertaking, however, was largely inadequate. The Amnesty Commission and the DDRT did not have the capacity to play a broader social role in the reintegration process and results were deficient. The Amnesty Commission and the DDRT were overwhelmed by a sudden influx of thousands of people without income who sought reintegration into the community. The programmes were under strain to provide projects that could sustain the reporters as there was insufficient funding to cater for the large number reporters who needed to be integrated back to ordinary life (ibid.).

Moreover, these DDR programmes focused on reuniting families and providing psychosocial care-activities to lessen psychological trauma and social dislocation (Blattman & Annan, 2008). DDR economic programmes tend towards keeping ex-combatants occupied after demobilisation so as to cut off their ties with the rebels. But economic and educational programmes remained small in scale. And, even if effective, the promotion of short-term activities only resulted in short-term solutions. But, an increased supply of services through increased vocational training and enterprise development programmes soon encountered lack of demand. This is because, establishment of enterprises such as numerous kiosks, tailoring shops sooner or later resulted in over-supply of services against the meagre economic base of camp economies. This rendered such activities unprofitable in the long run. Accordingly, these activities did little to help the youth recover their losses and increase their productivity. A comprehensive economic transformation would be more viable for sustainable stability in the region.

The outcomes of the amnesty initiative

The Amnesty Act had some immediate positive outcomes. Its existence encouraged hundreds of insurgents around the country to return to their homes. Some of the LRA's key members such as Brigadier Sam Kolo, a former chief spokesman for the LRA, took advantage of the amnesty law and surrendered (Ruaudel & Timpson, 2005). David Okwera, Albino Ongom, and Michael Okwar, ex-LRA combatants, who I interviewed, informed me that news of the amnesty they received through radio or by word of mouth motivated them and many of their fellow combatants to leave the bush and return home (A group Interview with three returnees, Interview, 17 March 2008). David Okwera said,

> Some of us in the bush wanted to escape and return back home, but we were afraid of being rejected or being arrested by the Government. The news of amnesty which we received through *Mega Radio* encouraged us to escape.

In Acholi, even before the arrival of the Amnesty Commission, the community, local government and other agencies had developed reception and reintegration programmes for those returning through the Acholi traditional system of justice. The Commission also retained the responsibility for the legal procedure of issuing amnesty certificates. By mid-2004, over 5,000 LRA soldiers had surrendered and applied for amnesty (Allen, 2006, pp. 75–6). By June 2005, more than 15,000 former combatants and abductees of the LRA had taken advantage of the Amnesty Act (Ssenyonjo, 2005). As a result of the apparent success of the amnesty legislation, some Ugandan political opposition groups, such as the

Forum for Democratic Change (FDC) and civil society organisations like the ARLPI, were supportive of amnesty as a plausible route to peace (Komakech, 2004). The Amnesty Act had political consequences because it allowed other initiatives towards dialogue and, on the whole, had the potential to enable further peace negotiations and reconciliation. The pardoning of war crimes, as understood in the framework of restorative justice, was to contribute to the achievement of the nobler social good of peace and stability.

Regardless of the restorative goal of the amnesty and the apparently positive response from many LRA combatants, the LRA leadership rejected the Amnesty Act and discouraged its fighters from benefiting from it since LRA representatives had not been party to the formulation of the law (Quinn, 2009). In their estimation, since the amnesty was extended without LRA consultation in negotiations, it amounted to a one-sided amnesty. There was no strong reason to believe the top LRA command would accept an agreement of which they had played no part in negotiation (Latigo, 2008, pp. 95–6). Amnesty was offered on the grounds that the rebels were guilty and that the Government was exercising mercy in the hope that the rebels would welcome the spirit of the pardon.

Hovil and Quinn (2005) suggest that the Amnesty Act of 2000 that prevailed in northern Uganda was different from other amnesties initiated in other situations of transitional justice. They point out that the amnesty granted in Chile, for instance, targeted military personnel after the conflict was over. The Chilean Amnesty provided blanket immunity for the military from being prosecuted in the trials that would follow. The amnesty granted in South Africa as part of the TRC initiative was a negotiated outcome granted in exchange for full disclosure of information regarding human rights abuse. The South African TRC was only set up after the apartheid government had left office. The amnesty in Uganda was declared before the end of the conflict (ibid.). It was meant to create an environment conducive to negotiations and put an end to the conflict.

Since the Amnesty Act of 2000 was not a negotiated agreement between warring parties, the willingness on the part of both sides of the conflict, especially the LRA leadership to engage in DDR was doubtful. Ordinarily, for parties to take part in a DDR programme there is a need for a peace agreement to govern the process. In the Ugandan situation, the armed groups such as the LRA had not willingly agreed that they be demobilised and disarmed, instead they were unilaterally offered pardon by the Government whose victory in the armed struggle was far from decided. Those among the rebels who benefited from amnesty, from the point of view of the rebel groups, were deserters. In this respect, the Amnesty Act did not fulfil its ultimate goal of bringing lasting peace and the LRA continued its strategy of abduction and looting. The situation remained precarious for those living in IDPs in the following years.

The Juba Peace Talks

Another notable local initiative which attempted to bring lasting peace to northern Uganda was the Juba peace initiative. The initiative began in 2006 and promised a more sustained peace process between the LRA and the Ugandan Government compared to previous attempts made since the beginning of the conflict in 1986. The intention of the initiative was to open a path for LRA rebels to surrender and to provide for the eventual execution of a traditional justice system.

The role of civil society in the Juba Peace Talks

The Juba Peace Talks were the brainchild of the Acholi Religious Leader's Peace Initiative (ARLPI). The ARLPI came into existence in 1997 as a response to the incessant conflict between the Government and the LRA. The initiative comprised an inter-faith collaboration of leaders from the Catholic Church, the Anglican Church of Uganda, the Orthodox Church and Muslims in the districts of Gulu and Kitgum in northern Uganda. Bishop Macleod Baker Ochola II, an Anglican cleric, points to the significance of this partnership of religious leaders, remarking that the ARLPI '[pooled] together moral authority, status and an extensive organisational anchor of churches, parishes and mosques' (Ochola, 2004, p. 4).

The ARLPI was formally inaugurated in February 1998 to proactively pursue a peaceful means of bringing an end to the conflict in northern Uganda. It pursued this goal through community-based mediation, advocacy, peaceful negotiation, community mobilisation and awareness creation. Thus, the main objectives of the ARLPI included uniting and mobilising the people especially from the Acholi region to pursue peace and development and to promote the advocacy of social justice and human rights in the conflict area (ibid.). It also sought to build capacity in conflict analysis and conflict resolution. It promoted the idea of peaceful co-existence and good neighbourliness for different communities in Uganda. Finally, the ARLPI sought to undertake any other activities which might contribute to the '[... creation and promotion] of love, harmony, forgiveness, reconciliation, healing and peace' (ibid.). It is on the basis of these goals that the ARLPI supported the Amnesty Act of 2000 and subsequent peace processes.

According to Matthew Odong, the Secretary General of ARLPI, the local religious leadership 'wanted to be part of the solution to the problem and to contribute towards ending the conflict and to provide an alternative to the parties who believe in the military option' (Odong, Interview, 27 March 2008). They likened the situation to the saying that '... when two bulls are fighting then it is the grass that suffers which, in this case, is the Acholi population' (ibid.). According to Matthew Odong, the ARLPI appealed to all parties involved in the conflict: the Government, the LRA and victims. On the Government side, they sought to highlight the fact that a military option was not a feasible solution to the problem and would only result in ever more carnage. For this reason, the ARLPI asked the Government to consider engaging the LRA in talks. The ARLPI appealed to the LRA to put down arms and seriously consider dialogue and to embrace forgiveness and reconciliation. To the victims, they pointed out that, in keeping with religious values, there could be no peace, nor a stable future, without forgiveness. Mathew Odong (ibid.) argued, 'Unless the victims forgive as Jesus forgave, the war will not end.' They also pointed out that those who were in the bush, even though they had committed all sorts of atrocities, were not strangers but brothers and sisters, sons and daughters of the community because they had been abducted from among the people. Underlying all these appeals was the notion of forgiveness and reconciliation.

As a consortium of religious organisations, the ARLPI sought to promote the values of the dignity of human life, of joy, of peace, of happiness and of the sanctity of life (ibid.). Odong (ibid.), remarked '... the values of preservation of human life is what is binding us together and leaving everybody happy'. He went further to say that, in modern terms justice meant prosecution and imprisonment if the defendant was found guilty, yet he reasoned that this could not be an appropriate mechanism in northern Uganda as prosecutions would not bring about lasting peace.

The role of the Acholi religious leaders' initiative was, thus, to persuade the people to move in a new direction. In this respect, the generally positive disposition towards the idea of forgiving the LRA that preceded the Juba Peace Talks was the product of lobbying and advocacy by the religious leaders. The impact of religious leaders cannot be underestimated given their influence at grassroots level, their simple message and the core human values which they advocated. In this respect, the Carnegie Commission (1997, p. 104) observes:

> Religious leaders and institutions are well-suited for promoting peace for a variety of reasons; a clear message that resonates with their followers; a long standing and pervasive presence on the ground; a well-developed infrastructure that often includes a sophisticated communications network connecting local, national and international offices; a legitimacy for speaking out on crisis issues; and a traditional orientation to peace and goodwill.

Conflicts in some parts of Africa like Sudan and Nigeria are linked to religious rivalry. Even in Uganda the association of religious identities in politics, as manifested in the rise of religious political parties such as the DP in post-independence Uganda, was associated with the protracted conflicts in Uganda. This notwithstanding, Christian institutions have played significant roles in terms of fostering human development in Africa since the Christian church is the most pervasive religious institution in most parts of sub-Saharan Africa (Gifford, 1999, p. 57). This dominance is necessitated by values and beliefs central to Christianity such as compassion, love, justice, sacrifice, trustworthiness, belief in the dignity of a human person and respect for fundamental human rights. Inspired by these fundamentals, Christian institutions have brought social development, especially in the fields of education, health services, guidance and counselling, food programmes, empowerment and the pursuit of peace and justice. Religious organisations, therefore, have filled the gaps left open by the negligence and incapacity of many African state structures. This was the case in the situation in northern Uganda. Since the situation in northern Uganda for the most part had not been in the international limelight, it was the religious bodies which were available and provided moral and practical support to their parishioners in this conflict-ridden zone. Church institutions became centres of support for thousands seeking shelter from violence. It is against this background that over time, a greater consensus emerged among church leaders regarding the need to be proactive in bearing witness to the conflict, and to engage directly in peacebuilding (Rodriguez, 2002, p. 58). The proximity of religious institutions to the people and the values for which they stood made their message of forgiveness palatable and powerful among the people.

Notwithstanding the fact that the ARLPI were at the forefront of initiating the Juba Peace Talks, the religious organisation only remained as observers during the formal talks. They continued, however, to play an important role even after having initiated the talks. For instance those who would wish to surrender following agreements were supposed to do so through ARLPI channels (Odwar, Interview, 16 March 2008).

The Juba Peace Talks process

On 16 May 2006, the President of Southern Sudan, Salva Kiir Mayardit announced that his Government would convene and broker peace talks between the LRA and the Government of Uganda, having agreed on terms with President Museveni and Joseph Kony. Thus, the Juba Peace Talks were formerly mediated by southern Sudanese Vice-President Riek Machar and former president of Mozambique and UN Special Envoy to northern Uganda, Joaquim Chissano (House of Commons Development Committee, July 2007, p. 13). Joaquim Chissano had been named by the UN Secretary General as his Special Envoy for the situation in northern Uganda, with a mandate to search for a comprehensive political solution to address the root causes of the conflict, including liaising with the ICC (ibid., pp. 13–14).

Negotiations began in July 2006 in Juba, the capital of southern Sudan. Taking part in the Juba Peace Talks were the Government of Uganda and the LRA. To create an environment conducive to peace talks, the Ugandan President Yoweri Museveni offered total amnesty to all LRA combatants including the top five LRA leaders in July 2006, on condition that the Juba Peace Talks met with success (Allen, 2006). The LRA/M on their part instituted a unilateral ceasefire on 4 August, 2006. Following the ceasefire, an agreement was signed between the Government of Uganda and the LRA/M, to cease hostilities which took effect on 29 August 2006. This was the first formal bilateral agreement between the parties in the two decades of the armed conflict (ICG, 14 September 2007, p. 5).

The ceasefire agreement called for all LRA fighters to assemble at and remain within 15 km of Ri-Kwangba, in South Sudan's Western Equatoria province for final disarmament and demobilisation. The LRA fighters were also assured of protection within the specified location. They were not technically in compliance, however, because they remained on the Congolese side of the border (ibid.). Kony and most of the LRA fighters were at a jungle base in Garamba

National Park in the DRC as of June 2007. There was also to be an official release of women and children associated with the LRA as part of the cessation of hostilities agreement.

The peace talks were seen to offer the best chance to end the 20-year civil war while the ICC arrest warrants were considered to be a complicating factor. In this respect, Vincent Otti, who was then the LRA second in command, was quoted as saying in October 2006 that the 'ICC was the greatest obstacle to the peace process' (Halera, 2006). Elsewhere, Otti was quoted as saying that 'as long as the ICC arrest warrants were still upheld then there would be no prospect of peace' since the LRA top commanders suspected that the Government's offer of amnesty could be meant merely to entice them out of the bush only to have them placed in ICC custody (Banya, 2006).

For a period at least, the talks were a success since they managed to remove most LRA combatants from Uganda and allowed thousands of civilians anguished by the protracted war to experience some sort of calm. Some returnees had been motivated by the talks to come out of the bush. They received the information from the media which encouraged them to escape (Group Interview, 17 March 2008). They had desired that the talks succeed. The former abductees and LRA combatants expressed their opinion that the talks would be the best way to resolve the conflict since they did 'not see any side defeating the other as Kony could not be as easily defeated as the Government had mistakenly believed' (ibid.). These sentiments were echoed by Joseph Okwera in an interview with a group of elders, who expressed the people's optimism about the Juba talks (Elders group, Interview 2 April 2008). He argued that for the sake of peace for the people, the Government needed to accept and put pressure on the ICC to withdraw the case against the LRA given that, from experience, military action had failed and could not solve the problem (ibid.). While he underlined the significance and the viability of the talks, he discounted the possibility that ICC intervention could solve the problem (ibid.).

As the talks progressed in Juba, there emerged signs of levels of trust and confidence conducive to reconciliation and to the resettlement of the displaced populations (Grono & O'Brien, October 2007). As a gesture of goodwill, the Government of Uganda had already offered a total amnesty to the LRA fighters. President Museveni considered this offer a golden opportunity for Kony and the LRA since, in his opinion, the LRA had been defeated militarily by the Government (Wasike, 28 August 2006). To reassure the LRA, President Museveni went against the ICC demands and stated that he would not hand Kony over to the ICC if the latter came out and personally apologised upon the signing of the Comprehensive Peace Agreement (CPA) that was to be negotiated in the Juba Peace Talks. Handing Kony over, for Museveni, would amount to betraying the indicted rebel leader (Rugunda, 2006).

LRA grievances at the Juba Peace Talks

Having been invited to the talks, the LRA acquired some legitimacy from the Juba Peace Talks. They began to be viewed in the talks not as criminal perpetrators of serious atrocities, responsible for thousands of deaths, but as a political voice speaking on behalf of northern Ugandans. The LRA demanded an end to the marginalisation of the Acholi, inclusion of the Acholi in government, political and economic processes, the development of the north and an end to the targeting of the Acholi for extermination (ARLPI Delegate in Juba Peace Talks, Interview, 31 March 2008). Regardless of the atrocities committed by the LRA, the grievances they raised were representative of the dissatisfaction of the wider Acholi population living in northern Uganda. This is captured in the remarks of Charles Olweny (Interview, 3 April 2008) below:

> The current government, a government of the southerners has not developed the north. All development goes to the south; government positions go to the south. The government looks at the LRA and the northerners as one, as government enemies, that the LRA and northerners are birds of the same feathers.

This sentiment reflects general perceptions about the Museveni administration. The Acholi also felt marginalised by Museveni's Government and demanded political, economic and social initiatives that would give them a higher stake in the decision-making process. They demanded participation in the central government. Some of the reasons for this perception include the fact that the economic and social prosperity in the south contrasted sharply with the situation in the north characterised by abductions, landmines, displacements.[2] Northern Uganda lagged behind most parts of the country in terms of human development. Loss of assets resulting from lootings and displacement, poor infrastructure, lack of social services and poor access to markets were responsible for retarding economic activities (Nannyanjo, August 2005, p. 9). From 1986, the NRM regime had engaged in peace and prosperity initiatives which saw the country gain stability and economic progress, but these improvements were largely felt in the southern part of the country.

Against the backdrop of perceived Acholi marginalisation by Museveni's regime, the LRA appeared to a section of the local community as the only remaining group able to face the UPDF's brutality and the marginalisation of northern Uganda by the Government. Though lacking outward popular support, Kony was a symbol of emancipation in the conflict between the people of Acholi and the Government. Kony and the LRA enjoyed some support from prominent Acholi people living both in Uganda and in the diaspora who offered him not only financial support but also legal and political advice, according to Patrick Okulu, an ex-abductee (Okulu, Interview, 30 March 2008). This recognition of the LRA needs to be understood in the context of the marginalisation of the Acholi people living in northern Uganda.

During my interview with Odong of the ARLPI, I asked whether the invitation of Kony to the peace talks amounted to the legitimisation of the LRA despite the atrocities that they had committed. His view was that, 'this was a unique situation calling for unique approach'. (Odong, Interview, 27 March

2008). He reiterated that the ARLPI did not recognise the legitimacy of the LRA, but emphasised that their activities destroyed life and that the talks represented a practical means of ending the violence. Odong (ibid.) disputed the LRA's claims that they were acting in defence of the Acholi and reasoned that this claim was not sincere, since 'if they were honestly fighting for the Acholi, why then do they kill the very innocent Acholi?'. However, while he agreed that the LRA were insincere and brutal, Odong maintained that they needed to be forgiven for the sake of future peace.

There existed an obvious paradox. The Acholi community felt marginalised; Kony claimed to be fighting to redeem the people from this marginalisation but his organisation committed atrocities against the very population it claimed to be protecting. Due to Kony's tactics, the people rejected his movement, but at the Juba Peace Talks supported the pardoning of his group. This paradox could be explained by the fact that, the Acholi people had been the principal victims of both the LRA and the UPDF. In addition to the violence of the LRA and the UPDF, the Acholi had experienced the disruption of their entire social, economic and cultural life during their long internment in IDP camps. Because of this, a deep-seated desire for peace appeared to shape their attitudes towards the situation in northern Uganda. Moreover, Acholi grievances against the government could not be nullified by the brutal means used by the LRA.

Although a portion of the population felt that they needed to forgive the LRA for the sake of peace, Kony himself treated the talks with contempt. In terms of generally accepted standards regarding international human rights and in light of their atrocities, the LRA were an illegitimate group and their place at the negotiation table could not be clearly justified; the criminal courts or tribunals seeming rather more fitting for an organisation of its type. The LRA leadership were no doubt aware of their crimes. And this is probably why, in the initial stages, neither Joseph Kony nor Vincent Otti were enthusiastic to attend the talks in Juba fearing possible arrest having been well advised by their 'very good lawyers and political advisors' (Okulu, Interview, 30 March 2008). Indeed, during these initial stages, the LRA negotiators at Juba were primarily from the diaspora. Kony and Otti did not directly join the talks but had been visited by Ugandan Government negotiators and maintained telephone contact with them (ICG, 14 September 2007, p. 2).

Kony was very well informed and knew he could possibly be arrested even after signing a peace deal and he would not take such a risk (Okulu, Interview, 30 March 2008). Indeed, the LRA demanded that the Ugandan Government publicly guarantee that they would not be surrendered to the ICC. Kony insisted during the talks that the ICC dropped the indictments against them (ARLPI Delegate in Juba Peace Talks, Interview, 31 March 2008). He was aware that he could be arrested later and charged as had happened to Sierra Leone's rebel leader, Foday Sankoh, whose forces had committed widespread atrocities. After Sankoh had been offered an amnesty and even appointed as the vice-president, he was finally arrested, and indicted by the Special Court for Sierra Leone for crimes against humanity (Doyl, 2006). Similarly, the former president of Liberia,

Charles Taylor, was indicted by the UN-backed Special Court for Sierra Leone (SCSL), before being offered asylum in Nigeria. Though Taylor was offered asylum in contravention of court orders, international pressure was placed on Nigeria to hand over Taylor to the court (HRW, 26 January 2006). Eventually, Taylor was arrested and charged by the SCSL for war crimes, crimes against humanity and other serious violations of international humanitarian law such as the use of child soldiers during Sierra Leone's armed conflict that spanned over ten years (HRW, June 2006). This could well have been Kony's fate.

The outcome of the Juba peace initiative

Amid fears and suspicions, the Juba Peace Talks continued and, on 2 May 2007, an agreement on a comprehensive end to the conflict was reached. On 29 June 2007 the Agreement on Accountability and Reconciliation (AAR) was signed between the Ugandan Government and the LRA (2007). The agreement also provided for reparations which would include rehabilitation, restitution, compensation, guarantees of non-recurrence of acts of violence and other symbolic measures such as apologies, memorials and commemorations (Latigo, 2008, p. 101). The LRA were expected to renounce their insurgency, sign a comprehensive peace agreement and submit their members to the process of disarmament, demobilisation and reintegration. The Government would reciprocate by striking the LRA off the list of terrorist organisations (ibid.). The parties expressed their commitment to honouring the suffering of victims by promoting lasting peace and justice, promoting a culture of accountability and redress in accordance with the constitution and international obligations, especially the requirements of the Statute of Rome which set up the ICC (ibid.).

The AAR, in part, stated that, traditional justice mechanisms as practised in the communities affected by the conflict would be promoted, with necessary modifications, as a central part of the framework for accountability and reconciliation. The debate on the use of traditional, restorative justice methods had been central to the Juba Peace Talks. To accommodate Kony and other LRA leaders, Uganda's negotiators proposed a mixture of *mato oput* (the traditional Acholi system of reconciliation ritual) for lesser crimes and recourse to a special Ugandan High Court for more serious offences (ARLPI Delegate in Juba Peace Talks, Interview, 31 March 2008). Article 4(4) of the Agreement stated that 'accountability mechanisms shall be implemented through the adapted legal framework in Uganda'. Article 6.3 stated that 'legislation shall introduce a regime of alternative penalties and sanctions which shall apply, and replace existing penalties, with respect to serious crimes and human rights violations committed by non-state actors in the course of the conflict'. The use of *mato oput*, which emphasised reconciliation rather than punishment, was favoured by Uganda's Chief Justice, Benjamin Odoki, as well as many Acholi leaders who were anxiously looking forward to an end to the protracted war, LRA terror tactics and the UPDF's ruthless revenge (McGregor, 2008). It was, however understood that the High Court could still charge Kony with various offences such as treason, murder and rape which carry with themselves death penalty (ibid.).

There was an anticlimax when the LRA leader Joseph Kony failed to show up on 10 April for the long-awaited signing of the Final Peace Agreement (FPA), designed to bring a negotiated end to years of brutal violence in north Uganda. Kony's failure to appear and sign the peace agreement marked a disappointing conclusion to two years of intensive negotiations. This, however, did not come as a surprise for a number of reasons. First, by the designated date for signing the FPA, the ICC had not yet withdrawn the warrants of arrest and indictments. Kony had maintained his position that a peace agreement was only possible if the ICC indictments against him were dropped. Second, it was still possible that Kony could be charged by the Ugandan criminal justice system even if the FPA were signed, according to the AAR. Kony seems to have been aware of this. There had been fears that the LRA's participation in the peace talks was merely tactical. Some observers expressed concern that the LRA could use the lull in hostilities, while in cantonment in Garamba, DRC, to rest and restore their fighting capacity and return with a renewed intensity (ICG, 14 September 2007, p. 2). The failure to sign the agreement disappointed many members of the Acholi population who had been hopeful that the Juba peace deal would finally bring peace.

Despite this obvious disappointment, there were positive outcomes following the talks. The Agreement on Cessation of Hostilities signed in August 2006 between the LRA and the Ugandan Government and the ceasefire which was part of the Juba Peace Talks resulted in somewhat of a lull in attacks in northern Uganda. This agreement forced the LRA commanders to flee their former sanctuary in Sudan for the jungles of the DRC and to negotiate a political deal in effect from May 2006 (UN IRIN, 25 May 2006). There developed a considerable calm in northern Uganda and those who had been living in the IDPs had started moving back to their homes or were able to work on their land free from the fear of attack unlike during the period before the talks. It, however, cannot be clearly determined whether the calm was primarily attributable to the ICC indictment that may have drawn the LRA to the negotiation table or to the talks or a combination of the two. A discussion of this will appear in Chapter 5.

Mato oput: the traditional Acholi system of peace and justice

If the Juba Peace Talks succeeded, then they were to be followed by *mato oput*, the traditional Acholi cleansing ritual. The ritual had come to be considered an alternative mechanism to promote peace and reconciliation. The ritual was considered by its advocates to hold the key to lasting peacebuilding following the long conflict. The value of *mato oput* was based on its widely acclaimed restorative dimension: a psychosocial value. The practice was something akin to the *Gacaca Courts* in the post-genocide Rwanda.

The idea of *Gacaca Courts* emerged in response to post-genocide Rwandan transitional situation where the international tribunal could not adequately deal with all the dimensions of the genocide. The number of suspects was far too large for the ICTR to handle. This motivated the post-genocide Rwandan Government to rediscover a traditional mechanism for dispute resolution and reconciliation, referred to as *gacaca*. *Gacaca* means 'judgement on the grass'. This model was applied in the precolonial periods to resolve disputes concerning land use and rights, cattle, marriage, inheritance rights, loans, damage to properties caused by one of the parties or animals and petty theft (Werchick, 2003). Thus the courts were meant to reintegrate suspects back into the community and restore harmony and social order in a given society, and to reintegrate persons who were the source of the disorder (Daly, 2002, p. 371). The courts had a community dimension. Participants in the *gacaca* included all those affected by the crimes and also those who would be affected by the suspect's return to the community. The courts were presided over by elders and judgements were settled only with consensus from all parties (Werchick, 2003).

Gacaca, as applied in post-genocide Rwanda, was meant to serve two purposes. The courts were meant to ease the congestion in Rwandan prisons by dealing with the large number of suspects which could not be handled by the national courts and the ICTR (Daly, 2002, p. 371). It was also intended to restore harmony and social order. In this respect *gacaca courts* were founded on the principle of restorative justice drawing from key elements such as reconciliation and reintegration.

Given their restorative principles and goals, *gacaca courts* were different from trials at the ICTR based in Arusha, Tanzania. The courts were closer to the people of Rwanda whereas the ICTR in Arusha was isolated from Rwanda in terms of its geography. This necessitated the involvement and participation of the people. In addition, as Daly (2002, p. 381) points out, whereas the ICTR focused on the elites who had organised the genocide, the *gacaca courts* focused on the community. The process of hearing the confessions and admissions of guilt of the accused and the forgiveness that followed was, in principle, a necessary step towards reintegration (Hamilton, 2000). In promoting the goals of restorative justice, decisions rendered by *gacaca courts* allocated compensation to victims. The Rwandan Government set up a genocide survivor's fund in 2003, which represented 8 per cent of the annual budget and assisted destitute survivors. Those convicted provided compensation through their prison services (Gabiro, 2002).

Just like the case of the *gacaca court*, the extraordinary character of the conflict in northern Uganda prompted a rediscovery of *mato oput*. The practice of *mato oput* as an instrument for conflict resolution and reconciliation among the Acholi was founded on their understanding of conflict in general and murder in particular. Among the Acholi, conflict was understood as a life-threatening phenomenon (Odong, Interview, 11 January 2008). Life, as such, was valued and celebrated. By life, among the Acholi, is meant a network of social relationships. Life outside the community was considered meaningless. Thus, an individual existed in and for the community. According to an elder, Matthew Odida living in Pabo camp, nobody could stand on his own and survive (Odida, Interview, 12

April 2008). As well as the living members of the community, the spirits of the dead were believed to play an important part in the life of the community and continued to be enjoined in the well-being of the community. Moral order was measured in terms of communal harmony and good relations with both the living and dead members of the community. Evil or immorality, crime or violence, therefore, was understood as an act of breaking societal harmony not only with members of one's own living community but also with the ancestral or spiritual world.

The value of community in African society was upheld not just among the Acholi but among most African communities as is demonstrated by available communitarian literature. In communitarian literature, the individual was regarded as a component of social relationships and not as an independent being. The individual is a being whose whole nature is constituted by the network of social relations of the wider community (Turner, 1968, p. 36). John Mbiti (1970, p. 141) captures this when he asserts that in Africa 'I am because we are, and because we are then I am'. The value of a person was defined within the framework of the community. People defined themselves in terms of group identity, as members of a clan, a tribe or a village and in terms of the specific duties they held within their communities (ibid., p. 108). According to Cobban (1987, p. 331), a person's dignity and honour proceeded from his or her transcendental role as a cultural being. These assertions underscore the significance of kinship the African sense of being and enshrines, according to Cobban, '[…] the general guiding principle of survival of the entire community and a sense of cooperation, independence, and collective responsibility' (ibid., p. 320). Thus, the self was considered as intrinsically connected to the community and personal welfare inseparably depended upon the welfare of the community.

Given the centrality of the community in the life of Acholi, according to Okot Okumu (Interview, 10 January 2008), post-conflict peacebuilding and conflict resolution formed an integral part of traditional patterns of societal harmony in the Acholi community. Societal structure in the Acholi community was characterised by mutual support in well-organised social units (ibid.). In the words of a former Secretary General of ARLPI, conflicts had to be solved since it was believed to have consequences for generations to come:

> It bounces back with consequences. These consequences turn back to haunt the children. It is not the two who will be affected. They see it as bringing sickness to the children. Reconciliation must come. The people must come to discuss the issue and press those involved in the conflict to agree.
>
> (A former ARLPI Secretary General, Interview, 18 March 2008)

The Acholi believed in *Jok*, the divine spirit or ancestors which guided their moral order. When a wrong was committed, ancestors would send *cen* or misfortune unless appropriate actions were taken by the elders and the offenders to restore the broken relations (Liu Institute, 2005). The 'phenomenon of *cen* illustrates the centrality of relationships between the natural and the supernatural worlds in Acholi, the living and the dead, [and] the normative continuity between an individual and the community' (ibid.). The 'living-dead' played an active role and had a great deal of influence in the world of the living. This meant the challenges of life extended beyond the world of the living and required consultation and reconciliation with the spiritual world (Okumu, Interview, 10 January 2008).

One of the crimes that contributed to breaking community relationships was that of murder. Acholi society strongly believed that human life is sacred and that human blood ought not to be spilled, thus the killing of a human being was strictly forbidden by their traditional beliefs (Latigo, 2008, p. 103). According to Callisto Otim (Interview, 10 January 2008), the crime of murder broke the social fabric of the community. This was because, in the event that a member of a family committed the crime, the person's whole clan bore the guilt. Similar sentiments were also echoed by Samuel Odong (Interview, 11 January 2008), according to whom, when one killed a member of another clan, the killing automatically severed the relationship between the clans. He said, 'when a conflict arose between two clans and there was a killing there must be abstinence from eating together because death did not allow people to eat together since the whole clan was involved' (ibid.). Food was a source of union. Ordinarily, people would beg millet from another clan or community in a reciprocal and distributive circle. This stopped when there was a killing. Reconciliation, thus, became imperative (A former ARLPI Secretary General, Interview, 18 March 2008). They could also not participate in any activities like hunting, marrying, trading, or worship or even shaking hands when a murder had been committed (Odong, Interview, 11 January 2008).

Accordingly, conflict among the Acholi, had both relational and moral dimensions. The collective responsibility and guilt which weighed heavily upon each and every member of the offender's community compelled them to accept collective responsibility. A collective repentance and remorse for the murder committed became necessary. Since there was no adversarial cross-examination as in a modern law court in Acholi society, judgement depended on truthfulness and ready acceptance of responsibility for one's actions. Telling the truth was a societal and moral obligation that everyone was bound to fulfil (Otim, Interview, 10 January 2008). According to Southwick, '[t]he process of sharing that burden also contributes to a process of reconciliation and prevention of future violence' (Southwick, 2005, p. 114).

Once somebody committed murder, the offender had to undergo a ritual cleansing ceremony in order to be allowed through the entrance of the village. It was believed that the vengeful spirit of the dead person would usually haunt the killer and his entire family. Accordingly, the rituals which were performed to cleanse the killer meant cleansing the entire community (Okumu, Interview, 10 January 2008). On this basis, the community were always vigilant to the effects of possession by *cen* or the effects of being disturbed by the spirit, like talking to oneself, having bad dreams, calling on the deceased and beseeching them not to harm him (Odong, Interview, 11 January 2008). Cleansing ceremonies were, therefore, meant to reconcile two families or clans that had been separated by an act of killing and to appease the spirit of the dead in order to prevent them from being haunted by the dead person's spirit (ibid.). In addition, the traditional healing was meant to let the bereaved see that justice was being carried out (Otim, Interview, 10 January 2008).

The Acholi traditional leadership and conflict resolution

The traditional Acholi conflict resolution system was an integral part of the area's indigenous system of governance. Before colonialism, the Acholi people had a traditional system of governance founded on religious beliefs, norms and customs. These values were maintained by the anointed chiefs of the Acholi people, known as the *rwot* or *rwodi* (plural for *rwot*) (Odong, Interview, 11 January 2008). During the colonial period a distinction was made between *rwodi moo* and *rwodi kalam*. The term *rwodi moo* was used to designate a chief anointed by oil (*moo*) and *rwodi kalam* was used to refer to those chiefs who acquired their power through official appointment or through pen (*kalam*). The latter acquired his authority from either colonial administrations or postcolonial administration. The *rwodi moo* were believed to have been chosen by supernatural powers and were enthroned to preside over traditional government of the Acholi people. The chiefs were anointed with fat (*moo*) preserved from the carcasses of lions in solemn religious ceremonies (ibid.). Once anointed the chiefs were believed to have acquired an esoteric relationship with the supernatural world. This elevated the chiefs to a position of respect and adoration (Latigo, 2008, p. 102).

Whenever there was conflict *rwodi* would intervene to promote reconciliation within the community (Afako, 2002). It was also the role of *rwodi* to intervene and calm tempers in the case of homicide (ibid.). In the course of dispensing their duties the traditional leaders ruled by consensus under guidance of a council of elders called the Grand Council (*Gure Madit*). Members who sat in the council of elders were chosen by their respective clans. The council of elders identified the problems and needs of the community and sought appropriate solutions to the problems of the society and ways of fulfilling its urgent needs. The Grand Council presided over cases arising from mass killings and land disputes between different clans. The aim of council of elders was to mitigate social problems that confronted the community. There were no written laws but decisions were taken in accordance with religious doctrines that were followed by the members of the society for the harmony and well-functioning of the community (Latigo, 2008, p. 103). This structure was, however, watered down by the British colonialists who replaced the *rwodi moo* with colonial administrators or chiefs, *rwodi kalam*. Although the 1995 Uganda constitution resuscitated cultural institutions, enshrined in the person of paramount chief, this was not founded on traditional beliefs and cultural norms of the Acholi (ibid.). The prominence of *rwodi moo*, however, was rejuvenated in the wake of the need to respond to the devastating conflict in northern Uganda.

The administration of mato oput

Conflict resolution processes were based on certain fundamental values that fostered the social fabric of Acholi society. These included acceptance of responsibility, repentance, forgiveness and compensation (Odong, Interview, 11 January 2008; Odong, Interview, 27 March 2008; Otim, Interview, 10 January 2008). These values among the Acholi, were embodied in the practice of *mato oput* (Afako, 2002). The term *mato oput* is composed of two words in Acholi language, '*mato*' meaning drinking and '*oput*' which is a type of tree with bitter herbs. Hence, *mato oput* literally means drinking a bitter herb made from the leaves of the *oput* tree. The drinking of this bitter herb means that the two conflicting parties accept the bitterness of the past and promise never to taste such bitterness again. In terms of its role in conflict resolution, *mato oput* is a traditional approach to justice and reintegration of offenders involving mediation of truth, accountability, and reconciliation through symbolic acts and spiritual appeasement (ibid.). Most of these principles emphasise the need to live in harmony with others and to restore social relations. As a practice, *mato oput* was a participatory process involving not only the victims and the perpetrators but also both the victim's community and the perpetrator's community in restoring the relationship broken by either an intentional murder or accidental killing. Thus the purpose of *mato oput* was to avoid revenge (Liu Institute, 2005). From a psychosocial standpoint, the ritual was a practical exercise aimed at fostering friendly relationships. Other such rituals included mock fights, the symbolic and actual sharing of food and drinks all of which were designed to make each of the hostile parties become hosts of the other. These procedures skilfully exploited cultural symbolism to show that relationships between two parties could effectively improve by involving them in joint rituals. *Mato oput* had symbolic importance but this symbolism had to be meaningful to the people it sought to reconcile for it to have an impact.

The ritual of *mato oput* normally followed a long process of mediation between the two parties involved and was complete only when the offender was willing to take responsibility. This consisted in what Villa-Vicencio referred to as 'cooperation among those involved in an endeavour to discern the best way to achieve peace' (Villa-Vicencio, 2004, p. 35). The actual enactment of *mato oput* began with acceptance of responsibility. The council of elders presided over by *rwodi moo* played a vital role as mediators in the process. Initially, in the aftermath of a dispute, the elders engaged with both sides of the conflict in order to ascertain the relevant facts of the crime. This was to set the stage for the administration of justice. Self-confession was out of the individual's volition and the commitment to do so was not so much a legal necessity but rather a moral imperative that was binding. Cheating was sacrilegious as it offended even the ancestors. As a requirement of moral accountability, according to traditional beliefs, a person who killed must, as soon as the act was committed, inform the community about the incident (Okumu, Interview, 10 January 2008).

If it was not clear who bore the guilt then a process of investigation had to be carried out to determine who was guilty. This could be achieved through testimony presented at interrogation or testimony gathered through informal processes set up by community elders presided over by *rwodi moo* (ibid.). Acknowledgement and acceptance of responsibility both on the side of the individual and the community allowed the people to begin to come to terms with the past. It also allowed the people to deal with their troubling past thereby allowing them to avoid dwelling on the past and thoughts of revenge (ibid.). Govier (2002, p. 87) highlights the need to confess to wrongdoings when he points out that

> to make sense of the idea that groups could be subjects and objects of forgiveness, it is required that groups be agents responsible for wrongdoings, suffer wrongful harm and that can have and can amend feelings, attitudes, and beliefs about various matters, including the harm they have suffered at the hands of others.

Acknowledgement was essential but not enough for rebuilding a social relationship. Forgiveness formed an essential and integral part of the process of reconciliation. Forgiveness and reconciliation are related intersubjective processes. Forgiveness is a transformation process within the victim, the overcoming of bitterness and anger as the offender acknowledges wrongdoing and expresses remorse. Reconciliation is the intersubjective acknowledgement of the need to let go and restore the relationship (Griswald, 2007). Forgiveness as encapsulated in *mato oput* should be seen as an internal process that is chosen freely by the victim. Through forgiveness, the victim acknowledges the wrong done to him but releases the resentment caused by such wrongdoing (Finnegan, 2005, p. 15). Govier captures this notion clearly when he says that 'for forgiveness to offer a way of healing ethnic and religious conflicts, it must first of all be possible for groups to forgive one another' (Govier, 2002, pp. 78–9). It is in this light that, after a genuine and wilful confession and repentance were received from the offender's community, that the victim's community would have to forgive in good faith. The assurance of forgiveness was a great relief and gave the offender's community a very real hope of peace. It was an assurance that the victim's community was on the path of reconciliation despite their loss (Otim, Interview, 10 January 2008). Shriver (1995, p. 28) observes that forgiveness as a human event means the commitment of members of a society to each other, because, in spite of the evil, only in that relationship does life make sense. He further points out that 'forgiveness is an act that joins moral truth, forbearance, empathy and commitment to repair a fractured human relation' (ibid.). The situation in northern Uganda shows that human relations were adversely severed since the protracted war destroyed everything that is human.

Once the victim's community chose to forgive the perpetrator, a settlement was agreed on and a form of compensation arrived at. The community from which the perpetrator came had a collective responsibility to collect the compensation and surrender it to the victim's community. The genuineness of repentance, says Callisto Otim (Interview, 10 January 2008), was measured by the willingness to pay compensation as required in traditional Acholi culture. The form of compensation depended on the circumstance and nature of the crime committed. The offender's community was required to pay ten head of cattle if the murder was not deliberately committed. But if it was proved that the murder had been a deliberate act, then compensation was to be in the form of a human person. In this case, the offender's community was required to give one of their young daughters between the ages of six and ten years to the victim's community (ibid.). The girl child given would become, by assumption, a daughter to the victim's community and in effect a replacement of the lost one. The willingness of the offender's community to sacrifice one of their daughters to the victim's community affirmed the genuineness of their commitment to peace and co-existence through the whole process of reconciliation (ibid.).

From the standpoint of modern human rights, the role of a girl child in compensation would be conceived as oppressive and a violation of the individual rights of the child who was being ransomed on behalf of the entire offender's community. She had to bear the pain of separation from her own family and taste the bitterness of violent conflict on behalf of the entire community, bearing the burden of collective responsibility. However, advocates of this practice argue that compensation was not a punitive imposition but was deemed as a process for healing and re-enhancement of life within the community (Group Interview, 23 March 2008). The presence of the girl child as a new member in the victim's community also became a channel for communication between both communities who were formerly aggrieved and cut off from each other. Her physical presence and her life guaranteed life to everyone in both communities. It was as if her presence and life was a recreation of both communities. That means the role of a girl child in compensation was understood as redemptive. In most African communities, the girl child was associated with the extension of life and friendship. Warring communities would marry their daughters to enemy clans or tribes. This was considered a gesture of friendship and the fostering of a relationship. In this case compensation in terms of a girl not only extended friendship, but more profoundly, meant the girl would bring more life to a community through her reproductive capacity.

After compensation, a third party invited both the offender and the offended parties for the important ceremony of *mato oput*. The cleansing ceremony of *mato oput* took place somewhere along the border between the conflicting communities. Goats and rams were exchanged and finally the victim and perpetrator's communities took the bitter herb, *mato oput*, from the same calabash. This was the culmination of reconciliation process. The very process of drinking the bitter herb from the same calabash was highly symbolic, depicting the bitterness in conflicts that ended in bloodshed (Pain, 1997, p. 82). The bitter drink also symbolised the sacred blood of a human being. Two people from each community took the *oput herb* with hands behind their backs. They would then sip the bitter juice simultaneously with their heads touching in the process. This would go on until every member from the victim community had shared the herb with another member from the perpetrator community (Odida, Interview, 12 April 2008).

The second phase of the process involved the sharing of meals together. After drinking the bitter herbs, animals were slain, cooked and eaten by both communities. Sharing meals in Acholi culture was always a profound fellowship that makes someone become part of family (ibid.). It was believed that this process took place in the presence of the ancestral living-dead and the creator as a witness to the covenant of peace. The taint that soiled their relationship became cleansed. The cleansing allowed normal social life between the two communities to begin again. At the end of the whole process, the perpetrator had acknowledged and confessed to that act and the victim's community forgave the crime and thus social relations were restored.

Mato oput *and the atrocities in northern Uganda*

Many advocates of *mato oput* believed that, when applied to the situation of northern Uganda, it could bring true healing, reconciliation and reconstruction in a manner that the international justice system could not (Liu Institute, 2005). According to one respondent who identified herself as Jennifer (Interview, 8 March 2008),

> Ultimately both the victims and perpetrators will have to stay in the same community. The case of northern Uganda is too complex to imagine that the problem can only be resolved by merely arresting the top LRA leaders and jailing them in Europe. Most of these perpetrators are members of the same families where the victims belong.

According to its advocates, one of the fundamental aspects of *mato oput* that makes it appropriate for post-conflict peacebuilding is that it is based on trust. Trust is one of the pillars of interpersonal peacebuilding. According to Hovil and Lomo (2005, p. 5), trust is important because it allows people within war-affected communities to engage in activities outside of their primary social groups, a participation that is essential in building and sustaining social cohesion. Social cohesion refers to those interrelated features of society, namely, the absence of covert conflict and the presence of strong social bonds manifested in terms of levels of trust, norms of reciprocity, abundance of association that bridge social division (Berkman & Kawachi, 2000, p. 175). For the case of northern Uganda, argue Hovil and Lomo (2005, p. 8), social bonds had been broken and appropriate processes had to start from the fact that the society was confronted by a situation of broken social trust. In this situation, the local population trusted neither the Government nor the LRA since each of these parties had caused them a great deal of harm. They did not even trust members of the communities in which they lived. An elderly woman who wished to remain anonymous commented regarding this as follows:

> Really, the war has spoilt everything that is human. Today you do not have a friend. Kony's soldiers have done very bad things to us; Museveni's soldiers have done equally bad things to us. You cannot say that even your closest neighbour is your friend; he may be a government spy or an LRA

> spy. How can you think of having a friend when our own sons come and loot from us?
>
> (Elderly Woman, Interview, 12 March 2008)

According to Fr Charles Odwar, the war destroyed basic social values traditionally valued by Acholi society. He said that, the value of life had become meaningless. Life in the bush and that in the camps destroyed social order, social cohesion and other values that reinforce harmonious social order, like forgiveness, the sanctity of human life, respect for elders and social responsibility (Odwar, Interview, 16 March 2008).

In the context of this social disruption, proper peace and reconciliation, according to Odwar (ibid.), could only be realised after restoring these values. This state of affairs, according to its advocates, made *mato oput* the appropriate mechanism given the value it places on forgiveness and trust building. Putzeys (2007), observes that without forgiveness, there can be no peace and justice in northern Uganda which can only be achieved through the restoration of basic building blocks of relationships such as trust, forgiveness and respect. And *mato oput*, according to its advocates, has the requisite symbolic influence to restore such values. During a group interview, Robert Kidega, a member of the group remarked that,

> Whatever had happened had already happened. People were too bitter to talk about what has happened and they would not wish to bring back those memories. There is no need of going to the past, instead we should focus on the future. Forgiveness is the most viable option.
>
> (Group of 8 Elders, Interview, 2 April 2008)

In line with this sentiment, the former Secretary General of ARLPI expressed what he considered as the ICC's inadequacy, remarking that,

> The ICC stresses punishing the individual. You punish the individual, what about the clan. By involving the clan everyone is reconciled. The whole clan won't be happy until reconciliation takes community dimension. The death of Slobodan Milosevic did not reconcile the whole society. Within a clan a conflict causes both social and spiritual separation, hence societal reconciliation is more important than legal procedures.
>
> (A former ARLPI Secretary General, Interview, 18 March 2008)

We can observe that, the LRA committed heinous crimes against their own people, the ICC offered to punish the culprits, but the religious leaders and community leaders were bent on convincing the people that it was better to forgive and rediscover *mato oput*. Did rediscovering *mato oput* with its fundamental values constitute a kind of vague serene disposition and uncritical mutual reconciliation that made the people appear as if they could not distinguish between the right and the wrong community values? Traditional *mato oput* seems to constitute a justice system that sought to go beyond social conformity, a system in which both restorative and retributive justice simultaneously are possible. As in the aftermath of the protracted conflict in northern Uganda, the endeavour to 'rediscovering' *mato oput* as a restorative form of justice sprang from the recognition of the complexities that characterised the conflict in northern Uganda. The term 'rediscovering' used here is consistent with the nature of the Acholi community as it was after over 20 years of social disruption by a protracted social conflict. As the Acholis reconstructed the *mato oput* ritual and its underpinning values, they were in a way constructing a new community which had never been there even before the war. The transfer of the Acholi population to the IDPs totally destroyed the traditional social fabric of the community with its lineages and values. The IDP phenomenon, a product of radical evil, destroyed the minimal threshold of social existence where the IDPs were reduced to what Giorgio Agamben refers to as *homo sacer*. Agamben (1995, p. 66) describes *homo sacer* as an individual who though has biological life, has no political existence and excluded from what gives an individual an identity. Agamben (ibid., p. 44) calls such an existence, *bare life*: a life where violence has bred a decay of all that is normative. The human condition of northern Uganda, which was characterised by torture, mutilation of body parts, dispossession, other gross human rights violations and marginalisation fit within Agamben's notion of bare life. Such a situation constitutes what Arendt (1967) refers to as radical evil, in reference to the Holocaust.

Indeed, one of the themes that prevailed in the majority of interviews carried out by this author was that Acholi society had lost many of its basic values. Accordingly, the dominant appeal for restorative justice as a key value seems to have been based on a desperate search for a lasting peace and a meaningful life and the restoration not merely of relationships with members of the LRA, but the restoration of worthwhile human existence. The rediscovery of *mato oput*, therefore, seems not to be based on any uncritical disposition among Africans to forgive too easily and to always submit to what their leaders think is right, but rather on a desperate search for peace and stability. Thus a better interrogation of the value of *mato oput* would need to go beyond its perceived relevance as has been advocated but also to interrogate fundamental elements that underpin its rediscovery. It is only once one has taken cognisance of the deplorable conditions which characterise life in northern Uganda that one can adequately assess the relevance of *mato oput*.

Accordingly, taking into consideration the issues raised above, a better evaluation of the proposed peace and justice instruments require that one considers the interwoven aspects of the conflict. First, was how crime, conflict and punishment are conceived traditionally from Acholi standpoint in relation to the existential situation that prevailed as result of the conflict. Crimes, as conceived by Acholi, were interpersonal. It is for this reason that truth becomes a key pillar in the process of restoring any broken relationships. The conflict in the north emerges as a case of broken relationship between the Acholi-dominated LRA and the Acholi as manifested in the manner the LRA committed grave atrocities on them. But equally significant is that, there was also a broken relationship between Acholi and the Government of Museveni manifested in terms of social and economic marginalisation and atrocities allegedly committed by the UPDF and the kind of life the people were subjected to in the IDP camps. But could *mato oput* adequately deal with the complex dimensions of the conflict in northern Uganda?

Conclusion

In order to adequately appreciate the capacity of alternative systems of justice considered in this chapter, one needs to consider the complex nature of the conflict and the deep-seated longing for peace and stability that exists in northern Uganda. The first, regards the conception of crime, conflict and punishment, from the traditional Acholi standpoint in relation the prevailing conflict situation. Crimes, as conceived in the Acholi context, were interpersonal. It is for this reason that truth was a key pillar in the process of restoring any broken relationships. The conflict in the north emerges as a case of the broken relationship between the Acholi-dominated LRA and the Acholi enemy in communities as manifested in the manner the LRA committed grave atrocities against them. However, there was also a broken relationship between Acholi communities and the Government of Museveni manifested in terms of social and economic marginalisation and atrocities allegedly committed by the UPDF and the kind of life the people were subjected to in the IDP camps. Did the advocacy of *mato oput* as a response to the two-decade conflict in northern Uganda capture a second dimension? Could *mato oput* deal with the conditions of bare life or radical evil and really restore meaningfulness to the live of the victims and their society? The next chapter examines how far these mechanisms would comprehensively respond to the interwoven dimensions of the conflict. In doing so, we analyse the assumptions for both retributive and restorative mechanism.

Notes

1 Commission of Inquiry into the Disappearances of People in Uganda since 25 January, 1971: Charter, The Commission of Inquiry (Cap 56) Legal Notice No. 2 of 1974, Published on 30 June 1974.

2 United Nations Humanitarian Coordination Unit, *Humanitarian Update*, *2*(9), 29 November 2000.

5 Transitional justice dichotomy in northern Uganda

Critical analysis

Introduction

Human rights advocates, lawyers and social scientists alike agree that atrocity crimes that define transitional societies confound the categories for ordinary moral assessment. Miriam Aukerman (2002, pp. 41–5) refers to such human rights violations as 'extraordinary evil'. There is also the agreement that the extraordinariness of such violations calls for extraordinary responses. Teitel (2000, p. 11) observes that transitional moments are times of massive paradigm shifts in understanding justice given that at such times societies are struggling with political, legal and economic transformation. The rule of law at these junctures appears deeply paradoxical with justice being re-conceptualised in terms of the goal of rebuilding broken communities (Teitel, 2000, p. 6). Law shifts from its ordinary role of providing order and stability to the role of enabling transformation in extraordinary periods of political upheaval (Teitel, 2000, p. 6). Experts also agreed that these crimes are so grave that they defy national boundaries in terms of their effects and obligation to intervene. There is, however, lack of agreement about what should precisely constitute the extraordinary responses. These observations constitute the crux of the dilemma that characterise societies making the transition to peace and stability. The challenge of dealing with the atrocity crimes against the civilian Acholi and the neighbouring populations living in northern Uganda falls within the above category. The LRA had committed gross human rights violations, thereby contravening international norms, punishable according to the standard of criminal justice. But in responding to the situation to bring justice to the victims of gross human rights violations, the ICC met with objections. Traditional leaders, civil society and even the Government which had referred the situation to the ICC in 2003 opposed the court in favour of alternative local models. This situation exposes the critical dilemma on how best a society can confront their past characterised by atrocity crimes. This chapter analyses competing assumptions of transitional justice in northern Uganda.

Retributive justice and post-conflict peacebuilding

The application of the principles of the international rule of law in response to the conflict situation in northern Uganda was based on the assumption that transition from conflict marked by gross human rights violations to peace and stability requires the application of universal legal and moral norms. The Preamble to the Rome Statute, the treaty that established the ICC, links criminal justice to the realisation of 'peace, security and well-being of the world' (UN Security Council, 1994). This was the principle that underpinned the ICTY in the wake of the Balkan war in the early 1990s. It also underpinned the ICTR following the 1994 genocide. In creating the ICTY and ICTR the UN Security Council believed that pursuing individual responsibility would make the repetition of the grotesque extermination, witnessed in the former Yugoslavia between 1991 and 1995 and during the 1994 genocide in Rwanda, impossible in future. When the ICC Prosecutor, Luis Moreno-Ocampo intervened in Uganda, he insisted that the indicted LRA leaders had to be made accountable for their crimes, as war crimes and crimes against humanity could not go unpunished. The Prosecutor dismissed any form of settlement that would preclude prosecution, as encouraging a culture of impunity over human rights. Accordingly, advocates of retribution hold the position that international criminal justice in post-conflict societies is the appropriate instrument for transitional justice. Various assumptions on the suitability of international rule of law in the post-conflict situation of northern Uganda can be identified.

Criminal justice and end to impunity

The first position is the view that criminal justice contributes to ending sovereign impunity by reinforcing societal values and preventing commission of crimes. From the time that the warrants of arrest were issued against the LRA there were indications that international criminal justice could go some way in bringing about peace and stability in northern Uganda. One of the indications that the ICC's intervention could have made some contribution is that the investigations and warrants of arrest discredited and destabilised individual members of the LRA top command. According to Akhavan (2005, p. 418), the investigations and charging of Kony and his top commanders upset the LRA structures and operations, making it difficult for them to regroup themselves. This drove them to the negotiation table and to gearing up towards a long-term peaceful outcome. Although one cannot point to hard evidence linking the indictments and the Juba peace negotiations, it is likely that the threat of prosecution sent shivers down the spines of the LRA military leadership, enticing them to the negotiating table in Juba (Grono & O'Brien, October 2007). The claim of linking the ICC indictments and peace initiatives can be corroborated by the observation that the LRA had avoided peace negotiations for years until the ICC released its warrants of arrest against Kony and the other LRA top command.

It is also claimed that the ICC's criminal investigation also restricted the flow of material support for the LRA from Khartoum. Sudan, a non-state party to the Rome Statute, had offered a safe haven and provided military support to the LRA in accordance with the pattern referred to as 'mutual interference', which was one of the complicating factors in the conflict and played a significant role in its longevity (Prunier, 2004, p. 359). The notion of 'mutual interference' is used by Lionel Cliffe (1999, p. 89) in his analysis of the regional dimensions of conflicts in the Horn of Africa. Referring particularly to the incessant conflicts that have plagued the Horn of Africa for about 30 years, Cliffe (ibid.) argues that regional factors contributed to the longevity of internal conflicts in African states. Within this scenario of mutual interference, opponents of existing regimes received some support from governments or other forces outside the countries of the region. The support from the Sudanese Government helped to sustain the LRA rebellion allowing them to operate with a free hand and take advantage of the protection, security and immunity and military support secured from the Khartoum Government (Kustenbauder, 2008, p. 8). But this pattern may have been disturbed when Khartoum signed an ad hoc agreement with the ICC committing itself to executing the warrants against the LRA commanders (Akhavan, 2005, p. 416; Moreno-Ocampo, 2006). This agreement is said to have forced the LRA commanders to flee their former sanctuary in the Sudan for the DRC jungles further from northern Uganda (UN IRIN, 25 May 2006). Moreover, since the ICC indictments had exposed the rebels to international limelight, Sudan may have been no longer capable of supporting the rebels in the same way as they had in the past.

The ICC's intervention is also believed to have deterred other actors from committing human rights violations as the indictment of the top LRA commanders '[sent] a powerful signal around the world that those responsible for such crimes would be held accountable for their actions'.[1] The UPDF, like the LRA, had allegedly committed crimes against the civilian population in northern Uganda, especially against the Acholi. In launching investigations against the LRA, even though the UPDF was not targeted by the investigations, the Court signalled that those who had acted against civilians with impunity were likely to face charges. Proponents therefore argue that the ICC indictments, by destabilising and generating fear among the LRA leaders, speeded up the pace of improving the security situation in northern Uganda and led to a reduction in attacks on camps (Akhavan, 2005, p. 418).

Linking criminal justice and end to impunity with respect to the ICC intervention in northern Uganda finds its explanation with legalist paradigms. First, that punishment through due process of the law restores social order. Bassiouni (2002, pp. 820–1) states that open trial processes of the ICC reinforce social values, and in turn contribute to the individual internalisation of these values, and redress harmful results that arise from crimes against humanity. The reasoning is that, a criminal, by committing an offence, creates an imbalance in the social order, and punishment restores this disorder. According to Murphy (1979, p. 77), the offender has unfairly gained advantages over the victim(s) and that punishment is meant to restore the equilibrium between benefit and burdens by ensuring that there is no profit in criminal wrongdoing. According to Michael Moore (1997, p. 747) retribution is based on a legal moralist theory of law according to which legislation ought to address morally wrongful behaviour. Punishment becomes a moral act in itself and justified on the basis that offenders deserve to be punished because he or she bears responsibility for his or her free and conscious actions. In this regard moral guilt is both a necessary and sufficient condition for punishment (Feinberg, 1995, p. 728). According to Kant (1965, p. 100), retributive punishment is a moral duty to ensure that the moral law is in effect.

Second, and in relation to the above reasoning, is the position that criminal justice has the prospect of deterring actors from committing atrocities and hence contributing to an end to impunity. The argument is that criminal law accuses multiple individuals, ranging from the highest authority to low-ranking soldiers, of single criminal acts. Thus trials have the capacity both to prevent and deter potential future conflicts (Orentlicher, 1991, p. 2540). Based on the deterrent perspective on punishment, trials are meant to instil in the minds of prospective abusers of human rights the awareness that they would be answerable as individuals for their actions. Deterrence seeks to discourage people from committing crimes by making them aware of the different forms of punishment and their severity. The preventive goal of punishment serves as a warning to those who may wish to do the same. A prospective criminal will assess the possibility of being caught and the cost of the consequences.

However, it is not possible to establish a clear and distinct correlation between the ICC intervention and the subsequent calm that was realised in northern Uganda following the indictments. It was equally difficult to state that the calm was an indication of the possibility of lasting peace and stability in the region. It is the case that some remarkable calm returned to the region compared to the period after the ICC indictment. A good number of those who had been living in the IDPs had moved back to their homes. However, it is not yet clear whether this calm was brought about by the ICC indictment or whether it was the Juba Peace Talks, or a combination of the two. Many of the statements about the contribution of the ICC intervention and the Juba Peace Talks were largely based on the sequence of events in the sense that the ICC intervention, then the LRA requested for negotiations and the subsequent Juba Peace Talks, followed by an unprecedented lull in attacks by the LRA.

Moreover, the claim that trials have the capacity to contribute the restoration of societal order hence conflict transformation remains debatable. The implication of this position is that if persecution does not take place then there is no conflict transformation. In the northern Uganda situation, there were no prosecutions until Dominic Ongwen was arrested and put to trial over ten years after indictment. Further implication regards the level of moral accountability in situations of complex post-conflict societies where there is a thin line between a victim and a perpetrator. During the conflict in northern Uganda some of the perpetrators were conscripted into the rebel forces after being abducted by the LRA. The LRA was largely comprised of children and adults who were initially abducted as children and forcibly conscripted as soldiers. These children were forced to commit crimes partly aimed at alienating them from their communities. For instance, Dominc Ongwen had been abducted by the LRA while on his way to school at about ten years old, and then trained as a soldier to fight against the UPDF. His actions followed an impaired moral formation. How can punishment make moral sense to him?

The second position is that there are links between individual accountability, rule of law and eventual democratic values, such as suppression of vested interest in favour of societal well-being, consensus building, tolerance and following the rule of law. The ICC investigations also brought the awful crimes in northern Uganda into the international spotlight, which in turn provided a springboard for regional and international support for the Juba peace process (Otim, 2007). Thus, the ICC indictment had the effect of increasing international support for ending the conflict in northern Uganda as it was only after the situation was referred to the court that the UN and a number of countries began providing significant support for peace in northern Uganda (Akhavan, 2005, p. 420). As part of the Juba Peace Talks, the Government and the LRA signed the Agreement on Cessation of Hostilities in August 2006 and a ceasefire accompanied the agreement (Ssenyonjo, 2007, p. 76). In line with the ceasefire agreement the LRA leadership decided to pull most of its troops out of northern Uganda, thereby reducing the frequency of attacks (ibid.). Both the ICC and the Juba Peace Talks seem to have complemented each other in achieving this lull in the conflict in northern Uganda. The ICC, which was thought to be a recipe for renewed atrocities, seems to have set the pace for subsequent peace initiatives. The court can be said to have demonstrated its dual potential of pursuing justice and securing the peace crucial to the reconstruction of a stable post-conflict northern Uganda and this represented at least some link between conflict resolution and the rule of law.

On the side of the Ugandan Government, some accountability initiatives subsequent to the ICC intervention were aimed at entrenching the Rome Statute aspirations within Uganda's domestic legal system. The government of Uganda began to incorporate some aspirations of the Rome Statute in its domestic legal system. These included the introduction of accountability-promoting laws and establishment of the International Crimes Division of the High Court of Uganda in 2008 with a bench of least three Judges, a Registry, an Office of the Prosecutor, and that of the Defense Counsel (Uganda Law Society, 2018).[2] The accountability-promoting laws enacted or amended following the ICC involvement included the International Criminal Court Act, enacted in 2010; the Accountability and Reconciliation Agreement with the LRA, and Transitional Justice Policy. The government also developed a Prevention of Genocide Bill, 2015 aimed at establishing an Independent National Committee to spearhead the fight against genocide. Thus, Malu argues that the ICC involvement may have informed the decisions to enact these laws and regulations (Malu, 2015). The assumption here is that peace and democratic culture accrue as dividends of the rule of law (Boed, 2002, pp. 487–98). Mayerfeld (2004, pp. 147–56) sees judicial intervention as an important tool for the consolidation and spread of democracy. He argues that the ICC protects democracies against anti-democratic forces since it can prosecute anyone who uses terror to seize or retain unconstitutional power, thereby transforming political culture.

The above development notwithstanding, determining the causal nexus between the ICC involvement in Uganda and the establishment of these legal instruments remains a significant question. What may seem a plausible claim is that these legal developments followed the ICC involvement, and that some of them reflect the international standards. Further, is whether the establishment of international rule of law promoting institutions and instruments would necessarily lead to the promotion of accountability at national level.

The third claim of prosecutorial approach is that it provides a link between the demand for accountability and the maintenance of peace by focusing on individual suspects while neutralising collective guilt, hence a key strategy for post-conflict recovery and prospects for peace (Sannerholm, 2006; Ratner & Abrams, 2001). Kofi Annan (21 September 2004) captures this in his comment that '[i]t is by introducing the rule of law and confidence in its impartial application that we can hope to resuscitate societies shattered in conflict'. It is on this basis that all the tribunals created in the post-Cold War era contain transformative objectives in respect of the ability of trials to heal societal wounds caused by mass atrocities. For example, the Resolution of the Security Council (1993) which established the ICTY proclaimed that the international tribunal '[w]ould contribute to the restoration and maintenance of peace'. The ICTR Statute states that prosecuting those who bore the highest responsibility for the Rwandan genocide would '[c]ontribute to the process of national reconciliation' and make sure 'that such violations are halted and effectively redressed' (Security Council, 1994). The Rome Statute links criminal prosecutions to the 'peace, security and well-being of the world'.

In Uganda, the involvement of the ICC could facilitate the process of reconciliation by neutralising conflict leaders, while exposing the real issues that had bedevilled the society (Fischer, 2010, p. 424). By reconciliation is meant establishment of strong patterns of social trust and cooperation across ethnic lines in post-conflict societies (Nalepa, 2012 p. 318). Reconciliation resulting from trial through the rule of law would mean healing of wounds of conflict, mistrust, prejudice and marginalisation. Based on this assumption the intervention of the ICC would contribute to reconciliation in the long-term in Uganda, by first isolating the LRA and their motivations and then creating conditions for the victim community and the country to examine the real issues as a basis for reconstruction. Trials, according to some of its advocates are held as 'the single most appropriate response to communal violence … the centrepiece of social repair' (Fletcher & Weinstein, 2002, p. 578). Thus, advocates of the prosecutorial process argue that addressing the legacy of past conflict during the crucial period of transition from violence or repression may be a key to reducing the possibility of future violence and increasing prospects of peace.

The link made between trials and societal peace and security is based on the idea that such an approach avoids imposing collective responsibility. International criminal justice, it is argued, contributes to peace by focusing on individual accountability in which mass atrocities perpetrated either by state or non-state actors are reduced to individual crimes. International criminal justice targets individuals, whether they are in the highest echelons of political leadership or foot-soldiers, insofar as each is personally complicit in serious human rights violation (Orentlicher, 1991, p. 2599). In this case judicial intervention reduces conflicts into individual crimes through individualised approaches such as arrest, detention and punishment. Since most ethno-political conflicts have a collective dimension, the individualised approach seeks to remedy collectivisation of guilt and responsibility by distinguishing the guilty from the innocent. Separating the guilty from the innocent is one of the major obstacles to reconstruction experienced by most post-conflict societies. Once guilt is collectivised, even the innocent are stigmatised as long as they belong to the perceived perpetrator group. This scenario is likely to lead to the collapse of trust and could weaken post-conflict reconstruction, further resulting in generational guilt. Thus international criminal justice pursues peace not by focusing on conflicts between groups, but by criminalising acts committed by individuals. In this way it neutralises inter-group tensions and contributes to reconciliation hence peace and stability.

The value of individual accountability notwithstanding, experience shows that intra-state conflicts always assume collective dimension and breaking through this domain is always very problematic. Experts point out that there is insufficient evidence to conclude that international justice contributes to national reconciliation (Drumbl, 2007, p. 150). Protracted social conflicts are associated with historical prejudices, divisions and exclusions; and conflict entrepreneurs claim to act in favour of their own ethnic, racial or religious groups.

The ethnic dimension of the protracted conflict in northern Uganda was also catalysed by ethnic stereotyping and tied to conflict structuration within the whole country. For instance, the British had promoted the stereotype of a martial ethnic group with reference to British military policy. This became a structural stereotype (Lwanga-Lunyiigo, 1989, pp. 24–43). One of the effects of structural stereotyping and discrimination is that '[i]ndividuals are assigned to specific types of occupations and other social roles on the basis of perceived cultural mark' (Hechter, 1974, p. 1154). According to this policy, one's ethnic group determined the particular job one was recruited for. Thus the Acholi were identified as warlike and suited to soldiering (Omara-Otunnu, 1987, p. 31). The myth was extended to the claim that because of their 'domination' of the army since colonialism, the northerners had 'dominated' politics since independence. Doornbos (1988, p. 265) maintains that the British favoured the northern 'martial tribes', especially the Acholi, in the armed forces at the expense of the more educated and economically more developed southerners, who were a potential threat to colonialism in Uganda. The Amin and Obote regimes basically maintained their sway over the economically more important south through their army support, which had been overwhelmingly recruited from the north (Doornbos, 1988, p. 265). The NRM leadership used these myths in whipping up the threat of the northerners in order to get support for the war in Buganda whose traditional king, the Kabaka, had been deposed by Obote in the years immediately following independence, creating a lasting resentment among the Baganda. Moreover, the myth that the Acholis were a martial tribe made the war in northern Uganda appear to be a northern problem (Rupesinghe, 1989). This partly explains why the war was never an important concern for southerners and further partly explains its longevity.

Another myth that has been used to explain the longevity of the conflict in northern Uganda is that the Acholi were not hard working, especially on their farms, which was why they depended on a military occupation for their livelihood. Pain (1987, pp. 47–50) points to the linking of this economic 'backwardness' with the massive recruitment of the Acholi in the armed forces and their 'looting' of the country during their counter-insurgency against the NRA. Museveni used the same myth to justify the marginalisation of the Acholi. In his biography, he states:

> the people in the area did not get in the habit of generating wealth through cash crop production … I always hear the cliché that the north was once prosperous and that it has declined in the last 10 years. I have never shared this opinion. I do not think that the north has ever been prosperous at any time. It is true that in the last 10 years there has been more human suffering than before, but to say that the area has ever been prosperous is to tell a lie.
>
> (Museveni, 1997, pp. 211–12)

Yet historians have shown that the Acholi were indeed productive and engaged in cash crop production. Acholiland was part of the cotton belt that provided Uganda with much needed foreign exchange (Pain, 1987, pp. 45–50). Pain further states that the Acholi were able to overcome the British colonial policy of economic marginalisation by engaging in agricultural production and that, between 1946 and 1953, the Acholi enjoyed an economic boom. According to Thompson (2003, pp. 33–4) during the 1950s, the Uganda National Congress gained popular support in that district because cotton farmers were concerned about cotton prices and marketing. By the time of independence in 1962, the Langi and Acholi were producing more cotton than was being produced in Buganda, and West Nile too became the leading producer of tobacco in Uganda (ibid.). Atkinson reasons that although the Acholi were considered 'backward' by the southern elite, their economic strengths lay in a form of agro-pastoralism that was well adapted to the ecological conditions of the region. This, in his view, made a very real and substantial contribution to Uganda's national economy (Atkinson, 1999). On the basis of these considerations, it is not accurate to claim that the protracted conflict in northern Uganda was sustained by laziness among the Acholi who depended on looting as a means to acquiring their material needs.

Contrary to the above claims it is more plausible to argue that it was not the Acholi's naturally warlike nature that caused them to dominate the army. A more cogent reason was the way that economic structures were constructed by the colonialists to build a militarily strong north. If it is possible to identify a militarised culture among the Acholi, this is not because they are naturally so inclined but stems rather from the systematic introduction of a 'military industry' among the northerners. Moreover, it is inaccurate to argue that the Acholi were the militarised section of the country. A militarised culture pervaded the whole of the country. Museveni, who launched a successful military campaign, had believed in the power of the gun in his pursuit of political leadership and yet, in the 1980 elections, he lost miserably especially to the DP's Paul Ssemogerere. On the basis of the above discussion, it is also illogical to infer that the Acholi dominated the military because they were not hardworking in other economic sectors and were therefore unable to derive their livelihood from any other source of employment. In contrast, one should argue that it was the systematic introduction of the 'military industry' that led to the Acholi domination of the military.

Moreover, Museveni suggests that the entire Acholi were responsible for the events in the Luwero Triangle, thus justifying the ensuing war as punishment for their atrocities. This can be deduced from Museveni's autobiography where he argues that the Acholi people as a whole had participated in the looting of the south by the northern soldiers. He claims that:

> You could not say that they were fighting to bring resources to the north, other than by way of looting and corruption, for social corruption had widely taken root in the region. Under previous regimes, the soldiers, most of whom came from the north, had been free to loot civilian property. Whenever they looted such things, for example corrugated roofing sheets, they would take them to their homes, and their parents would not ask where they obtained them, in spite of the fact that they could easily tell the difference between a new iron sheet and one that had been previously nailed to someone else's roof. In this way, the whole community in Acholi and Lango became involved in the plundering of Uganda for themselves.
>
> (Museveni, 1997, pp. 177–8)

The view expressed by Museveni points to the legitimation of group victimisation that had become so typical of ethnic-based conflicts in Africa. Gersony (1997, pp. 20–36) questions the justification for placing responsibility for the events in the Luwero Triangle exclusively on the Acholi elements in the UNLA. He admits that the Acholi were 'only one of several ethnic groups prominently represented in the armed forces', but he also underlines the fact that the Acholi in the army were subordinate in rank to senior officers of President Obote's Lango tribe. He further notes that the powerful figures in the security apparatus who influenced military policy, such as National Security Agency Director Chris Rwakasisi, were of Bantu and not Acholi background (ibid.). Gersony shows that the army relied upon North Korean technical advisors in its Luwero operations. Moreover the way politics was manipulated along ethnic lines by both sides in the war in the Luwero Triangle reveals Obote's mistrust of Acholi soldiers and officers, which eventually led to his overthrow (ibid.). Nyeko and Lucima (2002, p. 20) write that the Acholi officers in the UNLA, acting with the connivance of Paulo Muwanga, tried to stop the war by making overtures to Museveni's NRA after December, 1984.

Accordingly, placing the burden of responsibility on the entire Acholi community was quite unjustified. Gersony (1997, p. 30) asserts:

> The vast majority of Acholi civilians in Gulu and Kitgum participated in no way, were remote from events in Luwero, and had no immediate reason to be concerned about them at the time. Despite all of these mitigating factors, many Ugandans hold mainly the Acholi responsible for the Luwero atrocities because of the high proportion of Acholis in the armed forces at that time.

President Museveni's blaming the entire Acholi people for the wrongs done by the Acholi soldiers in the south after independence convicts the entire Acholi community of these gross human rights violations. The stereotypical claims, though wanting in rational justifiability, played a crucial role in forming the opinions of the various actors in the conflict and demonstrate the convoluted nature of the conflict. This raises questions about the ability of individual accountability to neutralise the collective guilt.

When conflict divisions seem to deeply-entrenched in the people's consciousness, it becomes complex for trial processes to deconstruct and lift such collective societal burdens. It complicates the ability of trials to act as neutralising agents of protracted social conflicts. In Uganda the pursuit of the LRA while leaving out the UPDF who also committed crimes against civilians would certainly undermine the people's perception on the ability of the ICC to contribute to reconciliation. The dissenting reactions to the ICC intervention among Acholi shows they could not isolate the criminality visited upon them by their own sons from the Ugandan complex conflict context. What emerges is that the nexus between trial, on the one hand, and end to impunity and sustainable peacebuilding on the other hand, is a conundrum. And the involvement of the ICC in northern Uganda demonstrates this. But, again, without such intervention impunity entrenches itself with the possibility of further conflicts and human rights violation. We shall revert to this issue in Chapter 6.

Transitional justice as restorative justice

The other antithetic claim is that restorative mechanisms are most suitable for societies making the transition from conflict to stability. Once again we begin with the assumption that has anchored the above discussion, namely that crimes which define transitional situations are extraordinary in nature thus requiring extraordinary responses. On this, as mentioned earlier, there is agreement between advocates of retribution and those who prefer alternative mechanisms. However, advocates of non-prosecutorial models contend that, given the widespread nature of such mass atrocity crimes, the adversarial approach is not effectively applicable in rebuilding societies shattered by such crimes. The approach to transitional justice that advocates non-prosecution and focusing on the restoration of social order is what scholars and practitioners have referred to as 'restorative justice'.

The notion of restorative justice emerged as international justice registered developments in the post-Cold War periods (Teitel, 2003b, p. 78). Restorative justice is applied in post-conflict periods and aims to repair harm, heal the victims and communities, and restore offenders to a healthy relationship with the community (Boraine, 2000, pp 152–3). The notion of restorative justice requires that crimes should be addressed by the community through many different processes such as rebuke and reintegration into the community of those offenders who admit their wrongdoing (Drumbl, 2000, p. 1258). Restorative justice focuses on the healing of the broader community and recognises that crime affects the entire community. In this respect, criminals are considered 'not as individuals that must be handled but as persons who, together with victims, are members of one community' (Etzioni, 1998, p. 374). Restorative justice has taken many forms, notably truth and reconciliation commissions and more localised traditional forms of justice.

Generally, advocates of restorative justice reject prosecution as a mechanism for post-conflict reconstruction. Many scholars in the field of political science such as Huntington (1991, p. 231) prefer to advocate an approach guided basically by the trajectory of political considerations. Acuna and Smulovitz (1997, p. 95) argue that prospects for democratic openings should be nurtured by pardoning leaders associated with authoritarian regimes for past human rights violations. General amnesty for all, according to O'Donnell and Schmitter (1998, p. 69), provides a far stronger base for democracy than prosecution. The ability of restorative approaches to bring lasting peace in northern Uganda remains contested.

The first point of departure for restorative approach is that peace comes before justice and can lead to democracy (Stepan, 1986, p. 64). In this light the ICC came to be seen as the central obstacle to ending the brutal civil war and its prescription as exacerbating conflict in Uganda, since the LRA had asked for talks with the Ugandan Government to end the 20-year civil war. Those who rejected the court's intervention argued that the need for peace justified engaging the LRA leaders in dialogue so that the people would have the opportunity to air their grievances, an element they considered important in the search for peace. Moreover, the LRA leadership had vowed not to surrender unless the prosecutor of the ICC withdrew the targeting of their top commanders (Liu Institute for Global Issues, 2006). Thus, the ICC intervention might have the effect of exacerbating the violence. By the time the ICC issued warrants of arrest for the five senior LRA leaders on 8 July 2005, preparations for talks aimed at peacefully resolving the conflict were underway in Juba. When the talks eventually started on 6 July 2006, one of the sticky issues that threatened to derail the talks was the demand by the LRA that the ICC withdraws the arrest warrants. The indictments posed a hindrance to the negotiations and threatened to scuttle the talks, which at the time looked promising. In fact, on 28 February 2008, the LRA set a condition for withdrawal of the indictments before it would sign any agreement and even requested a meeting with the ICC Prosecutor. Ocampo rejected the rebels' demands for a meeting, stating that the arrest warrants issued by the ICC remained in effect and had to be executed.

This perspective is informed by pragmatic considerations. Henry Kissinger (2001, p. 95) argues that flexible and prudent political judgement about when to advance peace and justice yields better outcomes than obstinately clinging to legalism. In this connection, opponents of prosecutions in post-regime change reason that amnesty for human rights abusers is a pre-requisite for a smooth political transition, since many transitional democracies do not have the power, popular support, legal tools or conditions necessary to prosecute effectively (van Zyl, 1999, pp. 647, 651; Landsman, 1996, pp. 81–4; Villa-Vicencio, 2000, pp. 205, 220). Van Zyl (1999) points to the South African case, in which the apartheid regime and its security forces would not have allowed the transition to a democratic order had its members, supporters and operatives faced a warrant of arrest. Landsman (1996, pp. 81–4), like van Zyl warns that prosecuting criminal leaders runs the risk of leading to renewed conflict, since these leaders could potentially use their military establishment to bring down the transitional government if they feel threatened. For Zalaquett (1995, pp. 203–6) peace is more important and should precede justice in the sense that peace provides the proper basis for justice. He argues that societal stability, actual political opportunities and constraints override the needs of victims and the ethical principles of justice. Roehrig (2002, pp. 186–8) argues that attempts to uncover the truth should follow successful efforts to secure peace and that only after a democratic culture has taken root should trials be considered. The stress is placed on a cautious approach to prosecution which is conducive to a smooth transition to peace (Roehrig, 2002, pp. 198–9; Huntington, 1991, p. 231).

The second significant point is that restorative justice applied in post-conflict regime transitions is also conceived as having inherent value of reconciliation over and above purely pragmatic considerations. For instance, truth commissions, amnesty and eventual reconciliation invoke the long-term aspirations of the political community as an alternative to revenge or victor's justice. It is in this respect that critics of the ICC contrasted it sharply with alternative local mechanisms such as the traditional Acholi system of justice, *mato oput*, which was understood to be communal and integrative in orientation. The local systems of justice were portrayed by its advocates as embodying a distinctly African form of natural justice necessary for social harmony. This harmony is constituted by consultation, consensus, communal participation and reconciliation. The criminal justice approach stresses the responsibility of individual perpetrators. Restorative justice is pursued through repentance, forgiveness and reconciliation. The promotion of these values is contrary to the application of basic principles of the rule law, according to which criminals should be punished once their guilt is determined through fair and transparent judicial process instead of being based on culturally conditioned moral norms. The cultural norms are not universal, instead they are based on historical circumstances. It is their particularity that causes their advocates to consider them to be suitable in transitional situations in the sense that they are more immediate and relevant to particular situations in the lives of the people who apply them.

In this respect, the traditional Acholi system of restorative justice, accordingly, was considered by its advocates as relevant since it stresses the communal aspect of justice by prioritising community responsibility over individual accountability. The process of the traditional justice system is also participatory, focusing on the healing of the community and reintegration of criminals back into the community. Mass atrocities assume societal and interpersonal dimensions because they are committed by a multitude of actors, and the atrocities affect mass victims. Given this community dimension, forgiveness becomes relevant because it 'prioritises relationships between people over dark feelings of revenge, no matter how natural, deserved or rational they may be' (Finnegan, 2005, p. 11). Jeong (2005, p. 164) observes that focusing on reconciliation can be faster in generating peace while providing the victims with the opportunity for catharsis when they come to know the truth through public confessions.

The concept of reconciliation, according to its advocates, incorporates features such as tolerance for political and ethnic diversity, respect for human rights and rejection of racial or ethnic stereotyping (Zalaquett, 1992, p. 1425; Wilson, 2001). Such values of restorative justice are relevant to the nature of societies making transitions from conflict to stability. This is so because, observes Miriam Aukerman (2002, pp. 41–5), massive human rights violations are an 'extraordinary evil' to which the response should be to focus on the society rather than individuals. She suggests that such crimes require an alternative model to protect the society against such horrors and to ameliorate the harm they cause, taking cognisance of the larger context within which widespread human rights abuses occur. Such a mechanism focuses on rebuilding societies by developing shared histories (ibid.). The overall purpose of restorative justice is the reintegration of victims and offenders who have resolved their conflict into their communities (Van Ness & Karen, 1997). This perspective separates criminal accountability from sustainable peace and consequently questions the link between upholding individual responsibility and the alleviation of human rights.

The third premise is that restorative justice processes are suitable for addressing traumas. Most intra-state violent conflicts with resultant human rights abuses imprint negative psychosocial legacies on society, rendering individuals susceptible to future conflicts (van der Merwe & Vienings, 2000, p. 345). Such conflicts destroy the fabric of society, which then needs to be repaired. Post-conflict reconstruction, according to its advocates of restorative justice, requires that cognisance be taken of these psychosocial and emotional dimensions of a given conflict. If post-conflict trauma is not dealt with it is likely that some of the victims of past violence may end up becoming the perpetrators of future conflicts (ibid., p. 344). In this respect, Zalaquett (1992, p. 1425) advocates the idea of a truth commission as being better than trials in addressing trauma, anger and fear. Dealing with post-conflict trauma is a significant element in sustainable peacebuilding since those who have experienced the horrors of violent conflict are in most cases psychologically and emotionally devastated. Post-conflict trauma healing is instrumental in reconstructing relationships that have been shattered on account of terrible crimes committed one against the other. Post-conflict societies are characterised by mistrust across various groups. International criminal prosecutions do not have the ability to reach the victims and meet their emotional concerns. Through restorative processes, such as truth and reconciliation, survivors, witnesses and presumed perpetrators all come together to witness and narrate, and perpetrators confess what they know about the past atrocities. This leads to a psycho-social healing (Lederach, 1997; Graybill, 2004). It is therefore necessary to deal with trauma in order to break the cycle of violence which may characterise a country's history. Socio-psychological approaches to peacebuilding emphasise relational aspects such as trust building. It seeks to minimise poorly functioning interactions and maximise mutual understanding between the previously conflicting groups (Lederach, 1997, pp. 81–3). If trauma is not dealt with, unhealed social losses and psychological trauma usually continue to dominate societies that have suffered conflict. A general consensus of the above views is that prosecutions threaten prospects for sustainable peace in post-conflict situations.

What emerges is that restorative justice is pursued as suitable for rebuilding societies which have been fragmented by violent conflicts. Such conflicts result in injuries to victims, communities and the offenders themselves. This situation has given rise to the assumption that the objective of transitional justice process should be to reconcile parties while repairing the injuries caused by crime (Auckerman, 2002). Restorative justice therefore attempts to accomplish several goals. First of all, justice needs to be served in respect to both the victim and the offender. Each party should feel that he or she has received fair treatment. Second, the relationship between the perpetrator and the victim needs to be addressed and an opportunity provided for reconciliation. Third, the process must also take into consideration the concerns of the community. Last, direction for resolution must be provided. Thus, restorative justice, in contrast to retributive justice, is concerned with the broader relationship between offender, victim and the community.

One of the underpinnings of restorative mechanisms in northern Uganda is that the Africans are communal by nature, a kind of dichotomy between African communalism and western individualism. This position is based on communitarian philosophy, which maintains that humans establish their value within the community where they are related in terms of duties and defined, in the form of group identity, as members of a clan, a tribe or a village (Mbiti, 1970). The community itself is not a mere collection of fundamentally isolated individuals, but an organic structure of relationships. Personal welfare is dependent on the welfare of the community, with the community carrying more weight than the individual. This position is disputable.

The position upholding the dichotomy between African communalism and western individualism is largely anthropological. Anthropology took a somewhat structural functionalist and ahistorical approach to African society – and therefore misunderstood the modernity of culture, so to speak, so that the western/African dichotomy became something of an invention which is, of course, used today as a kind of 'branding' exercise. It is not valid to argue that Africans were completely devoid of individualistic tendencies. There is no indubitable validity in the claim that individualism is inherent in western mentality whereas communalism is entrenched in the African consciousness. Indeed individualism is a modern idea, basically absent from ancient civilisation and medieval Europe. The notion emerged in Europe for the first time after the French Revolution (Schwab & Jeanneney, 1995). For most of human history, the well-being of the group mattered more than the well-being of an individual. Aristotle, one of the earliest classical political theorists, maintained that man is social by nature and cannot survive outside the community. Morris (1972, p. 2) points out, while the vocabulary of the Greeks is rich in words, they had no concept for an individual person and had what they referred to as a community of beings. The starting point was the *polis* which was the natural unit of society. Individualism and communalism are both aspects of all human beings and the prevalence of one over the other in a society at any given moment does not necessarily place that society within a given category of humanity vis-à-vis others. In making a comparative analysis of some African and western conceptions of morals, Kwasi Wiredu (1996, p. 72) remarks that '… the distinction between communalism and individualism is one of a degree only; for a considerable value may be attached to communality in individualistic societies just as individuality is not necessarily [trivialised] within communalism'.

If one proceeds from the premise that communal forms of justice are distinctively inherent in Acholi moral and legal norms, it would imply that the traditional Acholi system of justice discussed earlier in this work would appeal to Acholi in a more or less generalised manner. The Acholi population would embrace such values without difficulty. But this was not the case. The traditional mechanism did not appeal to some sections of the population. The Acholi were in no generalised way in support of or opposed to the reconciliatory approach to justice. Some held the strong view that those who committed atrocities against civilians needed to be punished (Ochar, Interview, 3 June 2008). *The Monitor* reported on 5 May 2005 that in that month a delegation of two local leaders from the Lira district in northern Uganda, the Local Council Five (LCV) Chairperson, Franco Ojur, and the Vice-Chairperson, Rebecca Atango, travelled to The Hague, Netherlands, for an audience with the ICC Chief Prosecutor to press for the arrest and prosecution of Kony and his top lieutenants (Wacha, 2005). An informant John Bosco, a Local Council leader of Pabo Sub-county and a resident of Pabo IDP camp, argued that

> [i]n a community, people don't have the same feelings. Some, especially those who have been hurt physically, disabled or maimed by the LRA, will find it very difficult to forgive them. We are always sensitising people to learn to forgive. But not all people can respond in the same manner and decide to forgive.
>
> (Bosco, Interview, 4 April 2008)

Some victims did not want to reconcile with offenders, and preferred prosecution for the LRA. While there was often sympathy for those who were abducted, some victims were firm that they would not accept former combatants including those who had been abducted (Five victims who sought anonymity, Interview, 4 April 2008). A field-based study to explore the victims' perceptions of accountability, reconciliation and transitional justice in northern Uganda was conducted by the Office of the UN High Commissioner for Human Rights (UNHCHR) from January to June 2007. The research revealed that respondents expressed their reservation about the 'capacity of domestic institutions of justice effectively to deliver on accountability in a fair and transparent manner' (UNHCHR, 2007, p. 69). It would, therefore, be inaccurate to claim that the Acholi wholeheartedly preferred traditional restorative justice to a retributive approach (Allen, 2006; Lamony, 2007, p. 53).

Moreover, some respondents were adamant that they would not wish to see Kony back in the community. This raises further questions about the claim that the Acholi population had forgiven the LRA. It is possible that the mobilisation and sensitisation of the Acholi population by civil society organisations and traditional leaders may have created the general impression of Acholi reconciliation with the rebels, individually they may not have been truly reconciled with the LRA depending on their personal experiences.

Strictly speaking, reconciliation is a personal decision. According to Cose (2004, p. 95) reconciliation is a complex psychological process that requires willingness on the part of those involved in a disagreement. Juan Méndez (2006) corroborates Cose's assertion when he observes that reconciliation between victims and their perpetrators is usually a misnomer since, although some victims may be ready to forgive, the choice ultimately remains a personal one that must always be free and voluntary. The fact that reconciliation is a personal undertaking is largely ignored in most peace agreements which are entered into a negotiation tables without proper representation of those affected. Such negotiations do not adequately appreciate the right of victims to help shape the trajectory of peace and justice (Méndez, 2006). Local peace initiatives assume that victims should be able to forgive in order to promote peace, but this ignores the rights of individual victims who end up being treated as if they were not personal beings.

Apart from a lack of broad acceptance of the Acholi system of justice, there were practical concerns regarding the efficacy of *mato oput* to engender real justice and the institutional reform necessary in northern Uganda. First, there was the problem of establishing responsibility. Establishing responsibility on the part of the accused is one of the important elements of *mato oput*. Knowing who is responsible for a crime is the first step in the process of reconciliation, but given the nature of the conflict in northern Uganda it was not easy to identify individual perpetrators and their corresponding victims. In the context of extraordinary crimes characterised by mass killing, displacement and the inability to determine who the victims and perpetrators were, it became difficult to differentiate between the domain of the victim's community and that of the perpetrator.

Regardless of the apparent popularity of *mato oput*, there was criticism brought against it in terms of its relevance as a system of peace and justice in the northern Uganda situation. Particular questions were raised about how the practice could be effective given the magnitude of the conflict where thousands of civilians both Acholi and non-Acholi had been killed and maimed. In the view of Thomas Odong, *mato oput* had been given too much value in its capacity to heal and restore social relationships. He pointed out that the practice in the past and among traditional Acholi people aimed at re-establishing relationships that had been suspended between two communities in response to either an act of killing done wilfully or that which happened accidentally (Odong, Interview, 18 March 2008). Odong added, however, that so much had changed in the course of the conflict that plagued the region for two decades. Odong's view was corroborated by Odwar's observation that, given the devastating effect of war, all systems and structures like education and religion had been affected and needed a reconstruction (Odwar, Interview, 16 March 2008). Other respondents observed that, morality itself had been transformed. Moreover, the cultural identity of the Acholi people had become very dynamic and was being reshaped by such factors as Christianity and modernity. Younger people in general who had grown up during a time of war had not been subject to such practices. Some Acholi had grown up in towns or the diaspora and had also lost touch with their traditions (Ongom, Interview, 11 January 2008).

Specific questions regarding *mato oput* focused on the practice of compensation. Compensation, as traditionally understood, was no longer possible for a number of reasons. First, in many instances people did not know the exact identities of either the victims or the perpetrators. Thus, even if compensation were possible, it was not easy to determine who would compensate whom. Second, in certain cases where a perpetrator was forced to kill his own parents or where a person killed ten people, the issue of retributive justice was complicated. In this case it would be difficult for compensation to be applied (Elderly woman, Interview, 12 March 2008). According to the former Secretary General of ARLPI,

> In the Acholi situation who is to pay for what? Many families have been affected, son and his father; brother and brother. Things have been meshed up. Victims and perpetrators are members of the same families. Victims are perpetrators at the same time. Who actually is afflicted by the atrocities is difficult to tell.
>
> (A former ARLPI Secretary General, Interview, 18 March 2008)

Another concern regarded the nature of the parties to the conflict. One interviewee who sought anonymity observed that any mediation process must include all the relevant actors (Anonymous, Interview, 24 March 2008). But as *mato oput* was presented, it appeared that the reconciliation would be between the LRA and its victims or the wider Acholi society. That means that the LRA and the Acholi population would be considered the only parties involved in the conflict. Yet the perpetration of human rights abuses had also occurred by the government army. According to a lecturer interviewed in Gulu University, there was no clear policy framework on how *mato oput* would include the Government which had also been a party to the conflict. Moreover there was a dimension of the conflict that placed the Government in opposition to the Acholi population according to popular perceptions. The Government of Museveni had itself been accused of targeting the Acholi for extermination (Lecturer in Gulu University, Interview, 10 March 2008). Such perceptions reveal that any peace and justice process that focused only on certain dimensions of the conflict or that ignored certain parties, risked being inadequate. According to an old man interviewed in Lapuje camp 'in the same manner as justice, reconciliation needs to take into account all the parties' (An old man, Interview, 25 May 2008). This sentiment was expressed more explicitly by a former ARLPI Secretary General (Interview, 18 March 2008) who said that, 'the case in northern Uganda involves killing. It is a larger conflict. The actual war is between the Government and the rebels. In this case, actual *mato oput* should be between the rebels and the government'. For *mato oput* to be properly applicable would require Museveni and Kony to participate in the ceremony as antagonising parties in the conflict. In this way it would have some impact. The observations point to the limitations of *mato oput* and indicate further that stressing the system at the expense of other instruments would not likely lead to sustainable peace.

Second, the traditional Acholi system of justice was not comprehensive enough to cater for the nature and extent of the conflict in northern Uganda. *Mato oput* was originally intended to resolve lesser cases of murder involving members of different clans or families. The traditional Acholi justice could not address the large-scale cases of murder committed by the LRA, let alone all other crimes committed in Acholiland or beyond. Since *mato oput* was initially meant to deal with murder cases, the practice did not articulate how it could deal with crimes such as rape, sexual harassment and gender-based violence that constituted part of the conflict in northern Uganda (Otim, 2007, p. 4). Not all the victims and perpetrators involved in the conflict were Acholi, and *mato oput* would not be meaningful to victims outside Acholiland. It is the case that Acholiland was the epicentre of LRA atrocities with the Acholi population bearing the greatest burden of the atrocities. It is also the case that the LRA were dominated by Acholis. However, given that the whole of northern Uganda in general had suffered decades of conflict, any transitional justice mechanism needed to be comprehensive and take all the various aspects of protracted conflicts in the entire region into consideration.

Third, we note that, a key component of *mato oput* is compensation. Many difficulties were encountered in the implementation of this practice. The requirement to provide ten cows for reparation was not possible in the IDP context. There was no measure to compensate for the cruelty, depravity and scale of the atrocities. The magnitude of the crimes was too great. Fulfilling the original requirement of *mato oput* – a girl child in compensation for a deliberate murder – would have been impossible and surely unjust, inhumane and a double violation.

The *mato oput* requirement that the victim's and the perpetrator's communities should come together could not to be achieved. Traditional villages had been replaced by expansive IDP camps inhabited by people from various clans and villages (Allen, 2006, pp. 53–60). The IDP phenomenon led to both physical and cultural dislocation, reducing the level of social and cultural cohesion. Moreover, the ceremonies had less appeal for the younger generation of Acholi who were unfamiliar with cultural practices. My research covering the Gulu, Amuru and Kitgum districts revealed that the majority of respondents in Acholi areas were unfamiliar with the traditional justice system. This made it difficult to perform ceremonies and diminished the cultural significance and viability of such ceremonies (Odwar, Interview, 16 March 2008).

A further reason challenging the capacity of *mato oput* to foster meaningful and effective reconciliation is that there was no clear policy framework on how the practice would include the Government which was actively involved in the conflict. As mentioned in Chapter 2, 'Museveni's government allegedly targeted the Acholi people' (Lecturer in Gulu University, Interview, 10 March 2008). This implies that for any fruitful resolution of the war, 'all dimensions of and parties [involved in the war] have to be catered for' (An old man, Interview, 25 May 2008). In this case, for *mato oput* to be properly applicable it would require that Museveni and Kony participate in the ceremony as antagonistic parties in the conflict.

Insofar as *mato oput* focused only on the relationship between the Acholi community and the LRA, ignoring atrocities committed by the Government, it worked well for Museveni. According to Okello Lucima (2008), since the war in northern Uganda was portrayed as an Acholi problem, *mato oput*, as a form of reconciliation of Acholi among themselves, served to reinforce the propaganda that the LRA insurgency was indeed an internal Acholi affair. Judging from the various strategies adopted by the President, some of which have been mentioned earlier in this work, Museveni clearly considered the insurgencies in Acholiland to be the result of the community's violent and irrational culture. In 1988, President Museveni established the 'Ministry of State for Pacification of Northern Uganda, Resident in Gulu' and appointed Betty Acan Bigombe, as the minister in charge (Nyakairu, 2008). Bigombe was tasked with convincing the LRA rebels to give up their struggle, following the failure of the NRA to defeat the rebels. The term 'pacification' was controversial in its connotations and denotation, which soon resulted in the revision of the title to 'Ministry of State in the Office of the Prime Minister, Resident in Northern Uganda' (ibid.). Either Bigombe overlooked the implications in the title of the ministry or she agreed to play into the hands of Museveni's *realpolitik*.

'Pacification' is an example of a political euphemism intended to mask notions like 'sanitise' and 'confer respectability' and to protect the user against being fully understood (Cohen, 2001, p. 107). According to George Orwell political speeches and writings employ figurative language to mask what is truly meant by the conveyor and to defend politically motivated actions which are otherwise indefensible (Young, 1991). During the Vietnam War, American soldiers employed the term 'pacification' to refer to the forced evacuation of Vietnamese from their huts, the rounding up of all males, the shooting of those who resisted, the butchering of domestic animals and the burning of dwellings (Bosmajian, 1997). According to Staub (2003, 1999) such terms, which have the effect of devaluing others and creating a sense of order, are common in societies with a history of marginalising a group of people, where violence is normalised and made acceptable, and with an ideology of antagonism. In Uganda, a legacy of violence and ethnic stereotyping was the result of colonialism and perpetuated by the post-independence leadership; it was characterised by such euphemistic references. These shaped the way people thought, devalued others and subordinated minority groups. In this respect, the term 'pacification', as used by President Museveni, was an example of euphemistic language which could have arisen out of the conventional conception that the Acholi people were warlike. Elsewhere James Ojara Latigo (2008, p. 89) claims that the president also referred to the Acholi and the LRA as grasshoppers in a bottle in which they would eat each other before they found their way out. In this respect *mato oput*, insofar as it was between the Acholi and the LRA, was well-suited to Museveni's matrix since it sought to reconcile criminals with their own community which they had victimised. The traditional practice placed the conflict further outside the national arena and in so doing absolved the state from playing any role with regard to the situation of the Acholi. This would mean that the LRA were not fighting the Ugandan state, but their own people. The Ugandan state, therefore, had no further responsibility vis-à-vis the rest of the war (Lucima, 2008).

Given the above, and the dynamics of the war in northern Uganda, *mato oput* was not an appropriate mechanism with which to handle the conflict in its broader aspects. The Acholi traditional practice might have had the capacity to achieve some level of psychosocial healing among the Acholi, as discussed above, but it would be inaccurate to maintain that the traditional system of justice held the key to solving the problem in northern Uganda as claimed by its supporters, despite its advocates' obvious fixation with it. As we have argued earlier, it is not accurate to regard the traditional practice as being the sum total of a peacebuilding process that would bring the long conflict to an end. Such a view overlooks the importance of addressing the deeper issues underpinning the conflict in northern Uganda and does not take cognisance of the real fault lines that might precipitate re-occurrences of similar conflicts in following years.

Conclusion

The foregoing discussion reveals that, although each of the mechanisms examined has some merit, none of them is sufficient. Confining transitional justice processes within retributive justice and non-prosecutorial parameters has exposed the limitations of these competing models. The two models do have a certain potential but they are not the only alternatives for transitional justice. These processes and debates have been based on a dichotomous approach to transitional justice. Discourses and practice of transitional justice should go beyond the dualist approach as is the case with the mainstream transitional justice. Promoters of amnesty base their argument on the pragmatic notion that punitive justice for those responsible for atrocities against humankind is contrary to the well-being of the very people whose rights are meant to be protected and that punitive justice is therefore not the preferred option. Pardoning perpetrators of human rights violations is acceptable as long as it serves the utilitarian goal of achieving greater social good. Social good is here understood as ensuring that the guns are silenced and must be achieved even at the cost of the more fundamental norms of the rule of law. These are the ideas underpinning the argument that pursuing the LRA for prosecution and punishment would cause them to harden their position, with the protracted spilling of blood. Peace is seen as being opposed to justice. The analysis reveals that as long as justice in transitional situations is reduced to prosecution and amnesty processes, peace and justice will remain in opposition to each other, thereby revealing a complex nature of transitional justice.

Notes

1 Annan Hails International Criminal Courts' Arrest Warrants for Five Ugandan Rebels, *U.N. News Service*, 14 October, 2005. Available at www.un.org/apps/news/printnewsAr.asp?nid=16243.

2 Uganda Law Society. (2018). The International Crimes Division of the High Court Of Uganda: Towards Greater Effectiveness, www.uls.or.ug/site/assets/files/1355/the_international_crimes_division_of_the_high_court_of_ugandatowards_greater_effectiveness.pdf.

6 Concluding remarks

Transitional justice as a vortex

The involvement of the International Court brought the debates on transitional justice in northern Uganda to unprecedented heights, highlighting dilemmas and complexities that have characterised situations making transitions from conflict to sustainable peace. This concluding chapter highlights some key learning points that can be drawn from the ICC intervention in northern Uganda. First, transitional justice situations are extraordinary, thereby complicating transitional justice mechanisms; second, the complex international system within which the ICC operates complicates the aspirations for transitional justice through the rule of law; the third point regards the Acholi question in the broader context of protracted conflicts in Uganda and its implications on transitional justice mechanisms in northern Uganda. Finally, I propose that transitional justice discourse should go beyond the peace and justice dichotomy to include sociological and economic reconstruction of such societies which are moving from conflict to peace and stability.

Extraordinariness of transitional situations and transitional justice dilemmas

At the conceptual level international criminal justice applied during transitional situations represents a novelty in the application of the rule of law. But this shift generates further complexities in already complex situations of political transitions. In this case transitional justice inhibits enduring dilemmas. International criminal justice as applied in transitional situations operates within the conceptual framework of classical notions of justice, according to which the criminal should be punished according to the rule of law, following a due process of the law but sharply distinct from the ordinary conception of justice (Crocker, 2000; Kritz, 1995, p. xx; Teitel, 2002). This elicits the question on whether the work of transitional justice requires revision of the basic principles of justice or is it more concerned with a modest inquiry into appropriate institutional arrangements to achieve peace (Ohlin, 2007, p. 52). In other words, where does the novelty reside given that the instruments operate according to the classical notions of justice? According to Posner and Vermeule (2004, pp. 762–4) international judicial instruments applied in transitional situations present no moral or legal dilemmas.

They refute the claim that '[t]transitional justice is a distinctive topic that presents a distinctive set of moral and jurisprudential dilemmas'. The position is that transitional justice is continuous with ordinary justice in that even the ordinary laws of consolidated democracies are equally dogged by jurisprudential dilemmas similar to those characterising transitional situations (ibid., p. 763). Accordingly, there is nothing new in transitional justice debates and that the problems raised in these debates should be reduced to ordinary moral and jurisprudential dilemmas that have always characterised the application of universal moral principles to particular situations. From this standpoint, international criminal justice applied as a mechanism for transitional justice does not present distinct dilemmas.

I argue, on the contrary, that although international criminal justice, as a mechanism for transitional justice, is based on the same legal and moral foundations of 'ordinary times', there is a new dimension that it imports in its application in transitional situations. This new dimension is shaped by the nature of crimes pursued by international criminal justice instruments in transitional situations. Crimes which are dealt with by international criminal justice instruments have the extraordinary nature of a collective character and threaten collective peace and security. In this respect, the ICC is more than a criminal court in the ordinary sense if it is required to prosecute cases when collective peace and security demands are its concerns (Ohlin, 2007, p. 62). Ordinarily, societies engage in the prosecution of individuals because criminals must be punished and the innocent go free, as required by the rule of law. At this point I wish to revert to an earlier assertion made in Chapter 5 on the nexus between prosecution and peacebuilding in that individual accountability has the potential of neutralising collective guilt by focusing on individual perpetrators. As indicated in this previous chapter, this claim remains problematic and one of the dilemmas central to transitional justice practice and debates. The problem here is tied to the nature of crimes that international justice is called upon to deal with.

Mark Drumbl (2007, p. 4) refers to crimes committed during relative peace as 'ordinary domestic crimes' which affect a small number of victims targeted in an indiscriminate manner. But crimes committed during extraordinary moments have both individual and collective character. Collective character means such crimes systematically threaten a significant proportion of the population. Drumbl (ibid., p. 11) refers to such crimes as 'extraordinary international crimes [... as opposed to] ordinary domestic crimes'. Extraordinary crimes include genocide and crimes against humanity involving large numbers of victims particularly targeted because of their group membership. To illustrate this distinction let us consider the case of rape, which is undoubtedly a crime against the person. As an isolated case, rape rests within the domain of ordinary criminal justice. However, the same act becomes an extraordinary crime – a subject of transitional justice – by virtue of it being perpetrated as a systematic means of intimidation, terror or genocide. As a crime against humanity, rape has an overwhelmingly destructive effect on the identity, integrity, peace and stability of the entire society (May, 2005, pp. 96–111). Thus, ordinary crimes like murder and rape acquire an extraordinary character – crimes against humanity or genocide – when committed as part of a 'widespread or systematic attack' on a civilian population. The extraordinariness of atrocity crimes render transitional justice, whichever the approach may be, very problematic presenting one of the dilemmas of transitional justice.

Apart from the collective target group, extraordinary international crimes are distinguished from ordinary crimes in terms of the complex agency in such crimes – the number of perpetrators. According to Drumbl (2007, p. 25), whereas ordinary crimes are committed by a small number of perpetrators, extra-ordinary crimes are committed by a large group constituting a multilevel pyramid. At the peak of the pyramid are the individuals who commandeer the plan. The planners are followed by mid-level officials who are 'ordered into ordering others' to kill while paying allegiance to conflict commandeers. Below the mid-level officials are those who do the actual killing. At the very bottom line are the 'hoi polloi' – multitudes who simply acquiesce and do nothing (ibid.). What matters in the case of extraordinary crimes during conflict is not the mind of the individual criminal (Robertson, 2006, p. 241). What is significant is the fact that the individual is part of a wider apparatus, which makes the crimes so horrific and locates them in a category outside ordinary criminality (ibid.). Moreover, the individuals acting as part of the wider apparatus are the ones considered to be conforming to social norms while those who choose to act otherwise are understood to be eccentric (Drumbl, 2007, p. 30).

Accordingly, during transitional moments the rule of law is applied to respond to events which defy our ordinary conceptual and moral categories (Friedlander, 1992, p. 3). Transitional justice is concerned with capturing what has been referred to as radical evil (Sarat et al., 2005). The notion of radical evil dates back to Emmanuel Kant, who described it as that which destroys the very foundation of moral possibility (Cherkasova, 2005, pp. 574–5). The notion was used by Arendt in the aftermath of the Second World War to describe the Holocaust. For Arendt and Jaspers (1992, p. 6), radical evil is that which makes '…human beings as human beings superfluous, not using them as means to an end, which leaves the essence as human untouched and impinges only on their human dignity; rather making them superfluous as humans'. Thus radical evil, for Arendt (1967, pp. 447–57), emerged in connection with a system that sought to reduce human beings to meaninglessness through total domination, epitomised by the concentration camps and the extermination of an entire people. Radical evil is about the strongest form of humiliation which destroys the very person, a fundamental assault against the most common denominator of being human. It is a direct onslaught against humanity as a moral community, a crime against humanity. In this respect, what sets radical evil apart from ordinary crimes is that, in some sense, humanity is harmed when these crimes are perpetrated (Arendt, 1967). Thus, insofar as transitional justice addresses events of radical evil or extraordinary crime, it becomes distinct from ordinary justice dispensed during ordinary moments and is bound to raise distinct moral and jurisprudential dilemmas.

A corollary to the nature of extraordinary crimes is the notion of international jurisdiction, which overrides national limits in the pursuit of justice in respect of such crimes. The notion of international jurisdiction, according to Sands (2004, p. 69), is based on a belief that certain crimes are so serious that they are treated by the international community as being international crimes. The relevance of international judicial intervention is that it has a universal character. The advocacy of a universal model of international justice is hinged on the controversial assumption that all nations subscribe to similar notions of justice and law. International judicial intervention, in these terms, is intervention inspired by the belief that transition to more stable and peaceful political systems implies upholding universal legal and moral norms. In this respect, transitional justice is conceived as criminal justice where the usual goals of rules of law and justice apply, namely, holding violators accountable for their actions and punishing them once their guilt is determined through a rigorous process before an impartial judge (Ohlin, 2007, p. 52). Accordingly, perpetrators of war crimes and crimes against humanity would be expected to be accountable for their crimes (Ratner & Abrams, 2001; Orentlicher, 1991, p. 2537). The pursuit of the human rights agenda is here conceived as moral conduct which is a matter of following rules, where duties and rights are determined by rules (Shklar, 1987, p. 1). The universal character of international accountability places it above alternative instruments for peacebuilding.

International criminal justice founds the notion of human rights in the global arena on the universalistic principle of the rule of law. This implies that certain crimes transcend national jurisdiction and that their commission immediately elicits a global response. Since the rule of law, especially in its substantive sense, is characterised by the feature of universality, it can be applied to safeguard human rights not only at national level, but also at international level. It is this aspect of the rule of law that gives the ICC its justified mandate to promote the moral vision of good life and respect for human dignity in societies characterised by violent conflicts and gross violations of human rights.

The obligation to prosecute and punish perpetrators of such crimes rests on the country having jurisdiction over these offences, but also applies to members of the international community (Méndez, 1997, p. 6). Given the international dimension of such crimes, Sands (2004, p. 69) argues, any state may claim jurisdiction over them. This implies a shift from pre-Nuremberg trials when the international laws of war were not concerned with the way a government treated its nationals. From the IMT of Nuremberg, the notion of individuals having concrete duties under international law, as opposed to national law, was clearly enunciated for the first time and later accepted by the international community of states. Until the Nuremberg trials, war crimes trials had been held at national level under national military law (Clapham, 2004, p. 31). This enunciation, though in retrospect, was a radical moment in the history of human rights and humanitarian law. The IMT set the beginning of a new way of thinking about international law attaching duties to individuals who committed massive criminal acts while acting on behalf of the state. Human rights law developed around the prohibition on genocide, torture, disappearances and summary executions, so that it became possible to consider individual responsibility for human rights violations, even in the absence of armed conflict (ibid., p. 33). The new understanding and application of crimes against humanity elevated human rights violations to the level of international crimes (ibid., p. 43). Thus, one of the novelties of international criminal justice applied during transitional moments vis-à-vis justice during ordinary times is that the former is based on an unprecedented doctrine of universal jurisdiction. This doctrine appeals to the conscience of mankind, based on the universal recognition of human rights and invokes ideals of justice, impartiality and fairness geared towards preservation of peace on a global scale (Kochler, 2006).

The notion of international jurisdiction is also relevant in situations making transitions from conflict to peace for practical reasons. Ordinary crimes are dealt with by a state judicial apparatus which cannot respond to evils of a radical nature given the context of transitional situations. In transitional situations it is likely that many of the judges will be the same judges who served in the old regime and so are thought to be deeply compromised from the start, as in the case of the Rwandan 1994 genocide. Second, many of the newly appointed judges are likely to be appointed because they were excluded from the old regime and they too would be possibly, or perceived to be, compromised or there may simply be no judges, as in the case of post-genocide Rwanda. Third, judges in a transition are often faced with having to hand down decisions on deeply political matters, thereby putting their independence in jeopardy. There is, therefore, a need for judges from non-interested parties and this can only be possible within the frame of international justice institutions.

The above universalism immediately meets critical opposition. The notion of universal jurisdiction has elicited the accusation that international standards of justice apply a one-size-fits-all and a decontextualised, normative remedy (Drumbl, 2005; Oomen, 2005). Universal jurisdiction, according to its opponents, prioritises what may not be pertinent in a particular situation and has the potential of usurping local initiatives. Adam Branch (2004, p. 5), referring particularly to the ICC's involvement in northern Uganda, asserted that insisting on prosecuting the LRA while the local community preferred to reconcile with the rebels amounted to paternalism and a new form of imperialism. Such views implied that the ICC was undermining local autonomy and self-determination since it failed to consider local demands (ibid.). A further implication is that it should have been up to Uganda to decide which direction was best for them in the pursuit of a peace process in northern Uganda (Afako, 2002, p. 8). The granting of amnesty to the top leaders of the LRA as an alternative to prosecution by the ICC was anchored on what was understood to be Uganda's right to political determination and the expectation that the ICC would refrain from interfering in its internal affairs. While making reference to Uganda's Amnesty Act of 2000, President Museveni claimed that Ugandans had discovered an internal solution (Ssenyonjo, 2005). The internal solution meant opting for negotiations with the LRA, granting amnesty to the rebels followed by the administering of *mato oput*, the traditional Acholi system of justice, as an instrument of integration. *The New Vision* reported President Museveni as asking the LRA to surrender and 'engage in internal reconciliation mechanisms put in place by the Acholi community such as *mato oput* or blood settlement' (*The New Vision*, 2004). Yet, when President Museveni referred the situation in northern Uganda to the ICC, it was because the crimes allegedly committed by the LRA required global intervention.

The contestation between the ICC's universal jurisdiction and the demands of self-determination in the context of gross human rights violation is entangled up in political considerations and this is one of the arenas where the rule of law encounters politics in an enduring puzzle. Notwithstanding the plausibility of international judicial intervention, it remains an arena of vested interested. When the US formally withdrew from the ICC in May 2002, it maintained that countries should be left to decide on their preferred way of responding to human rights abuses without any external, overriding prosecutorial model (Mayerfeld, 2004, p. 147; Morris, 2001; Bolton, 2001; Kissinger, 2001). The same USA has supported the ICC financially. These observations take us to another point, namely the nature of the international within which the ICC operates. In this respect, instead of claiming that the ICC intervention was likely to exercise unchecked power over Uganda, it would be more plausible to argue that the court was weighed down by sovereign powers and prevailing political realities.

The complex international system, the ICC and transitional justice

The arena within which an international justice system is instituted and operates is another aspect of the dilemmas of transitional justice. In this regard it is observable that critics have discredited the ICC for its dismal performance and inefficiency. We argue that the problem with the International Court is its inherent limitation in terms of power and scope. The ICC's efficacy is contingent upon the backing it should receive from domestic and international actors. The ICC does not have its own police force and relies for this on the governments in those countries in which it is carrying out its investigations. It is these governments that are expected to provide the court with the assistance it may need such as access to suspects and protection for investigators and witnesses. The reliance on governments' support represents a conundrum. On the one hand, without government support there would be no arrests, and without arrests there would be no trials, as Kirsch (2006) observes. In this case, the ICC turns out to be what Cassese (1998, p. 13) refers to as 'a giant without arms and legs – it needs artificial limbs to walk and work. And these artificial limbs are state authorities'. When the court issued warrants of arrests against the LRA, it shook the rebels prompting them to seek negotiations with the Government. Until that moment the court had received good cooperation from the Ugandan Government. However, the moment the Ugandan Government started warming to the proposed alternative initiatives, it became clear that, without the Government's assistance, the court was unlikely to bring the LRA leaders to justice.

Since the ICC's arrest warrants can only be effected through national jurisdictions, this means that the court's effective response to mass atrocities remains contingent upon the political will of states. This implies that the logic of the principle of complementarity can turn out to be an impediment to the ICC or, at least, problematic. According to the principle of complementarity, before the court could intervene in the situation of northern Uganda, it had to determine that the Ugandan authorities were unwilling or unable to prosecute those crimes. This means, the ICC's starting point was Uganda's inaction against the LRA crimes either in terms of inability or unwillingness. Yet, the Ugandan Government was complicit in human rights violations, even though it was the Government which initially referred the case to the court. How, therefore, could the court expect the Ugandan Government to cooperate with it by providing evidence, executing searches or arresting suspects? Moreover, the expectation that the Ugandan Government would effectively support warrants of arrest would prove to be problematic even if the Government were willing to do so. The Government had been unable to arrest the LRA and prosecute them and it was questionable how this would be possible. The principle of complementarity does not necessary lead to proper accomplishment of the court's effective operations, instead it might undermine the ICC operations which it is meant to foster.

More so, the politics of international criminal justice and particularly perceptions of partiality is yet another critical issue. The court seems to have focused predominantly on Africa, giving the impression that the court was using Africa as a guinea pig. The court's first referrals and investigations were in Africa, namely, northern Uganda, the DRC, and Sudan. The indictment of the Sudanese president, al-Bashir, elicited criticism from among African leaders. The court seemingly turned a blind eye to human rights violations in Iraq, Afghanistan, Chechnya, Gaza and Guantanamo Bay. In the context of the US war on terror following the 11 September 2001 attack on New York and Washington by Al-Qaeda, US officials sanctioned the coercive interrogation of terrorist suspects held under US authority at various detention sites such as Guantanamo Bay, Afghanistan and Iraq (Forsythe, 2005). Washington authorities *ipso facto* became violators of human rights and would be unwilling, in any serious manner, to investigate human rights violations sanctioned by them. The invasion of Iraq by the allied forces had been associated with the deaths of thousands of innocent civilians and led to severe insecurity, yet the actions of the US and the UK in Iraq did not constitute a central focus of the ICC. Other cases that could be mentioned include the actions of the Israeli Government in Gaza, which led to numerous deaths, injuries and destruction. Although the ICC had arrested some warlords involved in human rights violations in the DRC, the court did not consider the involvement of 85 companies implicated in the UN report of October 2002 in connection with human rights violations in the DRC conflict.[1] The court did intervene in the situation in Syria. In this regard, the fact that ICC intervention was overly focused on Africa not only brought into question its impartiality but also fostered the view that the court was a neocolonial instrument out to stifle Africa's self-determination endeavour. Okello (2007, pp. 2–3) contends that the ICC's interventions would be morally appealing if it had not concentrated its investigations in sub-Saharan Africa, making the continent appear to be the site for testing trial justice and new ideas. This brought about bad blood between African states and the ICC. The ICC threatened to withdraw en masse from the Rome Statute.

Upon its establishment, the ICC had been hailed as heralding a new era in the enforcement of international accountability, something which had been absent from international justice. With the coming into force of the Rome Statute, the International Court promised to be an authoritative institution with the power to enforce accountability in situations of massive human rights violation. Impunity would be a thing of the past. But from the dynamics that subsequently emerged it appears that those backing the court had placed too high a premium on an institution which, in the strictest sense, was still in its nascent stages of development. The expectations that impunity had been overcome were overtaken by the reality of international *politics* and the ICC was yet to reckon with the overbearing power of *realpolitik* in international relations. These observations reinforce the problem of transitional justice.

The Acholi question and transitional justice mechanisms in northern Uganda

A third critical issue is the Acholi question and transitional justice mechanisms. The primary goal of the ICC is to dispense justice through prosecutions and not to offer solutions for political stability. The role of the Prosecutor is to investigate and prosecute those he believes, on credible grounds, to be responsible for atrocious crimes. In northern Uganda, there were voices among the Acholi population who accused the Government of scheming to exterminate their cattle, to marginalise them economically and politically through the violence visited on them by NRA/UPDF. One old man captured this sentiment when he asked me:

> You have told me that you have travelled through Kitgum, Gulu and Amuru, have you seen any cattle grazing? But this used to be a land of cattle. Cattle used to be the source of our livelihood and our strength. The government knew that. In our language we say, when you want to kill a big tree you do not face the trunk; you begin by cutting its roots one by one and by doing that, you will have succeeded in terminating its lifeline.
>
> (Ben Ladit, Interview, 15 April 2009)

These perceived historical injustices require a politically-conscious redress. If these grievances were not addressed, prosecuting a handful of the LRA would not bring about lasting peace since it was unclear if the conflict would transmute. From the international criminal justice standpoint, the referral of the situation in northern Uganda to the ICC was in the best interests of the people of Uganda and the victims of the LRA atrocities. But the conflict in northern Uganda was a microcosm of sociopolitical issues that characterised postcolonial Uganda. Insofar as the Rome Statute did not include in its goals the values of structural transformation, part of the ICC's problem lay in its limited capacity to do anything about historical injustices. As a legal institution with a mandate to prosecute, the court does not make direct political decisions on what is necessary for post-conflict reconstruction and lacks the expertise necessary for post-conflict management or peacemaking (Blumenson, 2006, p. 816). The link that the ICC has with post-conflict peacebuilding and transformation is that of bringing about the rule of law and democratic culture.

Whereas the International Court cannot make political decisions, the ICC Chief Prosecutor is confronted with a need to meet the demands of the various interests and goals which are linked to a peaceful outcome. The ICC prosecutor has to contend with balancing these interests. Although the ICC is a legal instrument which should be completely depoliticised it does not function in a political vacuum. Every post-conflict justice has to deal with the contextual circumstances in which the crimes are committed; it has to gain access to evidence, which calls for the logistical and political cooperation of the state in which it is carrying out investigations.

Justice under transitional situations involves much more than judicial accountability meted out through prosecutions. In the context of massive scale violations, no criminal justice system can prosecute all those responsible. In the case of northern Uganda, the line between victim and perpetrator is vague. The LRA perpetrators were indeed victims before they were turned into abusers of human rights, making it difficult to effect justice through prosecution. Framing transitional justice in terms of jurisdictional mandate also falls short of interrogating what constitutes the key elements of the war in northern Uganda, especially its root causes, longevity and the reconstruction of the society. The ICC focused on the five commanders, and this was instrumental in sending out the message that no one can commit heinous crimes with impunity. However, insofar as it focused only on the few LRA commanders the court ignored two things, namely, the relationship between the Government and the Acholi population, and the fact that members of the LRA would come back and live in the community whose members they have tormented. It is also outside the domain of the ICC to deal with a number of critical questions such as the marginalisation of the Acholi.

Beyond dualism in transitional justice

Transitional justice in northern Uganda has been pursued and discussed within the mainstream frameworks of retributive and restorative justice. The ICC operates within a legal framework which defines transitional justice as that mode of justice which, according to Teitel (2003a, p. 893), '[... is] associated with periods of political change as reflected in the phenomenology of primarily legal responses that deal with the wrongdoing of the repressive predecessor regime'. The legal approach focuses on re-establishing the rule of law, but pays little attention to the broader needs of transitional societies. Standing in opposition to the legal approach is restorative justice, which responds to massive violations of human rights by seeking to repair harm, heal the victims and community and to reintegrate both the offender and the victim back into the community (Boraine, 2000, pp. 152–3; Drumbl, 2000, p. 1258). This approach is exclusive and narrow in the sense that it ignores other pertinent issues which merit consideration at times of transition. The scholarly and institutional aspects of transitional justice have so far sidelined issues of economic inequality, structural violence, redistribution and development (Miller, 2008, p. 266). Although dealt with in transitional justice discourse and practices, cases of inequality and structural violence are viewed as contextual backgrounds while economic concerns are reduced to discussions of reparation (ibid.). In contrast to such a limited approach to transitional justice, scholarship and practice, issues of inequality and structural violence should constitute the central object of transitional justice.

Framing transitional justice practice within a dichotomous approach led to a limited interpretation of violence and victimhood in northern Uganda. Violence in northern Uganda was understood to be limited to atrocities visited on the civilian population by the LRA. The violence should have been extended to include atrocities committed by both the LRA and the UPDF – historical grievances, extermination of the Acholi cattle by the UPDF, the dehumanising conditions of the IDP camps among a myriad of life-threatening phenomena associated with the conflict. Transitional justice in northern Uganda ought to have been conceived as encompassing processes that include negotiating to bring the conflict to an end, instituting criminal prosecutions and economic reconstruction, and focusing on gender-based grievances and broader structural transformation. This observation is important since it reinforces the thesis that limiting the transitional justice process in northern Uganda to a single mechanism ignores the multifaceted nature of ethno-political conflict.

A significant element of the conflict was the colonial legacy which bred inequality among ethnic groups and ethnic stereotyping which countered the prospects of national cohesion. These legacies were later exploited by postcolonial political leadership resulting in persistent instability in the country, and northern Uganda in particular. This inequality led to prolonged socio-economic and political exclusion in the northern part of the country. According to many respondents consulted by this researcher, the reason northern Uganda remained vulnerable to insecurity was its marginalisation from other parts of the country (Ogwal, Interview, 21 April 2009). A District Speaker of the Kitgum District, whose view I cited earlier in this discussion (see Chapter 2), corroborated the view that the prolonged war in northern Uganda had been considered to be an Acholi problem (District Speaker, Interview, 10 April 2008). This attitude reinforced the marginalisation of the Acholi.

Apart from the atrocities caused by the LRA, the uprooting of the people from their homes and their transfer to IDP camps, were in themselves extremely disempowering and created insecurity in the region (A Security Intelligence Officer, anonymous, Interview, 22 April 2009). Even after the people had been moved to camps, the LRA followed them and, in fact, the camps made it even easier for the LRA to attack and abduct people (Okiri, Interview, 28 April 2008). The IDP dwellers were barred from accessing their farmland to work the land and produce food. But even if they were able to access their land for cultivation purposes, they still needed the protection of the UPDF to work on their farms. In most cases the UPDF failed to protect them (Odhiambo, Interview, 5 May 2009; Oyella, Interview, 18 April 2009). The squalid camp conditions raised both social and health concerns. The close proximity of shelters to one another fostered widespread malaria and cholera. This, combined with malnutrition, caused high child mortality in the camps (Agnes Achayo, Interview, 5 May 2009). Within this context, opportunities for education were remote. Moreover, the camp set-up destroyed the pre-existing family and communal structures together with their value systems. As a result some people resorted to unhealthy and unacceptable means of survival, such as prostitution.

Accordingly, the social condition of the Acholi, resulting from violent conflict and structural violence should have been included within the scope of transitional justice in northern Uganda. A transitional justice process that did not radically correct such discriminatory structures could not achieve sustainable peace. A relevant example is a case of the West Nile region where the Government of Museveni signed an agreement with the Uganda National Rebel Front II (UNRF II) in 2002 after four years of negotiations. This agreement led to the rebels receiving amnesty in exchange for surrendering their struggle. Though the agreement survived, the local community continued to express their concern about what they considered to be a lack of justice and perpetual economic marginalisation (Refugee Law Project, 2004; Okello, 2007). Similarly, a number of respondents were sceptical about Museveni's commitment to peace in northern Uganda since most humanitarian activities had been undertaken by foreign non-governmental organisations, a sign of gross marginalisation (Kasirani, Interview, 7 June 2008). The need to initiate fundamental economic and political transformation remained key to realising sustainable peace in northern Uganda.

Transitional justice ought to grapple with political and economic deprivation because such deprivations are intricately tied to intra-state conflicts. A pattern of specific violations may, if left unchecked, gradually become a structural condition in itself and fuel further conflict (Parlevliet, 2002, p. 5). Experience shows that economically and politically stable countries with firm structures and institutions for the distribution of resources do not experience conflict. In countries that lack such structures, political power is violently contested since access to resources is usually tied to political power. In such societies a particular social group may, on the basis of its identity, be systematically barred from participating in the political processes. In most African societies for example, injustice, repression and exploitation are built on the fundamental structures of society, with differential access to social resources. This is likely to result in deep social cleavages and rivalries, which are conditions for protracted conflicts. According to Nherere and Ansah-Koi (1990) many conflicts are due to limited political participation, the pursuit of self-determination, limited access to resources, exploitation and discrimination. Such structures are likely to result in conflict because, once a section of society has been excluded, liberation is likely to be violent. The pursuit of economic and political liberation is likely to threaten the political and economic dominance of the ruling group leading to the counter response of systematic suppression and serious human rights violations.

In this respect structural discrimination is logically connected to human rights violations as captured by Parlevliet (2009, p. 5) who argues that the

> [d]enial of human rights is embedded in the structures of society and governance, in terms of how the state is organised, how institutions operate and how society functions. For example, a state may be characterized by a consistent lack of development in those regions where the majority of citizens are members of a social group other than the politically dominant group. Alternatively, a country's legislative and policy framework may be biased against certain identity groups resulting in their exclusion and marginalisation from political, economic and social spheres of life. Such conditions create structural fault lines in society that may be less visible at first sight, but provide fertile ground for the outbreak of violence.

There is a relation between social exclusion, human rights violations and conflicts. The denial of rights implies the frustration of needs related to identity, welfare, freedom and security, which are fundamental for human survival, subsistence and development. If human rights are denied and needs are subverted, the potential for violent conflict is greater as individuals or groups will seek to address their needs. In this regard, as long as disempowering structural conditions remain in place in a society and as long as these structures remain the matrix for power and economic distribution, then the prospects of violence persist (Nathan, 2001).

Thus, transitional justice processes and discourse ought to be concerned with how to explore a range of options such as accountability, without compromising broader and deeper transformative objectives (Simpson, 2008). The pursuit of international justice and respect for human rights ought not to be seen as detached from the greater need for peace and human security in its broadest sense. The linkage between poverty reduction and post-conflict peacebuilding has not been adequately explored in the literature on transitional justice, and poverty reduction has not constituted a central part of transitional justice. Transitional justice should, therefore, extend its scope beyond that of prosecution, reconciliation, psychosocial healing and related goals to grapple with the social and economic sources of the violation of economic, social and cultural rights. By broadening the scope of transitional justice to include violations of economic, social and cultural rights governments within transitional states would be obliged to deal with the conditions that brought such violations about. Such a process would also provide a platform for various actors, such as the aggrieved parties and international and national civil society with its legitimate demand to redress pertinent grievances. Failure to redress the socio-economic structures that underpin conflict means that sustainable peace cannot be realised. Within the framework of such a broadened approach, instruments such as commissions would be able to play the diagnostic role of exposing the extent and nature of the social and economic causes of conflict and the ensuing human rights violations. From such a process would emerge recommendations that would shape national political agendas geared to addressing poverty and structural inequalities.

It is significant to reconsider the manner in which transitional justice is conceptualised in contemporary transitional discourse and practice. Transitional justice practice and scholarship should seek to constitute transitional justice in terms of its moral, political and legal components. Transitional situations raise not only legal but also political and moral dilemmas. Such processes cannot be limited simply to exercising criminal justice or balancing politically contending interests, but must include reforming deep-rooted socio-economic, cultural, environmental, institutional and other structural causes that underlie the overt political symptoms of violent conflicts (Annan 2001; Barsalou, 2005).

This means that a reductionist approach to transitional justice may not be sufficient and effective enough. Since theory usually defines practice, narrow conceptualisation will limit the practical initiatives that may be constructed within a given conceptual framework. Transitional justice as a response to global insecurity cannot continue to be limited in its approach. Transitional justice needs, therefore, to shift towards a more holistic approach of transformative restoration such as protecting peace, security and the human rights of individuals. This would require understanding human rights in the broadest sense. Generally, in post-conflict society where serious crimes have been committed, most aspects of a social system, such as the legal, the political, the economic, the moral and the social, have broken down as is evident in the situation of northern Uganda. Economic reconstruction is transformative on the economic plane and political reconstruction is transformative on the political plane. Judicial accountability is transformative on the legal plane. The same logic applies to psychosocial reconstruction. The ultimate starting point of transitional justice is that social order has broken down and that any transitional justice instrument would seek to transform this broken order into structures conducive to sustainable peace. Transitional justice should therefore be guided by certain ultimate goals of human well-being. The important element in the 20-year conflict in northern Uganda is to provide resources for development and more pertinently for socio-economic and political transformation.

Note

1 See for instance United Nations. (2002). *Report of the panel of experts on the illegal exploitation of natural resources and other forms of wealth of the Democratic Republic of Congo. Security Council.* S/2002/1146. 15 October.

References

Books

Acuna, C. & Smulovitz, C. (1997). Guarding the guardians in Argentina – Some lessons about risks and benefits of empowering the courts. In J. A. McAdams (Ed.), *Transitional justice and the rule of law in new democracies* (pp. 93–122). Notre Dame: University of Notre Dame.

Afako, B. (2002). Reconciliation and justice: 'Mato oput' and the Amnesty Act. In L. Okello (Ed.), *Protracted conflict, elusive peace: Initiatives to end the violence in Northern Uganda.* London: African Centre for Constructive Resolution of Disputes.

Agamben, G. (1995). *Homo sacer: Sovereign power and bare life*. New York: Free Press.

Allen, T. (2006). *Trial justice: The international criminal court and The Lord's Resistance Army*. London: Zed Books.

Apter, D. E. (1961). *The political kingdom in Uganda: A study in the bureaucratic nationalism*. Princeton: Princeton University Press.

Arendt, H. (1967). *Origins of totalitarianism*. London: Allen & Unwin.

Arendt, H. & Jaspers, K. (1992). *Correspondence, 1926–1969*. L. Kohler & H. Saner (Eds). New York: Harcourt Brace Jovanovich.

Asowa-okwe, C. (1994). Politics in Uganda 1962–1992. In E. M. Khiddu, V. M. Mwaka & P. G. Okoth (Eds), *Uganda: Thirty years of independence 1962–1992* (pp. 133–64). Kampala: University Printers.

Atkinson, R. R. (1999). *The roots of ethnicity: The origins of the Acholi of Uganda before 1800*. Kampala: Fountain Publishers.

Bassiouni, M. C. (2002). The universal model: The international criminal court. In M. C. Bassiouni (Ed.), *Post-conflict accountability* (pp. 813–28). Ardsley: Translational Publishers.

Behrend, H. (1991). Is Alice Lakwena a witch? The Holy Spirit Movement and its fight against evil in the north. In H. B. Hansen & M. Twaddle (Eds), *Changing Uganda: The dilemma of structural adjustment and revolutionary change* (pp. 162–77). London: James Currey.

Behrend, H. (1999). *Alice Lakwena & the holy spirits: War in Northern Uganda 1985–1997*. Nairobi: East African Educational Publishers.

Berkman, L. F. & Kawachi, I. (Eds). (2000). *Social epistemology*. New York: Oxford University Press.

Blattman, C. & Annan, J. (2008). Child combatants in northern Uganda: Reintegration myths and realities. In R. Muggah (Ed.), *Security and post-conflict reconstruction: Dealing with fighters in the aftermath of war* (pp 103–26). New York: Routledge.

Boed, R. (2002). The international criminal tribunal for Rwanda. In M. C. Bassiouni (Ed.), *Post-conflict accountability* (pp. 487–98). Ardsley: Translational Publishers.

Boraine, A. (2000). Truth and reconciliation in South Africa: The third way. In R. I. Rotberg & D. Thompson (Eds), *Morality of truth commissions: Truth vs. justice* (pp. 141–57). Princeton: Princeton University Press.

Bosmajian, H. A. (1997). Dehumanizing people and euphemizing war. In G. Goshgarian (Ed.), *Exploring language*, 8th edition (pp. 215–20). New York: Longman.

Brett, R. & Specht, I. (2004). *Young soldiers: Why they choose to fight*. Boulder: Lynne Rienner Publishers.

Cassese, A. (2006). International criminal law. In M. D. Evans (Ed.), *International law* (pp. 265–73). Oxford: Oxford University Press.

Clapham, A. (2004). Issues of complexity, complicity and complementarity. In P. Sands (Ed.), *From the Nuremberg to the Hague: The future of international criminal justice* (pp. 30–67). Cambridge: Cambridge University Press.

Cobban, H. (2007). *Amnesty after atrocity?: Healing nations after genocide and war crimes*. Boulder: Paradigm Publishers.

Cohen, S. (2001). *States of denial: Knowing about atrocities and suffering*. Cambridge: Polity Press.

Conso, G. (1999). Looking to the future. In S. L. Roy (Ed.), *The international criminal court: The making of the Rome statute, issues, negotiations, results* (pp. 471–7). The Hague: Kluwer Law International.

Cose, E. (2004). *Bone to pick: Of forgiveness, reconciliation, reparation, and revenge*. New York: Atria Books.

Crocker, D. A. (2000). Truth commissions, transitional justice, and civil society. In R. I. Rotberg & D. Thompson (Eds), *Truth v. justice: The morality of truth commissions* (pp. 99–121). Princeton: Princeton University Press.

Denza, E. (2006). The relationship between international and national law. In M. Evans (Ed.), *International law*, 2nd edition (pp. 423–48). Oxford, Oxford University Press.

Dolan, C. (2009). *Social torture: The case of Northern Uganda, 1986–2006*. New York: Berghahn Books.

Doornbos, M. R. (1988). *Not all the King's men: Inequality as a political instrument in Ankole, Uganda*. The Hague: Mouton Publishers.

Drumbl, M. A. (2007). *Atrocity, punishment and international law*. New York: Cambridge University Press.

Ernesto, V. (2004). Institutional responses to genocide. In A. Jones (Ed.), *Genocide, war crimes and the West: History and complicity* (pp. 329–30). London: Zed Books.

Etzioni, A. (1998). Community justice in a communitarian perspective. In D. R. Karp (Ed.), *Community justice: An emerging field* (pp. 373–8). Lanham: Rowman & Littlefield Publishers.

Feinberg, J. (1995). What, if anything, justifies legal punishment?: The classic debate. In J. Feinberg & J. Coleman (Eds), *Philosophy of law* (pp. 613–17). Belmont, CA: Wadsworth.

Finnström, S. (2003). *Living with bad surroundings: War and existential uncertainty in Acholiland, Northern Uganda*, Uppsala Studies in Cultural Anthropology (Vol. 35). Uppsala: Uppsala University Press.

Forsythe, D. P. (2005). *The humanitarians: The international committee of the Red Cross*. Cambridge: Cambridge University Press.

Forsythe, D. P. (2006). *Human rights in international relations*. Cambridge: Cambridge University Press.

Friedlander, S. (Ed.). (1992). *Probing the limits of representation: Nazism and the final solution*. Cambridge: Harvard University Press.

Gifford, P. (1999). *African Christianity: Its public role in Uganda*. Kampala: Fountain Publishers.

Govier, T. (2002). *Forgiveness and revenge*. New York, NY: Routledge.

Gowlland-Debbas, V. (2000). Functions of the security council. In M. Byers (Ed.), *The role of international politics: Essays in international relations and international law* (pp. 277–313). Oxford: Oxford University Press.

Griswald, C. L. (2007). *Forgiveness: A philosophical exploration*. Cambridge: Cambridge University Press.

Hansen, H. B. & Twaddle, M. (Eds). (1995). *Religion and politics in East Africa: The period since independence*. London: James Currey.

Huntington, S. P. (1991). *The third wave: Democratization in the late twentieth century*. Norman: University of Oklahoma Press.

Jeong, H. (2005). *Peacebuilding in postconflict societies: Strategy and process*. London: Lynne Rienner Publishers.

Jones, B. (2009). *Beyond the state of rural Uganda*. Edinburgh: Edinburgh University Press.

Kant, E. (1965). *The metaphysics of justice*. Translated by John Ladd. London: Macmillan.

Keitetsi, C. (2002). *Child soldier*. London: Souvenir Press Ltd.

Kisamba-Mugerwa, W. (1991). Institutional dimensions of land tenure reform. In H. B. Hansen & M. Twaddle (Eds), *Changing Uganda: The dilemmas of structural adjustment and revolutionary change* (pp. 311–21). London: James Currey.

Kritz, N. J. (1995). Dilemmas of transitional justice. In N. J. Kritz (Ed.), *Transitional justice: How emerging democracies reckon with former regimes* (Vol. 1, pp. xix–xxx). Washington, DC: United States Institute of Peace Press.

Lederach, J. P. (1997). *Building peace: Sustainable reconciliation in divided societies*. Washington, DC: United States Institute of Peace Press.

Lee, R. S. (Ed.). (1999). *The international criminal court. The making of the Rome statute: Issues, negotiations, results*. The Hague: Kluwer Law International.

Lukwago, I. K. K. (1982). *The politics of national integration in Uganda*. Nairobi: Coign Publications.

Lwanga-Lunyiigo, S. (1989). The colonial roots of internal conflict. In K. Rupesinghe (Ed.), *Conflict resolution in Uganda* (pp. 24–43). Oslo: International Peace Research Institute.

May, L. (2005). *Crimes against humanity: A normative account*. Cambridge: Cambridge University Press.

Mbiti, J. S. (1970). *African religions and philosophy*. London: Heinemann.

Méndez, J. E. (1997). In defence of transitional justice. In J. A. McAdams (Ed.), *Transitional justice and rule of law in new democracies* (pp. 1–26). Notre Dame: University of Notre Dame Press.

Moore, M. (1997). *Placing blame: A general theory of the criminal law*. Oxford: Clarendon Press.

Morris, C. (1972). *The discovery of the individual: 1050–1200*. New York: Harper & Row Publishers.

Morris, V. & Scharf, M. P. (1998). *The international criminal tribunal for Rwanda* (Vol. 1). New York: Transnational Publishers.

Mudoola, D. M. (1996). *Religion, ethnicity and politics in Uganda*. Kampala: Fountain Publishers.

Mungeam, G. H. (1966). *British rule in Kenya 1895–1912: The establishment of administration in the East African protectorate*. Publisher Oxford: Clarendon Press.

Murphy, J. G. (1979). *Retribution, justice and therapy: Essays in philosophy of law*. London: Reidel Publishing Company.

Museveni, Y. K. (1997). *Sowing the mustard seed: The struggle for democracy in Uganda*. London: Macmillan.

Mutibwa, P. (1992). *Uganda since independence: A story of unfulfilled hopes*. New Jersey: Africa World Press.

Nalepa, M. (2012). Reconciliation, refugee returns, and international criminal justice: The case of Bosnia and Herzegovina. In M. Williams & R. Nagy (Eds), *Transitional justice* (pp. 315–59). New York: New York University Press.

Nherere, P. & Ansah-Koi, K. (1990). Human rights and conflict resolution. In G. Lindgren, P. Wallensteen & K. Nordquist (Eds), *Issues in third world conflict resolution* (pp. 3–42). Uppsala: Department of Peace and Conflict Research, Uppsala University.

O'Donnell, G. & Schmitter P. C. (1995). Transition from authoritarian rule: Tentative conclusions about uncertain democracies. In N. J. Kritz (Ed.), *Transitional justice: How emerging democracies reckon with former regimes* (Vol. 1). Washington, DC: United States Institute of Peace Press.

O'Donnell, G. & Schmitter, P. C. (1998). *Transition from authoritarian rule: Tentative conclusions about uncertain democracies*. Baltimore: Johns Hopkins University Press.

Odongo, O. (2000). *A political history of Uganda: Yoweri Museveni's referendum 2000*. London: WICU Publishing Press Ltd.

Ofcansky, T. P. (1996). *Uganda: Tarnished pearl of Africa*. Boulder: Westview Press.

Omara-Otunnu, A. (1987). *Politics and the military in Uganda*. London: Macmillan.

Pain, D. (1997). *The bending of the spears: Producing consensus for peace & development in Northern Uganda*. London: International Alert.

Politi, M. & Gioia, F. (Eds). (2008). *The international criminal court and national jurisdictions*. Aldershot: Ashgate Publishing Company.

Ratner, S. R. & Abrams, J. S. (2001). *Accountability for human rights atrocities in international law: Beyond the Nuremberg legacy*. Oxford: Oxford University Press.

Robertson, G. (2006). *Crimes against humanity: The struggle for global justice*. New York: New Press.

Rodriguez, C. (2002). Acholi civil society initiatives. In L. Okello (Ed.), *Protracted conflict, elusive peace initiatives to end the violence in Northern Uganda* (pp. 58–59). London: The African Centre for Constructive Conflict Resolution.

Roehrig, T. (2002). *The prosecution of former military leaders in newly democratic nations: The cases of Argentina, Greece, and South Korea*. London: McFarland.

Rotberg, R. I. (2000). Truth commissions and the provision of truth, justice and reconciliation. In R. I. Rotberg & D. Thompson (Eds), *Morality of truth commissions: Truth vs. justice* (pp. 3–21). Princeton: Princeton University Press.

Rupesinghe, K. (Ed.). (1989). *Conflict resolution in Uganda*. Ohio: Ohio University Press.

Sanchez, J. (2007). *Terrorism & its effects*. Delhi: Global Media.

Sands, P. (2004). After Pinochet: The role of national courts. In P. Sands (Ed.), *From the Nuremberg to the Hague: The future of international criminal justice* (pp. 68–108). Cambridge: Cambridge University Press.

Sannerholm, R. (2006). Beyond criminal justice: Promoting rule of law in post-conflict societies. *Conference on Globalisation and Peacebuilding*, Department of Cultural Anthropology & Ethnology, Uppsala University, Sweden.

Sarat, A., Douglas L. & Umphrey, M. M. (Eds). (2005). *The limits of law*. California: Stanford University Press.

Schabas, A. W. (2004). *An introduction to the international criminal court*. Cambridge: Cambridge University Press.

Schabas, A. W. (2007). *An introduction to the international criminal court*. Cambridge: Cambridge University Press.

Schwab, M. G. & Jeanneney, J. R. (Eds). (1995). *The French revolution and its impact.* Westport: Greenwood Press.

Selbourne, D. (1997). *The principle of duty*. London: Abacus.

Shatzmiller, M. (2005). *Nationalism and minority identities in Islamic societies*. Montreal: McGill-Queen's University Press.

Shklar, J. N. (1987). Political theory and the rule of law. In A. C. Hutchinson & P. Monahan (Eds), *The rule of law: Ideal or ideology* (Vol. 1, No. 1, pp. 1–16). Toronto: Carswell.

Shriver, D. W. (1995). *An ethic for enemies: Forgiveness in politics*. New York: Oxford University Press.

Simpson, G. (2008). One among many: The ICC as a tool of justice during transition. In N. Waddell & P. Clark (Eds), *Courting conflict?: Justice, peace, and the ICC in Africa* (pp. 73–9). London: Royal African Society.

Starba, J. P. (Ed.). (1991). *Morality and practice*, 3rd edition. Belmont: Wadsworth Publishing Company.

Stepan, A. (1986). Paths toward redemocratization: Theoretical and comparative Considerations. In G. O'Donnell, P. Schmitter & L. Whitehead. (Eds), *Transitions from authoritarian rule: Comparative perspectives* (pp. 65–84). Baltimore, MD: Johns Hopkins University Press.

Teitel, R. G. (2000). *Transitional justice*. Oxford: Oxford University Press.

Teitel, R. G. (2002). Transitional justice as liberal narrative. In O. Enwezor & A. Jaar (Eds), *Experiments with truth: Transitional justice and process of truth and reconciliation* (pp. 241–57). Ostfildern-Ruit: Hatje Cantz Publishers.

Thompson, G. (2003). *Governing Uganda: British colonial rule and its legacy.* Kampala: Fountain Publishers.

Van der Merwe, H. & Vienings, T. (2000). Coping with trauma. In L. Reychler & T. Paffenholz (Eds), *Peace-building: A field guide* (pp. 343–51). Colorado: Lynne Publishers.

Van Ness, D. & Karen H. S. (1997). *Restoring Justice.* Ohio: Anderson Publishing Company.

van Zyl, P. (2000). Justice without punishment: Guaranteeing human rights in transitional societies. In C. Villa-Vicencio & W. Verwoerd (Eds), *Looking back/reaching forward: Reflections on the truth and reconciliation commission of South Africa* (pp. 42–57). Cape Town: University of Cape Town Press.

Villa-Vicencio, C. (2003). Restorative justice in social context: The South African truth and reconciliation commission. In N. Biggar (Ed.), *Burying the past: Making peace and doing justice after civil conflict* (pp. 239–50). Georgetown: Georgetown University Press.

Villa-Vicencio, C. (2004). Restorative Justice. In C. Villa-Vicencio & E. Doxtader (Eds), *Pieces of the puzzle: Keywords on reconciliation and transitional justice* (pp. 33–8). Cape Town: Institute for Justice and Reconciliation

Welch, D. (1993). *Justice and genesis of war.* Cambridge: Cambridge University Press.

Wilson, R. A. (2001). *The politics of truth and reconciliation in South Africa* Cambridge: Cambridge University Press.

Wiredu, K. (1996). *Cultural universals and particulars: An African perspective.* Bloomington: Indiana University Press.

Wrigley, C. (1988). Four steps towards disaster. In H. Bernt & M. Twaddle (Eds), *Uganda now: Between decay and development* (pp. 27–35). London: James Currey.

Young, C. (1994). *The African colonial state in comparative perspectives*. New Haven: Yale University Press.

Young, C. (1998). The African colonial state and its political legacy. In D. Rothchild & N. Chazan (Eds), *The precarious balance: State and society in Africa* (pp. 25–66). Boulder: Westview.

Young, J. W. (1991). *Totalitarian language: Orwell's newspeak and its Nazi and communist antecedents*. Charlottesville: University Press of Virginia.

Zalaquett, J. (1995). The dilemma of new democracies confronting past human rights violations. In N. J. Kritz (Ed.), *Transitional justice: How emerging democracies reckon with former regimes* (Vol. I, pp. 203–6). Washington, DC: United States Institute of Peace Press.

Journal articles

Akhavan, P. (2005). The Lord's Resistance Army case: Uganda's submission of the first state referral to the international criminal court. *American Journal of International Law*, *99*(2), 403–21.

Allen, T. (1991). Understanding Alice: Uganda's Holy Spirit Movement in context. *Journal of International African Institute*, *61*(3), 370–99.

Apuuli, K. P. (2005). Amnesty and international law: The case of the Lord's Resistance Army insurgents in northern Uganda. *African Journal on Conflict Resolution*, *5*(2), 33–61.

Apuuli, K. P. (2006). The ICC arrest warrants for the Lord's Resistance Army leaders and peace prospects for Northern Uganda. *Journal of International Criminal Justice*, *4*(1), 179–87.

Auckerman, M. J. (2002). Extraordinary evil, ordinary crime: Transitional justice. *Harvard Human Rights Journal*, *15*, 40–97.

Bassiouni, M. C. (2006). Where is the ICC heading? The ICC – Quo vadis? *Journal of International Criminal Justice*, *4*(3), 421–7.

Bekou, O. & Shah, S. (2006). Realising the potential of the international criminal court: The African experience. *Human Rights Law Review*, *3*, 499–544.

Bhargava, A. (2002). Defining political crimes: A case study of the South African truth and reconciliation commission (TRC). *Columbia Law Review*, *102*, 1304–35.

Blanton, R., Mason, T. D. & Athow, B. (2001). Colonial style and post-colonial conflict in Africa. *Journal of Peace Research*, *38*(4), 473–91.

Blumenson, E. (2006). The challenge of a global standard of justice: Peace, pluralism, and punishment at the international criminal court. *Columbia Journal of Transnational Law*, *44*(3), 795–867.

Bolton, J. R. (2001). The risks and weaknesses of the international criminal court from America's perspective. *Law and Contemporary Problems*, *64*, 167–80.

Branch, A. & Mampilly, Z. C. (2005). Winning the war, but losing the peace? The dilemma of SPLM/A civil administration and the tasks ahead. *Journal of Modern African Studies*, *43*(1), 1–20.

Brett, E. A. (1995). Neutralising the use of force in Uganda: The role of the military in politics. *Journal of Modern African Studies*, *33*(1), 129–52.

Burke-White, W. (2003). A community of courts: Toward a system of international criminal law enforcement. *Michigan Journal of International Law*, *24*(1), 1–102.

Carver, R. (1990). Called to account: How African governments investigate human rights violations. *African Affairs*, *89*.

Cassese, A. (1998). On the current trends towards criminal prosecution and punishment of breaches of international humanitarian law. *European Journal of International Law*, *9*(1), 2–17.

Chaney, K. R. (1995). Pitfalls and imperatives: Applying the lessons of Nuremberg to the Yugoslav war crimes trials. *Dickinson Journal of International Law*, *14*(1).

Cherkasova, E. (2005). On the boundary of intelligibility: Kant's conception of radical evil and the limits of ethical discourse. *The Review of Metaphysics*, *58*(3), 571–84.

Cliffe, L. (1999). Regional dimensions of conflicts in the Horn of Africa. *Third World Quarterly*, *20*(1), 89–111.

Cobbah, J. A. M. (1987). African values and the human rights debate: An African perspective. *Human Rights Quarterly*, *9*(3), 309–31.

Crocker, D. A. (1998). Transitional justice and international civil society: Toward a normative framework. *Constellations*, *5*, 492–517.

Daly, E. (2002). Between punitive and reconstructive justice: The Gacaca courts in Rwanda. *New York University Journal of International Law and Politics*, *34*(2), 355–96.

Deng, F. M. (September 1995). Egypt's dilemmas on the Sudan. *Middle East Policy*, *4*, 50–6.

Doom, R. & Vlassenroot, K. (1999). Kony's message: A new Koine? The Lord's Resistance Army in Northern Uganda. *African Affairs*, *98*(390), 5–36.

Drumbl, M. (2000). Punishment, post-genocide: From guilt to shame to 'civis' in Rwanda. *New York University Law Review*, *75*(5), 1221–326.

Drumbl, M. (2005). Law and atrocities: Settling accounts in Rwanda. *Ohio Northern University Law Review*, *31*(41), 41–74.

Fletcher, L. E. & Weinstein, H. M. (2002). Violence and social repair: Rethinking the contribution of justice to reconciliation. *Human Rights Quarterly*, *24*(3), 573–639.

Gaeta, P. (2004). Is the practice of 'self-referrals' a sound start for the ICC? *Journal of International Criminal Justice*, *2*, 949–52.

Graybill, L. S. (1998). South Africa's truth and reconciliation commission: Ethical and theological perspective. *Ethics and International Affairs*, *12*, 43–62.

Graybill, L. S. (2004). Pardon, punishment and amnesia: Three African post-conflict case studies. *Third World Quarterly*, *25*(6), 1117–30.

Greenawalt, A. K. A. (2007). Justice without politics? Prosecutorial discretion and the international criminal court. *Journal of International Law and Politics*, *39*, 583–673.

Hamilton, H. (2000). Rwanda's women: The key to reconstruction. *Journal of Humanitarian Aid*. Available at www.jha.ac/greatlakes/b001.htm

Happold, M. (2007). The international criminal court and the Lord's Resistance Army. *Melbourne Journal of International Law*, *8*(1), 159–84.

Hayner, P. B. (1994). Fifteen truth commissions – 1974 to 1994: A comparative study. *Human Rights Quarterly*, *16*(4), 597–655.

Hechter, M. (1974). The political economy of ethnic change. *American Journal of Sociology*, *79*(5), 1151–78.

Jackson, P. (2002). The march of the Lord's Resistance Army: Greed or grievance in Northern Uganda? *Small Wars and Insurgencies*, *13*(3), 29–52.

Kissinger, H. (2001). The pitfalls of universal jurisdiction. *Foreign Affairs*, *80*(4), 86–96.

Kress, C. (2004). 'Self-referrals' and 'waivers of complementarity': Some considerations in law and policy. *Journal of International Criminal Justice*, *2*(4), 944–8.

Landsman, S. (1996). Alternative responses to serious human rights abuses: Of prosecution and truth commissions. *Law and Contemporary Problems*, *59*(4), 81–92.

Mayerfeld, J. (2004). The democratic legacy of the international criminal court. *The Fletcher Forum of World Affairs*, *28*(2, 1), 47–156.

McGregor, A. (2008). Leadership bloodbath marks failure of Uganda's LRA to sign peace treaty. *Terrorism Focus*, *5*(15). Available at https://jamestown.org/program/leadership-bloodbath-marks-failure-of-ugandas-lra-to-sign-peace-treaty/

Miller, Z. (2008). Effects of invisibility: In search of the 'economic' in transitional justice. *The International Journal of Transitional Justice*, *2*, 266–91.

Morris, M. (2001). The disturbing democratic deficit of the international criminal court. *Finnish Yearbook of International Law*, *12*, 109–18.

Mose, E. (2005). Appraising the role of ICTR: Main achievements. *Journal of International Criminal Justice*, *3*(5), 920–43.

Mwenda, A. M. & Tangri, R. (2005). Patronage politics, donor reforms and regime consolidation in Uganda. *African Affairs*, *104*(416), 449–67.

Nardin, T. (2000). The moral basis of humanitarian intervention. *Ethics and International Affairs*, *16*(1), 57–70.

Nathan, L. (2001). 'The four horsemen of the apocalypse': The structural causes of crisis and violence in Africa. *Peace & Change*, *25*(2), 188–207.

Nouwen, S. M. H. & Werner, W. G. (2010). Doing justice to the political: The International Criminal Court in Uganda and Sudan. *European Journal of International Law*, *21*(4), 941–65. Available at https://doi.org/10.1093/ejil/chq064

Obote-Odora, A. (September 1999). Competence of the international criminal tribunal for Rwanda. *International Humanitarian Law*, *6*(3).

Ohlin, J. D. (2007). On the very idea of transitional justice. *The Whitehead Journal of Diplomacy and International Relations*, *8*(1), 51–68.

Oomen, B. (2005). Donor-driven justice and discontents: The case of Rwanda. *Development and Change*, *36*(5), 887–910.

Orentlicher, D. F. (1991). Settling accounts: The duty to prosecute human rights violations of a prior regime. *Yale Law Journal*, *100*, 2537–48.

Parlevliet, M. (2002). Bridging the divide: Exploring the relationship between human rights and conflict management. *Track Two*, *11*(1), 8–43.

Philipp, C. E. (2003). The international criminal court – A brief introduction. *Max Planck Yearbook of United Nations Law*, *7*, 331–9.

Posner, E. & Vermeule, A. (January 2004). Transitional justice as ordinary justice. *Harvard Law Review*, *117*(3); 761–825.

Prunier, G. (2004). Rebel movements and proxy warfare: Uganda, Sudan and the Congo (1986–1999). *African Affairs*, *103*(412), 359–83.

Punyasena, W. (2006). Conflict prevention and the international criminal court: Deterrence in a changing world. *Michigan State Journal of International Law*, *14*, 40–57.

Quinn, J. (2009). Getting to peace? Negotiating with the LRA in Northern Uganda. *Human Rights Review*, *1*, 55–71.

Razmetaeva, Y. (2014). The right to resist and the right of rebellion. *Jurisprudence*, *21*, 758–84.

Robinson, M. (2003). From rhetoric to reality: Making human rights work. *European Human Rights Law Review*, *1*, 1–8.

Schwelb, E. (1949). Crimes against humanity. *British Yearbook of International Law*, *23*(8), 178–226.

Singer, P. W. (Winter 2002). Caution: Children at war, *Parameters*, *31*(4), 40–56.

Southwick, K. (2005). Investigating war in Northern Uganda: Dilemmas for the international criminal court. *Yale Journal of International Affairs*, *1*(1), 105–19.

Ssenyonjo, M. (2005). Accountability of non-state actors in Uganda for war crimes and human rights violations: Between amnesty and the international criminal court. *Journal of Conflict and Security Law*, *10*(3), 405–34.

Ssenyonjo, M. (2007). The International Criminal Court and The Lord's Resistance Army leaders: Prosecution or amnesty? *Netherlands International Law Review*, *54*(1), 51–80.

Staub, E. (1999). The roots of evil: Personality, social conditions, culture and basic human needs. *Personality and Social Psychology Review*, *3*, 179–92.

Staub, E. (2003). Preventing violence and generating humane values: Healing and reconciliation in Rwanda. *International Committee of the Red Cross*, *85*(852), 791–806.

Teitel, R. G. (2003a). Theoretical and international framework: Transitional justice in a new era. *Fordham International Law Journal*, *26*(4), 893–906.

Teitel, R. G. (2003b). Transitional justice genealogy. *Harvard Human Rights Journal*, *16*, 69–94.

Teitel, R. G. (2005). The law and politics of contemporary transitional justice. *Cornell International Law Journal*, *38*(3), 837–62.

Tomuschat, C. (2006). The legacy of Nuremberg. *Journal of International Criminal Justice*, *4*, 830–44.

Turner, T. S. (1968). Persons' concept of 'generalized media of social interaction' and its relevance for social anthropology. *Sociological Enquiry*, *38*, Spring, 121–34.

van Zyl, P. (1999). Dilemmas of transitional justice: The case of South Africa's truth and reconciliation commission. *Journal of International Affairs*, *52*(2), 648–64.

Villa-Vicencio, C. (2000). Why perpetrators should not always be prosecuted: Where the international criminal court and truth commissions meet. *Emory Law Journal*, *49*, 205–22.

Werchick, L. (2003). Prospects for justice in Rwanda's citizen tribunals. *Human Rights Brief*, *8*(3), 15–18.

Westbrook, D. (2000). The torment of Northern Uganda: A legacy of missed opportunities. *The Online Journal of Peace and Conflict Research*, *3*(2). Available at www.trinstitute.org/ojpcr/p3_2westbrook.htm

Wood, S. & Scharffs, B. (2002). Applicability of human rights standards to private corporations: An American perspective. *American. Journal of Comparative Law*, *50*, 531–66.

Zalaquett, J. (1992). Balancing ethical imperatives and political constraints: The dilemmas of new democracies confronting past human rights violations. *Hastings Law Journal*, *43*, 1425–38.

Reports/working papers/conference papers

Agreement on Accountability and Reconciliation between the Government of the Republic of Uganda and the Lord's Resistance Army/Movement, Juba, Sudan, 29 June 2007.

Ahere, J. & Maina, G. (March 2013). The never-ending pursuit of the Lord's Resistance Army: An analysis of the regional cooperative initiative for the elimination of the LRA. *Policy & Practice Brief*, Issue No. 24. African Centre for Constructive Resolution of Disputes, Durban South Africa.

Amnesty International. (2004). Uganda: First steps to investigate crimes must be part of comprehensive plan to end impunity. Public Statement, AFR 59/001/2004. *News Service*, No: 022. Available at https://reliefweb.int/report/uganda/uganda-first-steps-investigate-crimes-must-be-part-comprehensive-plan-end-impunity

Barsalou, J. (2005). Trauma and transitional justice in divided societies. United States Institute of Peace, Special Report, No. 135. Washington, DC.

Carnergie Commission. (1997). Preventing deadly conflict. Final Report. New York: Carnegie Corporation of New York.

Coalition to Stop the Use of Child Soldiers. (2004). Child soldiers global report 2004. London: Coalition to Stop the Use of Child Soldiers. Available at www.child-soldiers.org/resources/global-reports?root_id=159&category_id=165

Finnegan, A. C. (2005). *A memorable process in a forgotten war: Forgiveness within Northern Uganda* (Master's Thesis), The Fletcher School, Tufts University, MA.

Fischer, M. (2010). Transitional justice and reconciliation: Theory and practice. Available at www.operationspaix.net/DATA/DOCUMENT/4036~v~Transitional_Justice_and_Reconciliation__Theory_and_Practice.pdf

Foundation for Human Rights Initiative. (January 2007). Northern Uganda: Peace at last? Report for the Period July–December 2006-FHRI.

Fuller, G. E. (June 2003). *The youth factor: The new demographics of the Middle East and the implications for U.S. policy.* Washington, DC: Saban Center for Middle East Policy, Brookings Institution.

Gabiro G. (2002). Rwanda genocide: Paying for reconciliation. *Foundation Hirondelle.* Available at www.hirondelle.org/en

Geneva Convention. (1949). Relative to the protection of civilian persons in time of war. Art. 3. Available at www.unhchr.ch/html/menu3/b/92.htm

Gersony, R. (1997). The anguish of Northern Uganda: Results of a field-based assessment of the civil conflicts in Northern Uganda. Kampala: U.S. Agency for International Development.

Glassborow, K. (2006). *Peace versus justice in Uganda.* Africa Report No. 77, 27 September 2006. Available at iwpr.net/?p=acr&s=f&o=324160&apc_state=heniacr200609

Gleichmann, C., Odenwald, M., Steenken, K. & Wilkinson, A. (2004). *Disarmament, demobilization and reintegration: A practical field and classroom guide.* Clementsport: Pearson Peacekeeping Centre.

Global IDP Database. (18 December 2003). Profile for internal displacement: Uganda. Norwegian refugee Council/Global IDP Project. Geneva, Switzerland.

Grono, N. (November 2006). *The Role of the international criminal court in African peace processes: Mutually reinforcing or mutually exclusive?* Institute of Public Policy Research, Briefing Paper. Available at www.ippr.org/files/images/media/files/publication/2011/05/Role_of_ICC_1583.pdf

Grono, N. & O'Brien, A. (October 2007). *Justice in conflict? The international criminal court and peace processes in Africa.* Comment Paper. Royal African Society, London.

House of Commons Development Committee. (July 2007). *Prospects for sustainable peace in Uganda.* Ninth Report of Session 2006–07. Available at www.parliament.the-stationery-office.co.uk/pa/cm200607/cmselect/cmintdev/853/853.pdf

Hovil, L. & Lomo, Z. (2005). *Whose justice? Perceptions of Uganda's Amnesty Act 2000: The potential for conflict resolution and long-term reconciliation.* Refugee Law Project, Working Paper No. 15. Available at https://allafrica.com/.../main/.../00010394:ad20eceb262e2b1268108ea5971c2783.pdf

Hovil, L. & Quinn, J. (2005). *Peace first, justice later: Traditional justice in Northern Uganda.* Refugee Law Project Working Paper No. 17. Kampala, Uganda.

Human Rights Focus. (February 2002). *Between two fires: The human rights situation in protected camps in Gulu District.* Gulu, Human Rights Focus.

Human Rights Focus. (October 2003). *The hidden war: Forgotten people – War in Acholiland and its ramifications for peace and security in Uganda*. Kampala, Human Rights Focus.

HRW. (1997). *The scars of death: Children abducted by the Lord's Resistance Army in Uganda*. Human Rights Watch Report. Available at www.hrw.org/legacy/reports/1997/uganda/

HRW. (1999). *Leave no one to tell the story: Genocide in Rwanda*. Available at www.hrw.org/reports/1999/rwanda/Geno15-8-05.htm#TopOfPage

HRW. (2003a). *Abducted and abused: Renewed conflict in Northern Uganda*. Human Rights Watch Report, *15*(12A). Available at www.hrw.org/reports/2003/uganda0703/uganda0703.pdf

HRW. (2003b). *Covered in blood: Ethnically directed violence in Ituri region*. New York, Human Rights Watch.

HRW. (2003c). *Uganda, stolen children: Abduction and recruitment in Northern Uganda. 15*(7A). Available at http://hrw.org/reports/2003/uganda0303/

HRW. (2003d). *Uganda: Child abductions skyrocket in North*. Geneva. Available at www.hrw.org/news/2003/03/28/uganda-child-abductions-skyrocket-north

HRW. (September 2005). *Uprooted and forgotten: Impunity and human rights abuses in Northern Uganda*. New York, Human Rights Watch.

HRW. (26 January 2006). *The letter to Liberian President Johnson-Sirleaf urging prompt action to ensure Taylor's surrender*. Available at www.hrw.org/news/2006/01/26/letter-liberian-president-johnson-sirleaf-urging-prompt-action-ensure-taylors

HRW. (June 2006). *Trying Charles Taylor in The Hague: Making justice accessible to those most affected*. Available at www.hrw.org/backgrounder/ij/ij0606/ij0606.pdf

HURIPEC. (3 May 2004). *Listen to the people: Peace and reconciliation in Northern Uganda*. Kampala: Human Rights and Peace Centre.

ICG. (2004). *Northern Uganda: Understanding and solving the conflict*. International Crisis Group Africa Report No. 77, April.

ICG. (23 June 2005). Building a comprehensive peace strategy for Northern Uganda. *International Crisis Group Africa Briefing*, No. 27.

ICG. (14 September 2007). Northern Uganda peace process: The need to maintain momentum. *Africa Briefing* No. 46. Available at www.crisisgroup.org/africa/horn-africa/uganda/northern-uganda-peace-process-need-maintain-momentum

Kirsch, P. (2006). Address to the United Nations General Assembly, 9 October the International Criminal Court, The Hague, The Netherlands. Available at https://www.icc-cpi.int/NR/rdonlyres/53692E4E-2B35-41BD-8B90-91828D55880A/278543/PK_20061009_en.pdf

Kochler, H. (2006). Universal jurisdiction and international power politics: Ideal versus real. *Yeditepe'de Felsefe*, *1*(5), 1–16.

Kustenbauder, M. (2008). *Advantages and limits of protracted low-intensity civil war: Northern Uganda and the Lord's Resistance Army*. Paper prepared for the 3rd Annual Graduate Student Conference on Order, Conflict and Violence, Yale University, Connecticut.

Lamony, S. A. (2007). Approaching national reconciliation in Uganda. Working Paper. Available at http://iccnow.org/documents/ApproachingNationalReconciliationInUganda07aug13.pdf

Latigo, J. O. (2008). Northern Uganda: Tradition-based practices in the Acholi region. In *Traditional Justice and Reconciliation after Violent Conflict: Learning from African Experiences*. Stockholm: International Institute for Democracy and Electoral Assistance.

Liu Institute for Global Issues. (2006). Accountability and reconciliation and the Juba Peace Talks: Beyond the impasse. Institute of Global Peace, Gulu District NGO Forum. *Field Notes*, No. 3. Available at https://sppga.ubc.ca/news/accountability-reconciliation-juba-peace-talks-beyond-impasse/

Liu Institute for Global Issues and Gulu District NGO Forum. (2005). *Roco Wat I Acoli*: Restoring relations in Acholi-land: Traditional approaches to reintegration and justice. Available at https://sppga.ubc.ca/news/roco-wat-acoli-restoring-relationships-acholi-land-traditional-approaches-justice-reintegration/

Lomo, Z. & Hovil, L. (March, 2004). *Behind the violence: The war in Northern Uganda*. Institute of Security Studies Monograph, No. 99.

Lucima, O. (2008). *Mato oput is a cloak for impunity in Northern Uganda*. Friends for Peace in Africa, Houston, Texas, USA.

Lumwaka, C. (2002). *The peace process in Northern Uganda*. African Centre for Constructive Resolution of Disputes, ACCORD, Durban, South Africa.

Maepa, T. (February 2005). *The truth and reconciliation commission as a model of restorative justice*. In T. Maepa (Ed.), *Beyond retribution prospects for restorative justice in South Africa*, No 111. Pretoria: Institute for Security Studies Monograph Series.

Malu, L. N. (2015). *The international criminal court and conflict transformation in Uganda: Views from the field*. African Centre for Constructive Resolution of Disputes. Available at www.accord.org.za/ajcr-issues/the-international-criminal-court-and-conflict-transformation-in-uganda/

Manjunath, K. S. & Sharma, S. (December 2005). *The need for the international criminal court?* Institute of Peace and Conflict Studies, Special Report, No. 5.

Mckay, S. & Mazurana, D. (2004). *Where are the girls? Girls in fighting forces in Northern Uganda, Sierra Leone and Mozambique: Their lives during and after war*. Montreal: Rights & Democracy.

Méndez, Juan E. (2006). 'Peace, Justice and Prevention: Dilemmas and False Dilemmas', in Mô Bleeker (Ed.), *Dealing with the Past and Transitional Justice: Creating Conditions for Peace, Human Rights and the Rule of Law*. Bern: Political Affairs Division IV, Federal Department of Foreign Affairs, FDFA, pp. 15–19.

Museveni, Y. K. (7 April 1987). Speech on the opening of the National Resistance Council Session at the National Assembly, Kampala.

Museveni, Y. K. (1990). Theoretical justification of NRM struggle. In *Mission to Freedom: Uganda Resistance News 1981–85*. Kampala: Directorate of Information and Mass Mobilization, NRM Secretariat.

Nannyanjo, J. (August 2005). *Conflicts, poverty and human development in Northern Uganda*. United Nations University, Helsinki, Finland.

Neu, J. (2002). Restoring relations between Uganda and Sudan: The Carter Center process. African Centre for the Constructive Resolution of Disputes, ACCORD. Available at www.c-r.org/our-work/accord/northern-uganda/carter-center.php

Norwegian Refugee Council/Global IDP Project (12 December 2005). 'Uganda: Relief Efforts Hampered in One of the World's Worst Internal Displacement Crises'. Available at www.unhcr.org/refworld/docid/4455ce834.html

Nyeko, B & Lucima, O. (2002). Profiles of the parties to the conflict. In Okelo Lucima (Ed.), *Protracted conflict, elusive peace: Initiatives to end violence in Northern Uganda*. The African Centre for Constructive Resolution of Disputes, ACCORD, Durban, South Africa.

O'Kadameri, B. (2002). *LRA/Government negotiations 1993–94*. African Centre for the Constructive Resolution of Disputes. Available at www.c-r.org/our-work/accord/northern-uganda/negotiations-1993-94.php

Ochola, M. B. (April 2004). *Hope in the storm: Experience of ARPI in conflict resolution of Northern Uganda armed conflict*. Paper presented at the Swedish Seminal on Northern Uganda organised by the Mission Church of Uppsala, 15 April 2004.

Okello, M. C. (2007). The false polarisation of peace and justice in Uganda. *Refugee Law Project*. Available at www.refugeelawproject.org

Omach, P. (2003). *The state, insurgency, and international relations: The case of Uganda* (PhD Thesis). International Relations, University of the Witwatersrand.

Otim, M. (2007). *Challenges in the pursuit of transitional justice in Northern Uganda*. Justice and Reconciliation project, Gulu District NGO Forum, Liu Institute for Global Issues.

Otunnu, O. (2002). Causes and consequences of the war in Acholiland. In L. Okello (Ed.), *Protracted conflict, elusive peace: Initiatives to end the violence in Northern Uganda*. The African Centre for the Constructive Resolution of Disputes.

Pain, D. (1987). Acholi and the Nubians: Economic forces and military employment. In P. D Wiebe & C. P Dodge (Eds), *Beyond crisis: Development issues in Uganda*. Makerere Institute of Social Research, Makerere University, Kampala.

Parlevliet, M. (2009). Rethinking conflict transformation from a human rights perspective. *Berghof Research Center for Conflict Management*.

Refugee Law Project. (February 2004). *Behind the violence: Causes, consequences and the search for solutions to the war in Northern Uganda*. Working Paper No. 11. Kampala, Uganda.

Refugee Law Project. (2006). *Only peace can restore the confidence of the displaced*. Geneva: Internal Displacement Monitoring Centre.

Ruaudel, H. & Timpson, A. (12 December 2005). *Northern Uganda – from a forgotten war to an unforgivable crisis – the war against children*. Institute for Security Studies, Situation Report.

Schomerus, M. (2007). *The Lord's Resistance Army in Sudan: A history and overview*. Small Arms Survey Human Security Baseline Assessment, Working Paper 8, Graduate Institute of International Studies.

UN IRIN. (30 November 2005). Uganda: LRA rebels ask for peace talks with government. *IRIN*, 30 November 2005. Available at http://allafrica.com/stories/200511300106.html

UN IRIN. (25 May 2006). Uganda: LRA rebels ready to talk peace. *IRIN News*, Kampala, Uganda. Available at www.irinnews.org/report.aspx?reportid=59108

Van Acker, F. (2003). *Uganda and the Lord's Resistance Army: The new order no one ordered*. IPDM-UA Discussion Paper, 2003.

Wallis, D. (July 2005). *Rebels kill 19 in northern Uganda as attacks worsen*. Reuters, Kampala.

Weeks, W. (2002). *Pushing the envelope: Moving beyond 'protected villages' in Northern Uganda*. New York: Office for the Coordination of Humanitarian Affairs.

World Food Programme. (21 October 2005). *World food programme emergency report*. Available at https://reliefweb.int/sites/reliefweb.int/files/resources/3DC9C84960D3DA6B852570A1005B30C9-wfp-emergency-21oct.pdf

World Health Organization. (July 2005). *Health and mortality survey among internally displaced persons in Gulu, Kitgum and Pader districts, Northern Uganda*. Available at www.who.int/hac/crises/uga/sitreps/Ugandamortsurvey.pdf

Official documents

Amnesty Commission. (n.d.) A handbook for implementation of the Amnesty Act 2000: Procedures and principles of operation. Amnesty International.

Annan, K. (2001). *Prevention of armed conflict*. Report of the Secretary General to the United Nations General Assembly and Security Council. Document A/55/985-S/2001/574. New York: United Nations.

Annan, K. (2004). Address to the United Nations General Assembly. Available at www.un.org/sg/en/content/sg/statement/2004-09-21/secretary-generals-address-general-assembly

Commission of Inquiry. (1974). (Cap 56) Legal Notice No. 2 of 1974, Published on 30 June 1974.

ICC. (September 2003). *Paper on some policy issues before the Office of the Prosecutor: Referrals and communications*. Policy Paper, September 2003.

ICC. (January 2004). President of Uganda refers situation concerning the Lord's Resistance Army (LRA) to the ICC. 29 January. Available at www.un.org/press/en/2004/afr821.doc.htm

ICC. (July 2004). *Prosecutor of the international criminal court opens an investigation into Northern Uganda*, 29 July 2004. Available at www.icc-cpi.int/pages/item.aspx?name=prosecutor+of+the+international+criminal+court+opens+an+investigation+into+nothern+uganda

ICC. (8 July 2005). Decision on the prosecutor's application for warrants of arrest under Article 58, Prosecutor v Kony (Pre-Trial Chamber II) ICC-02/04-01/05-1-US-Exp. Available at www.worldcourts.com/icc/eng/decisions/2005.07.08_Prosecutor_v_Kony1

ICC. (27 September 2005). Warrant of arrest for Joseph Kony, issued 8 July 2005 as amended 27 September 2005. Situation in Uganda ICC-02/04-53. Available at www.icc-cpi.int/CourtRecords/CR2006_01096.PDF

ICC. (13 October 2005). *The situation in Northern Uganda*. Pre-Trial Chamber II, Case 01/05, The Prosecutor v. Joseph Kony, Vincent Otti, Okot Odhiambo and Dominic Ongwen, The International Criminal Court-ICC-02/04-01/05-268-tENG.

ICC. (14 October 2005). *Statement by Chief Prosecutor Luis Moreno-Ocampo*. Press Briefing, 14 October 2005. Available from www.icc-cpi.int

ICC. (14 October 2005). Warrant of arrest unsealed against five LRA Commanders. ICC-CPI-20051014-110, Press Release. Available at www.icc-cpi.int/pages/item.aspx?name=warrant+of+arrest+unsealed+against+five+lra+commanders

ICC. (2006). The International Criminal Court: Situations and cases. Available at www.icc-cpi.int/cases.html

ICC. (15 September 2006). *Situation in Uganda*. In the case of the Prosecutor v. Joseph Kony, Vincent Otti, Okot Odhiambo, Raska Lukwtya, Dominic Ongwen, ICC-02/04 01/05, Pre-Trial Chamber II.

ICC. (September 2007). Policy paper on the interest of justice. ICC-OTP-2007. Available at www.icc-cpi.int/library/organs/otp/ICC-OTP-InterestsOfJustice.pdf

Moreno-Ocampo, L. (September 2003a). *Paper on some policy issues before the Office of the Prosecutor*. Office of the Prosecutor, the International Criminal Court.

Moreno-Ocampo, L. (2003b). *Report of the Prosecutor of the ICC*, Second Assembly of States Parties to the *Rome Statute of the International Criminal Court*.

Moreno-Ocampo, L. (24 October 2005). *Statement by Luis Moreno-Ocampo, Prosecutor of the International Criminal Court*. Statement, Informal Meeting of Legal Advisors of Ministries of Foreign Affairs.

Pre-Trial Chamber I Decision on the Prosecutor's Application for Warrants of Arrest (ICC-01/04-01/06-8), 10 February 2006.

Security Council. (1994). Security Council Resolution 808, Preamble. U.N. Doc. S/RES/808, 22 February.

Uganda Government. (2000). *Amnesty Act 2000.*

Uganda Law Society. (2018). The international crimes division of the High Court of Uganda: Towards greater effectiveness. Available at www.uls.or.ug/site/assets/files/1355/the_international_crimes_division_of_the_high_court_of_ugandatowards_greater_effectiveness.pdf

UN. (1998). Diplomatic Conference of Plenipotentiaries on the Establishment of an International Criminal Court (1998). Rome Statute of the International Criminal Court. UN Doc A/CONF.183/9 of 17 July 1998, entered into force 1 July 2002. New York, United Nations, available at www.icc-cpi.int

UN. (October 2002). Report of the panel of experts on the illegal exploitation of natural resources and other forms of wealth of the Democratic Republic of Congo. *Security Council.* S/2002/1146.

UNDPA. (19 December 2004). Uganda: Child soldiers at the centre of mounting humanitarian crisis. Available at www.unis.unvienna.org/documents/unis/ten_stories/01uganda.pdf

UNICEF. (2005). *Child soldiers trapped in vicious cycle of war*. Available at http://origin-www.unicef.org/infobycountry/uganda_25184.html

UN General Assembly. (1970). Basic principles for the protection of civilian populations in armed conflicts. 9 December. Available at www.refworld.org/docid/3b00f1c961.html

UNHCHR. (January 1999). *Abduction of children from Northern Uganda*. Report of the Secretary General, E/CN.4/1999/69.

UNHCHR. (2003). *State of human rights in Northern Uganda*. UHRC 6th Annual Report. Available at www.ohchr.org/Documents/AboutUs/annualreport2003.pdf

UNHCHR. (August 2007). *Making peace our own: Victims' perceptions of accountability, reconciliation and transitional justice in Northern Uganda*. Available at www.unhcr.org/refworld/docid/46cc4a690.html

UN Humanitarian Coordination Unit. (29 November 2000). Humanitarian Update, *2*(9).

UN News Service. (14 October 2005). Annan hails international criminal court's arrest warrants for five Ugandan rebels. Available at https://news.un.org/en/story/2005/10/156842-annan-hails-international-criminal-courts-arrest-warrants-five-ugandan-rebels

UN Security Council. (1994). *Statute of the International Criminal Tribunal for Rwanda*, 8 November 1994.

World Bank (2006). World development report 2007: Development and the next generation. *World Bank.*

Newspapers/news agencies/magazines

Allio, E. & Moro, J. (2005). Uganda: LRA kills seven in Adjumani. *The New Vision*, Kampala, Uganda, 11 March.

Banya, C. (2006). Otti wants trial in Uganda. *Sunday Vision*, Kampala, Uganda, 15 October.

BBC. (21 December 2007). Otti 'executed by Uganda rebels'. Available at http://news.bbc.co.uk/2/hi/africa/7156284.stm

BBC News. (9 January 2015). LRA's Dominic Ongwen 'capture': Seleka rebels want $5m reward. Available at www.bbc.com/news/world-africa-30743647

BBC News. (14 January 2015). LRA commander Dominic Ongwen 'in Ugandan custody'. Available at www.bbc.com/news/world-africa-30810501

Branch, A. (Summer 2004). International justice, local injustice: The International Criminal Court in Northern Uganda. *Dissent Magazine*, *51*(3), 22–6.

Daily Nation. (13 January 2015). *Ugandan LRA rebel commander Dominic Ongwen to be tried at ICC: army*. Available at www.nation.co.ke/news/africa/LRA-Dominic-Ongwen-Uganda-Capture-ICC/-/1066/2587956/-/13bt2aj/-/index.html

Doyl, M. (2006). Mixed amnesty precedents. *BBC News*, 4 July. Available at news.bbc.co.uk/1/hi/world/africa/5148226.stm

Halera, P. (2006). LRA's Otti vows to kill ICC captors. *Daily Monitor*, Kampala Uganda, 13 October.

Kirunda, K. A. (2005). Kolo [former LRA commander] explains LRA attacks. *The Monitor*, Kampala, Uganda, 11 March.

Komakech, R. (2004). Reform speaks against Amnesty Act changes. *The New Vision*, Kampala, Uganda, 22 April.

Moreno-Ocampo, L. (2006). Sudan to execute Kony arrest warrant. *Daily Monitor*, Kampala, Uganda, 12 June.

Mugabi, F. (2009). Three LRA rebels surrender. *The New Vision*, 7 October.

Mukasa, H. (2006a). Interpol issues red notice for Kony. *New Vision*, Kampala, Uganda, 1 June.

Mukasa, H. (2006b). LRA assemble as deadline closes. *The New Vision*, Kampala, Uganda, 17 September.

Musinguzi, B. (2004). Amnesty group rejects ICC trial of Kony rebels. *The East African*, 16 February.

Nyakairu, F. (2005). Guns forced Kolo out, says Museveni. *The Monitor*, Kampala, Uganda, 18 February.

Nyakairu, F. (2008). Uganda the making of Joseph Kony: Failed peace. *The Sudan*, Kampala, Uganda, 13 January.

P'lajur, J. M-O. (2005). Acana warns world court on the LRA. *The Monitor*, Kampala, Uganda, 18 February.

Rugunda, R. (2006). Government position on Kony peace talks in Juba. *The New Vision*, Kampala, Uganda, 18 July.

The Monitor. (3 February 1998). Kampala, Uganda.

The Monitor. (11 November 2003). Uganda: Kony War a Forgotten Crisis. Kampala Uganda.

The New Vision. (15 November 2004). Kampala, Uganda.

The New Vision. (13 August 2006). Lukwiya death angers LRA. www.newvision.co.ug/new_vision/news/1142962/lukwiya-death-angers-lra

Wacha, J. (2005). Lira leaders off to the Hague. *The Monitor*, Uganda, 5 May.

Wasike, A. (28 August 2006). Museveni warns LRA on breaking truce. *The New Vision*, Kampala, Uganda.

List of interviews

10 January 2008: Callisto Otim, a retired secondary school teacher, 68 years old; Gulu.

10 January 2008: Okot Okumu, an ex-soldier during Obote's reign, early 60s; Gulu District.

11 January 2008: Samuel Odong, a cultural leader, 72 years old; Gulu District.

11 January 2008: Quirine Ongom, a Catholic priest, 45 years old; Gulu District.

6 March 2008: Jacinta Apola a community worker, 45 years; Gulu District.

8 March 2008: Cultural leader who sought to be anonymous, 65 years old; Gulu District.

8 March 2008: Jennifer, Lacor IDP camp Amuru District.

10 March 2008: University Lecturer, anonymity, 47-year-old, Gulu University.
11 March 2008: Group of Elders; Gulu District.
12 March 2008: Elderly woman, anonymous, middle aged; Lacor IDP Camp, Amuru District.
13 March 2008: Peter Onega, 56 years old; Gulu District.
16 March 2008: Charles Odwar, a Catholic priest, 42 years old; Amuru District.
17 March 2008: Group interview with three returnees, Lacor IDP camp, Amuru District.
18 March 2008: A former ARLPI Secretary, 62 years old; Lacor, Amuru District.
18 March 2008: Thomas Odong, 52 years; Amuru District.
20 March 2008: Benson Otto, camp resident, 46 years old; Lacor IDP camp, Amuru District.
23 March 2008: Group interview; Lacor IDP camp, Amuru District.
23 March 2008: Christine Labogo, 35 years old; Secretary for Women and Children Affairs, care giver for those who are on ARV; Lacor IDP camp, Amuru District.
24 March 2008: A man who sought anonymity; Lacor IDP camp, Amuru District.
25 March 2008: Betty Akello camp resident, 40 years old; Lacor, Amuru District.
27 March 2008: Matthew Odong, Secretary General of ARLPI; Lacor Seminary, Amuru District.
30 March 2008: Patrick Okulu, a former abductee, 23 years old; Pabo IDP Camp, Amuru District.
31 March 2008: ARLPI Delegate in Juba Peace Talks; Amuru District.
2 April 2008: Group Interview with eight Local Elders (camp residents); Pabo IDP camp Amuru District.
3 April 2008: Fr Charles Olweny, a Catholic priest, 30 years old; Christ the King Parish, Pabo Amuru District.
4 April 2008: five victims who sought anonymity; Pabo IDP camp, Amuru District.
4 April 2008: John Bosco, Government representative, Council Leader of Pabo-sub County and a resident of Pabo IDP Camp, 40 years old; Pabo IDP camp, Amuru District.
5 April 2008: A mother of abducted girl; Amuru District.
10 April 2008: District Speaker for Amuru District; Amuru.
12 April 2008: Matthew Odida, a resident of Pabo IDP camp, a retired civil servant, 84 years old; Pabo IDP camp, Amuru District.
15 April 2008: Anonymous Man (a); Amuru District.
23 April 2008: Charles Abok Kitgum.
28 April 2008: John Okiri 58, years old; Kitgum District.
16 May 2008: Abel Ojara; Kitgum District.
17 May 2008: Patrick Okidi, 26 years old; Kitgum District.
17 May 2008: Ex-abductee, anonymous, 23 years old; Kitgum.
18 May 2008: JB an ex-abductee; Kitgum District.
18 May 2008: Anonymous woman ex-abductee; Kitgum.
18 May 2008: Two anonymous returnees (young men), Kitgum.
24 May 2008: Anonymous Man (b); Kitgum District.
25 May 2008: An old man, 68 years old; Labuje IDP camp, Kitgum.
25 May 2008: A young man; anonymous, 26 years old; Labuje IDP camp, Kitgum.
29 May 2008: Crispin Opio, a counsellor working with ex-abductees, 48 years old; Kitgum.
31 May 2008: Caroline Auma, 50 years old, camp resident; Lapuje, Kitgum.
2 June 2008: Ochola 24, years old; Gulu.

3 June 2008: Dominic Ochar, 54 years old; Gulu District.
7 June 2008: John Mundua Kasirani, 27 years old; Gulu District.
15 April 2009: Ben Ladit, about 68 years old; Gulu District.
18 April 2009: Margaret Oyella, 50 years old; Gulu.
21 April 2009: Justine Ogwal, mid-forties; Gulu District.
22 April 2009: A Security Intelligence Officer who sought strict anonymity; Gulu district.
5 May 2009: Kizito Odhiambo; Kitgum District.
5 May 2009: Agnes Achayo; Kitgum.

Index

Page numbers in *italics* denote figures.